SITUATIONS
A Casebook of Virtual Re the English Teach

Betty Jane Wagner
National-Louis University
and
Mark Larson
Evanston Township High School

Boynton/Cook Publishers
HEINEMANN
Portsmouth, NH

Boynton/Cook Publishers, Inc.
A subsidiary of Reed Elsevier Inc.
361 Hanover Street
Portsmouth, NH 03801-3912
Offices and agents throughout the world

LB
1631
.W22
1995

Every effort has been made to contact the copyright holders and students for permission to reprint borrowed material. We regret any oversights that may have occurred and would be happy to rectify them in future printings of this work.

The authors and publisher wish to thank those who have generously given permission to reprint borrowed material:

"The Journey" by Anneliese Arénas-Bowman from *Monday Magic Abacadabra*, published by the Chicago Area Writing Project, 1992. Reprinted by permission.

"Stopping by Woods on a Snowy Evening" from *The Poetry of Robert Frost* edited by Edward Connery Lathem. Copyright 1951 by Robert Frost. Copyright 1923, 1969 by Henry Holt and Copmpany, Inc. Reprinted by permission of Henry Holt and Company, Inc.

"The Story of the Hour" by Kate Chopin was originally published by the Louisiana State University Press. Reprinted by permission.

Excerpts from the *Writing Assessment Handbook, High School,* including the Rhetorical Effectiveness Scoring Guides for Interpretation and the Reflective Essay, were previously published by the California Department of Education, P.O. Box 271, Sacramento, CA 95812-0271. Copyright © 1993. Reprinted by permission.

Excerpts from What I'd Tell, an unpublished manuscript by Eileen Shakespeare. Printed by permission.

Library of Congress Cataloging-in-Publication Data
Wagner, Betty Jane.
    Situations: a casebook of virtual realities for the English teacher / Betty Jane Wagner, Mark Larson.
        p. cm.
    Includes bibliographical references.
    ISBN 0-86709-345-5
    1. English language—Study and teaching (Secondary)—United States.
2. Language arts (Secondary)—United States. 3. English teachers—United States.
I. Larson, Mark. II. Title
LB1631.W22 1995
428'.0071'273—dc20   94-28627
                                                          CIP

Editor: Peter R. Stillman
Production: J. B. Tranchemontagne
Cover design: Darci Mehall

Printed in the United States of America on acid free paper.
99 98 97 96 95 **DA** 1 2 3 4 5 6 7 8 9

To Durrett and Mary

CONTENTS

INTRODUCTION

You are holding in your hands a "virtual reality" of the English class-room. Think of this book as serving the function of the virtual-reality cockpit that future airline pilots enter in their flight simulation training. As they sit in a confined space that looks like a real cockpit, potential disasters are presented through videotapes projected onto their windshields, while the pilots respond at the controls in the safe milieu of simulated dangerous developments in the air before they are confronted with actual ones. Increasingly, doctors and nurses are also being trained for emergency situations with interactive video or reality simulators.

This text is your set of eyephones and data gloves.[1] You will be neither flying, nor zapping simulated enemies, nor facing emergency-room decisions, but you will find yourself in the cockpit of an English classroom facing the challenges teachers face there. Like the airline pilot's flight simulator, which physically moves as an airborne plane would, you have in this book a virtual reality. Although the potential disasters are not presented on interactive videotapes, we try to create as palpable a simulation as we can with words alone. What you will find here is everything from mild teaching difficulties to downright disasters.

This book is organized a bit like a hypertext[2]: you may enter it at any point; the order in which you read this book depends on what interests you. Although we have clumped the situations into four rough categories (teacher, curriculum, students, and school), there is no need to start with the first and read through to the last. Instead, we suggest you look at the table of contents, decide which situation you are most likely to encounter, and read that one first; and continue in any sequence that interests you.

---

[1]Interactive computer software and hardware used in virtual reality, including three-dimensional graphics, to create a realistic simulation of an environment.

[2]A method of storing data by means of a computer program that permits the reader to create and link fields of information so they can be called up to the screen nonsequentially.

The situations you enter are as much as possible like those you will encounter in middle school and secondary classrooms. The cases we present here are not made-up. Rather, they are all actual situations gathered from a variety of schools—urban and suburban, large and small—although the names of the participants have been changed and some of the dialogue has been recreated.

We assume you are already an English teacher or hope to become one. You want to share your knowledge of and enthusiasm for the rich literary traditions of our multicultural heritage with a new generation of readers. Yet, of course, you have concerns. The purpose of this book is to address and reflect on those concerns in the process of presenting as realistically as possible what is "out there." Good teachers are those who have not only a vision of what students need to know, but also the capacity to respond appropriately to the students who walk through their classroom doors, no matter how at variance these might be from the ideal students they might hope to teach. Success as a teacher always depends on the quality of the connections you make with your students. You want to inspire teen-agers to become fully literate—to read perceptively, to relish at least some of the literature you prize, and to become accomplished writers. The challenge is bracing.

The two authors of this book—one a university English education professor and the other a secondary school teacher—offer this book as a bit of virtual reality, dropping you into the territory of English teaching as fully as is possible in a mere text.

We suggest you read this book in the context of discussions with your peers. We intend for it to stimulate dialogue. Read a situation, or, better yet, assign parts and read it aloud together, and then talk about that case and brainstorm ways the teacher might respond and deal with the situation described. These cases have no clearly "correct" responses: they are presented as representative challenges contemporary English teachers are likely to face. After your group has together come up with a list of possible actions, read the perspectives that follow. In the perspectives we have presented either a way to think about the situation or a set of options a teacher might consider. However, none of our proposals may fit a particular problem. Some of the situations we describe are too far gone for any action with that particular group of students to have the positive effect we envision. Our goal is to provide suggestions that may be implemented before a situation gets beyond redemption. Each teaching situation is unique, and although there are some representative types, which we have tried to offer you here, there is no simple, sure-fire strategy for dealing with any one of them. You will probably be able to think of alternate ways to cope with these challenges—and often better ways than we offer.

The value of this virtual reality is its "virtual-ness." Under the pressure of real situations, you have to make quick decisions, you have little time to consider alternatives, and, worst of all, you have to live with the consequences of bad decisions. By entering these virtual realities now, you will have the luxury of time to consider the best course of action and the advantage of suggestions of your peers, free from the often overwhelming but inevitable hazards of teaching.

Everyone who knows anything about teaching in this decade owns the job is tough. The well-being, even in some cases the actual physical safety, of groups of human beings is in your hands: their whole attitude toward written culture can be shaped by your teaching. Often they come to you with grievously unmet needs; most of these you cannot meet. But as one secondary English teacher in Boston put it:

> Our mission with urban kids is an intellectual mission. No one else will ever teach your students ninth-grade English. . . . Someone else might nurture them through a personal crisis, might add a sweet and loving touch to their day, and you should too. But you can't do *only* that. You have to teach your discipline well, too, because you are the only one in their lives who is assigned that job.[3]

UNDERLYING ASSUMPTIONS

We see this book as part of the growing body of casebooks built on practitioner knowledge in teaching and in teacher education. They are in the tradition of Shulman's[4] close-to-the-classroom casebooks. A case is not just a narrative of what went on in a particular English classroom, but rather a representative example typifying a larger class of classroom events. Thus, in Chapter 1, "Defending a Grade," although the case presented is a dialogue over a grade for a paper, this interchange represents a larger class of interchanges between student and teacher. It is an instance or a "case" of evaluation, one that is representative of a class of dialogues of this type. Because all

---

[3]Eileen Shakespear, "What I'd Tell A White Gal," in the Multicultural Collaborative on Literacy and Secondary Schools (M-Class) teacher research project sponsored by the National Center for the Study of Writing, University of California, Berkeley, Cal. 1993.

[4]Judith H. Shulman, ed. *Case Methods in Teacher Education.* (New York: Teacher's College Press, Columbia University, 1992).

of the situations presented in this book are representative, the book is broadly applicable to practicing or future English teachers. It is particularly apt for students on the cusp of their teaching internship.

The English teaching profession is not as problem-ridden as the virtual reality you will find in this book might lead you to believe. Every day far more teaching strategies succeed than fail. Of course, there are also situations that are even worse than any we have taken you into here. There are classrooms where students come to class so high on drugs that they have to be rushed to the emergency room; where because of the high absentee and transient rate, teachers rarely meet the same group two days in a row; and where students come armed with guns. Such situations cannot be "fixed" without community action that goes far beyond what any single teacher can do. In this book we have concentrated on types of situations with problems for which teacher response is very likely to make a critical difference.

Like all educators, the two authors of this book plan our instructional strategies, relate to our students, and conduct our teaching on the basis of values and assumptions about what is important to learn and how learning happens. We make some of these assumptions explicit here.

The three guiding principles of classroom practice that we subscribe to are individualization, interaction, and integration.[5]

1. Although it is traditional to bring groups, often large ones, into the same confined space to be educated, our teaching focus has to be on *individuals*. It is individuals who learn, not classes. Each student learns differently. Each has a different set of values and interests, a different home, community, and ethnic heritage—a different way of being in the world. The more options we can give these individuals to choose what they will read and write about, to sequence their own learning, and to reflect on and evaluate their own progress, the better teachers we will be.

No two individuals construct knowledge in exactly the same way. They bring to any classroom not only different prior experiences, but also their own set of goals. We teachers must design classroom experiences that facilitate the student's own struggle to learn and operate competently in the increasingly complex society in which we all live.

2. Without *interaction* among individuals, the potential of the classroom as a learning setting is largely lost. Education is at bottom an intentional conversation between the more experienced and the

---

[5]For a full treatment of these principles, see James Moffett and Betty Jane Wagner, "Individualization, Interaction, and Integration," in *Student-Centered Language Arts, K–12* (Portsmouth, N.H.: Boynton/Cook, 1992), 20–47.

less experienced. It is because individuals differ that this conversation has a rich potential for expanding the range of one's insights. It is not a simple case that the teacher is the only one who is more experienced and whose experience "counts," and the others are all inexperienced: every individual in the classroom brings experience and perspective. The teacher in most cases has had more experience with the literature at hand, but whatever he or she contributes is effective to the degree that it meshes with the experiences the learners bring.

Although the acts of reading and writing are engaged in alone, we see them both as profoundly social. Most teen-age readers enjoy talking about their favorite books, and the range of their interests expands as they listen to the responses of their peers.

The practice of talking about literature, however, is not without its problems. When students start talking about their feelings about the books they read, they often get into heated arguments about their differences. One Chicago public school teacher found that when her eighth graders were encouraged to read and discuss in literature circles[6] texts that explore the themes of racism and prejudice, the students divided uncomfortably along racial and gender lines.[7] The arguments became heated, and often the students resorted to verbal attacks on each other as representatives of their different races or genders.

Writing improves when students talk about it. So does reading. Students need ample opportunity for feedback from readers—peers as well as the teacher. Writing in the classroom starts out as personal and private, but as students read their drafts to each other, it becomes social. Critical to the decisions that every writer must make is the tension to produce something that is both true to what the writer wants to say and that also communicates to the reader.

Students need experience in interpreting texts, and like most adults they find this process more stimulating and effective if they do a great deal of it orally rather than in writing. The feedback they get is immediate and energizing. Through the process of talking about

---

[6]Literature circles are small groups of students who meet simultaneously in the classroom to discuss texts they have read. Some teachers have each student assume a different role in the small group, such as: the one who writes a list of questions to discuss, the one who keeps the discussion on track, the one who writes down what participants say, and the one who summarizes and reports on their discussion to the rest of the class.

[7]Griselle M. Diaz-Gemmati, "And Justice for All," in Sarah W. Freedman, Elizabeth Radin Simons, and Alex Casareno, eds., *Multiculturalism is the Mainstream: Teacher Research in Urban Multicultural English and Social Studies Classrooms*, from the Multicultural Collaborative on Literacy and Secondary Schools (M-Class) teacher research project sponsored by the National Center for the Study of Writing, University of California, Berkeley, Cal., in progress.

texts, they learn much more about the limitations of their own vision than they do when they read literature only for right answers and information to spew back to a teacher on a test.

3.   The third principle on which we base our practice is *integration,* binding school learning with home and community experience, connecting the literature students read with the lives they lead. Because we believe that most students learn best in heterogeneous groups, we have serious reservations about the common practice of tracking students on the basis of test scores. Except for those with severe learning disabilities, or an occasional outstandingly gifted individual, most students learn from those who differ from themselves. Also, it is a rare student who is not good at something that at least his peers, if not the teacher, value, so students with limited literacy can contribute to class discussion in other valuable ways.

It is because the American student body is so diverse that rich opportunities for cross-teaching occur. Imagine the opportunities for learning about languages and cultures in any major city in the United States. For example, there are currently 103 languages spoken in the Chicago public schools. As examples, here are those that begin with *A* and *S:* Afrikaans, Ahmedabad, Akan, Albanian, Algonquin, Amharic, Apache, Arabic, Aramaic, Armenian, Assyrian; Serbo-Croatian, Shona, Sindhi, Sinhalese, Slovak, Slovenian, Sotho, Spanish, Swahili, Syriac. Imagine how much a class might learn about the culture and the literature of other peoples if they were each to read a major literary work—in translation—from the culture in which the first language of each of the students is spoken. Diversity itself is a powerful teacher.

Throughout history the great centers of learning have always been at the crossroads of cultures where peoples from varied heritages met and learned about one another. The United States is now facing the second great wave of immigration in its history. We have the potential for stimulating classroom conversations if we integrate the culture of our students into our curriculum.

No matter how well-educated the teachers, the classroom is a limited milieu. In our rapidly expanding information age, students also need to be integrated with the world beyond the classroom. Current technology can link students with their counterparts throughout the world via electronic mail. When the persons who read their writing have less in common with them than their classmates do, writers need to elaborate and expand and explain. Nothing improves student writing faster than having genuine readers somewhere in the world who need or want to find out what the students have to tell them.

If we integrate the students' learning with the world outside the classroom, we will bring into the classroom much real-world material to read and to use as models for writing. Instead of focusing their reading only on fiction and poetry and asking them to write essays, we need to expand the range of genres students can read and write and listen to and speak about. (See Appendix F for a model of the range of these types of discourse.) In any genre, students can read, write, listen, and speak. Although there is much overlap, purpose generally determines genre, and the more experience students have with a wide range of genres, the better they understand how their own purposes indicate appropriate forms for their discourse.

Teaching is a bit like the film *Groundhog Day*. In that movie, Phil Connors, the character played by Bill Murray, kept waking up in Punxsutawney, Pennsylvania, on February second. Each morning he had a chance to relive that one day until he got it right. Each fall we teachers face a new group of students—eager innocents who have not yet learned our limitations. We have a fresh chance to "get it right." Teachers are never going to get it right once and for all. Our hope is that this book will help you to envision a better way to teach, to strengthen your resolve to try new instructional strategies, and to commit yourself to your own growth as a teacher.

Welcome to what we hope is a stimulating, professional adventure.

PART I

FOCUS ON THE TEACHER

CHAPTER 1

DEFENDING A GRADE

SITUATION

"But you said that was good."
"Well, it—yes, it showed a good sense of how to organize a paper, but . . ."
"So why did I get a C-minus?"

Laura gave the class the following assignment:

> Write a one-paragraph essay in which you tell what makes your family unique. Be sure to have a strong topic sentence, mention all your immediate family members, stay on the topic, and end with a solid conclusion.

In response, Jeffrey wrote:

> There are four people in my family but I only live with three. I have one sister and one brother. We live with my dad most of the time but sometimes we spend a vacation with my mom. She's busy. My sister is a senior and will graduate soon. I think she will go to a school near my mom. And live with her. I still have two years to go. I might or might not go to college. I'd like to be a lawyer because they make a lot of money. My brother is only seven. He doesn't know what he wants to do yet. But he has a lot of time. My dad is an architect. My mom is a decorator. That's how we live.

When the papers are returned, Jeffrey asks to see the teacher in private to discuss his grade of C-minus. The following conversation ensues:

Laura begins in her most encouraging teacher manner: "I like this essay because it sticks to the point about what everyone is either doing or planning to do. You show a good sense of how to make a paper cohesive."

Jeffrey doesn't smile. "So why did I get a C-minus?"

"Well, the assignment asked that you tell what makes your family *unique*."

"I did that."

"Without looking at the paper, tell me what is unique about your family."

"I don't know. My dad's an architect."

"What kinds of things does he design?"

"I don't know. He designs stores mostly."

"Does that take him out of town often?" Laura asks.

"No."

"Is there anything unusual about his work?"

Jeffrey shrugs, "No."

"Let's go back to my original question. What is unique about your family? Every family is unique in some way."

"I don't know if it's unique, but we don't live together."

"That's something you could have written about," Laura prompts.

"I did."

"But you didn't say much about it. You focused on what everyone is doing or plans to do."

"But you said that was good."

"Well, it—yes, it showed a good sense of how to organize a paper, but . . ."

"So why did I get a C-minus?"

"Because you didn't really focus on what the assignment asked for."

"Like what?"

"Like how your family is unique."

"I told you! We live apart."

"But you didn't explore it."

"You didn't say I was supposed to *explore* it. Look, here's a topic sentence, then I mention each member of my family, and then there is a conclusion. I don't understand why I got a C-minus."

QUESTIONS TO CONSIDER

1. Why is Laura having difficulty getting through to this student?

2. What could she do differently?

3. Would you have given this paper a different grade? Why or why not?

4. Is this a good assignment? If not, how would you make it better?

5. How would you role play a different dialogue between the teacher and student?

PERSPECTIVES

If you identified with Laura in this demoralizing exchange, you see how she is sinking deeper and deeper into a no-win hole. The student's question, "Why did I get a C-minus?" dominates the dialogue: little opportunity arises to move into a fruitful teaching moment in which the student gets a more mature insight as to what this paper needs. The crux of the problem is that it is too late for the student to see how to improve this particular paper. This draft is dead. The student needed to sense the value of apt detail and elaboration as he began the process of writing this paper, not at the point at which he is arguing for a better grade. In the dialogue above, he is putting the teacher on the defensive. He is the one who initiated this conference, and his goal was not to learn how to write a better paper, but rather, to get the teacher to change the grade. As you can see, he keeps coming back to his original question. To try to defend the grade is to sink deeper into a quagmire; the student legitimately claims he has done exactly what the teacher told him to do, and thus he deserves a better grade.

The Dialogue

So what is Laura to do? One alternative is to give up trying to make this a teachable moment. Obviously, this teacher created a problem by first complimenting the student on what is good about the paper and then later saying that the student "didn't really focus on what the assignment asked for." From the student's point of view, he did exactly that, and he has no vision of anything more he could have done. Instead of complimenting Jeffrey, as Laura might have done earlier in the writing process, she should consider simply answering his question about the grade by acknowledging that grades are determined in part by how this particular paper ranks in comparison with all the other papers in the class or in other classes she has taught, and that this paper ranks low in its degree of development and elaboration.

If Laura had kept a file of model student papers for each of the assignments she regularly gives, she could pull out an illustrative one at a time like this and show Jeffrey the level of writing that merits an A. If Laura has not taught long enough to have such a file, she might advise the student with this C-minus paper to ask another student whom she knows has written well if Jeffrey could read his or her paper for comparison. Or she might refer the student to James Moffett's *Active Voices III*,[1] which is a rich source of student written papers in a variety of modes of discourse. (An appropriate student written piece for Jeffrey would be "Making Do" on page 51.) After Laura has suggested pieces for the student to read to compare with his own, she should drop the subject. She can invite the student to come back in for another conference to talk about the differences he notices between his paper and the others she has asked him to read.

Another term, Laura might introduce a writing assignment by having the students read a set of essays by anonymous students from other classes. They then rate them on a 0-to-5 scale, with 5 being the highest score. This exercise could begin a discussion of what good writing is and help the students develop standards for quality. The students can keep these rated essays in their folders as touchstones for comparison with their own pieces of writing.

The Assignment

Is this a good assignment? From the dialogue, you can see that the assignment reflects Laura's belief that "every family is unique in some way." If the word *unusual* were used instead of *unique*, she might have been better able to defend her belief. Since teachers can count on having at least one student in any class who cannot resist challenging even the most obvious of assumptions, it would be wise for Laura to word assignments so that they are open-ended and invite a range of responses. That way a student might show how his or her family is a typical rather than a unique representative of American families.[2] Such an alternative might keep students from making perfunctory statements they don't actually believe. One of the criteria for good student writing Diederich presented in his classic book[3] is that it sound as if the author believes what he or she is writing. The voice is authentic.

Perhaps the biggest problem with this assignment, however, is not the assumption that each family is unique, but the assumption that a writer can treat this topic in a single paragraph. To deal with such a subject in more than a superficial way, a writer needs more scope. Suppose an able student decides to "show rather than tell," as the commonly repeated maxim for writers insists. Suppose the student starts, "The best way to show the uniqueness of our family is to

---

[1] Portsmouth, N.H.: Boynton/Cook, 1987.

[2] (As Tolstoy quipped, all happy families are alike, but an unhappy family is unhappy after its own fashion.)

[3] Paul Diederich, *Measuring Growth in English* (Urbana, Ill.: National Council of Teachers of English, 1974), 55.

let you overhear a typical late evening conversation as we all stand around in our kitchen nibbling on cold snacks." This indirect presentation of the topic does not necessarily meet the formal demands of the assignment, but it may evoke a family aura far more effectively than an essay in a single paragraph. Backing into one's subject can be very effective because the reader can be surprised into a discovery.

Further, there is the topic sentence problem: As Braddock[4] has noted, most paragraphs in published writing do not have a clearly identifiable topic sentence. This does not mean they necessarily lack focus. Instead, the topic may overarch several paragraphs, and other devices are used to maintain coherence rather than a topic sentence for each paragraph. It is common practice, among secondary English teachers especially, to assign one-paragraph essays, and in such cases the formula for success, in the teacher's eye at least, is to have a clear, strong topic sentence. In the case of the teacher presented in this chapter, she probably expected a topic sentence that ideally would begin with words such as, "My family is unique in that . . ." Such writing meets the teacher's expectations of language and format, not the students' need to express something significant about their own experience, and that is why the result is often of a painfully C-minus quality. The best writers often leave the solid conclusion to the reader to formulate, but they lay the groundwork so deftly that the reader is subtly led to build the apt conclusion the writer had in mind all along.

So what is to be done? How could this assignment be worded to avoid the pitfalls cited above? Stop now and try a rewording; share it with a peer or with the class . . .

Did you suggest that the paper might be longer than a paragraph? Did you omit the suggestion that the writer mention all of the family members? These two suggestions could lead the student toward a more powerful focus. Suppose, for example, that there are a lot of immediate family members, too many for a tight focus, or several step-siblings who are not currently living with the immediate family. Or suppose that what is unique about a family is the relationship between the parents, and that that is the desired focus. The inescapable problem of wording writing assignments is to make them clear and specific enough to give the student something to go on and yet ambiguous enough to stimulate a variety of authentic responses.

Usually the least helpful advice is to stipulate format. Yet it is precisely this information students ask for most often. "How long does it have to be?" "Should we mention the topic in the first

---

[4]Richard Braddock, "The Frequency and Placement of Topic Sentences in Expository Prose," *Research in the Teaching of English* 8 (1974) 287–302.

sentence?" Such questions are stirred by lack of interest, insecurity, and passivity, not to mention the inappropriate directions they may have received from previous teachers. The more precise your responses to their questions, the more passive the students become. You are assuming the initiative for writing, and leaving fewer decisions for the student to make. Writing what one chooses, in what manner, in what format and diction, at what length, at what level of specificity—all breed energy. Students cannot write unless they are somehow in charge, or can claim their own turf. Somehow, and this is admittedly tricky, the teacher has to stand aside and let the students assert themselves, and at the same time stay involved and nudge them toward better performance.

When to step aside and when to nudge? This has to be played by ear, and differently for each student. Laura will never know for sure when she is needed, but whenever a student is floundering for an idea and awash in the possibilities seems passive and confined by the specifics, she needs to intervene and coach. Her job with some students is to provide a simple starting point, and with others it is to free them to start on their own, decide their tack for themselves, and go it alone.

The Process

One of the tenets of good composition teaching is that students write best on those topics with which they have the greatest familiarity. But how is Laura to help them sense the richness of their own experiences? One way is to have them keep journals of their responses to what is happening to them. She can encourage them to jot down in these journals reactions to events, moods and feelings, and ideas for future writing. One way to help them sense that they have in their memories a vast storehouse of ideas for writing is to have them make time lines of memorable events in their lives. On the first day of class, Laura could have her students draw the configuration in Figure 1.1 on the first page of their writing journals.

Figure 1.1: Time Line

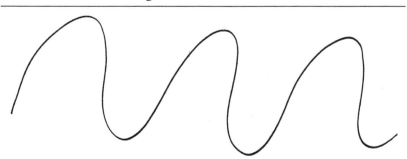

She can tell them this is a time line of their lives, and ask them to go back to their earliest memory and put a note or diagram to themselves somewhere along the first curved vertical line, as in Figure 1.2.

Figure 1.2:
Time Line with student's earliest memory indicated

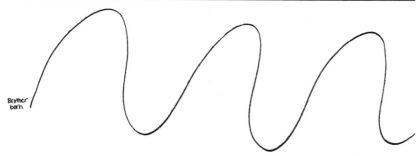

Then Laura can have them decide on a second memory and put in a word or phrase or a diagram to remind them of that event. This note goes above the first on the undulating line. They continue to mark their line until it looks something like Figure 1.3.

Figure 1.3: Time Line filled with memories

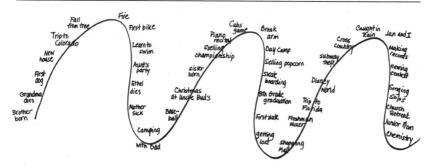

Laura tells them this diagram can be their trigger for memory writing, their source of topics. Then she asks them to select one memory that interests them—one they can remember fairly vividly and would like to explore through writing. They write that event at the top of the next page of their journal. Then she can lead them in a guided meditation, asking them either to close their eyes or to go back to that time in their minds. She may decide to have them quiet themselves for a moment, breathing deeply and relaxing. As she guides with her leading questions, the students remember as many details as they can. Laura reminds them that good writers often generate a lot of ideas at the beginning of a project and then have the luxury of choosing the best ones to use in their draft.

- What is the sharpest image you now see in your mind?
- What time of day is it?
- What is the weather like?
- Where are you?
- Look around you. What do you see to the left? To the right?
- Are there any colors that stand out?
- Do you notice any particular smells?
- What do you hear?
- Are there any textures you are aware of?
- Who else is in the scene with you?

When they open their eyes, they quickly list as many details as have come to them, not worrying now whether they will want to incorporate them in a later piece of writing.

She asks the students to try to capture the moment when the memory of the event they have chosen is the most vivid. Then, as they are jotting notes to themselves, she periodically introduces questions and prods such as these:

- What would you likely have been talking about, if anything?
- Now let the event you remember happen slowly in your mind, just as if you were watching a slow motion movie.
- When did you first realize something important was going to happen?
- How did you feel?
- What did you do?
- Were there snatches of conversation you remember or could recreate?
- Describe the scene as vividly and completely as you can, remembering to watch it unfold slowly. Describe in as much detail as you can that moment at which your feeling about what was happening was the most intense.
- How did you react?
- What is the most significant thing you remember about what happened?

When Laura has done everything she can think of to help the students remember a particular scene, she then asks them to reread their list of notes to themselves or to a partner and use them as material for writing a draft they would be willing to share with her or with other students. If they have some notes they would rather not read to another classmate, she assures them that is all right. As they write their drafts, they stay with the incident they chose, using as many of their notes as they find useful or suitable to share with others. It is up to them to decide what, if anything, they want to leave out.

As the students are writing this first draft in class, Laura can conduct short conferences with them. As she walks from student to student, each selects his or her best paragraph so far to read aloud quietly to her. She comments on, but does not judge, the content, asks a question or two to evoke elaboration, and then goes on to another student, so that as many students as possible get some feedback from her during the class period(s). At this stage in the writing process, she tries to give as few evaluative comments as possible, concentrating instead on assuming the role of trusted adult or partner in dialogue to use Britton's phrase.[5]

The next day, or whenever these first drafts have been completed, Laura has the students read them in triads, if they choose.[6] Those who opt not to read can continue to work on their drafts while she conducts short conferences doing all she can to keep their drafts alive and interesting to the students. She tries to help each student delay closure. Then all the students hand in their first drafts to Laura for written feedback. Because this is a first draft, she should not give advice on matters of mechanics, such as spelling, punctuation, or capitalization. Instead, she responds to the content with prompts like these: "Your first sentence did not pique my interest as much as this later one. Can you think of a way to get your reader interested sooner? By the third paragraph, you seem to hit your stride. I was very interested by then."

The Grade

Laura can help students become aware of what merits a good grade by reading aloud two or three of the best first drafts (with the students' permission) and commenting on why she selected them. This can help the weaker students improve their own drafts and

---

[5]James Britton, Tony Burgess, Nancy Martin, Alex McLeod, and Harold Rosen, *The Development of Writing Abilities (11-18)* (Urbana, Ill.: National Council of Teachers of English, 1979), 58–73.

[6]The value of telling one's own stories is eloquently illustrated in Robert Coles, *The Call of Stories: Teaching and the Moral Imagination.* (Boston: Houghton Mifflin, 1989.)

understand why their grades are lower than other students'. Since everyone knows the teacher is reading first drafts, Laura might make a public suggestion or two for improving even these best papers, and then hand them all back for revision, editing, and final draft writing. A general comment about all of the papers, such as that most were not elaborated enough, may stimulate better final papers.

When is it time to assign a grade? Remember that a grade is a gravestone for a paper: it marks the death of the draft. If the grade is good, the student will see no reason to continue to work on it; if it is bad, the student either will be discouraged or will try to defend the quality of his paper, as the student quoted in this chapter did. Laura needs to encourage students to work on a draft as long as possible. Research has shown that greater attention to instruction and to solving writing problems during the writing of a *limited* number of papers is more effective than the hurried production of a great number of papers.[7] Assign a grade only to a paper a student has decided is complete or has been forced to abandon because of a deadline.

Better yet, Laura might try the practice of portfolio assessment. She would simply assign a grade to a body of work—a portfolio of papers selected by the student in consultation with Laura from all the papers collected during a particular marking period. With portfolio assessment, she avoids the problem, posed in this chapter, of having a student question a particular grade for a specific paper. (See Chapter 11, "The Writing Competency Test," and Appendix B, "Memo to the English Department," for more on portfolio assessment.)

Portfolio assessment will create a new problem, however: students will probably find it difficult to get used to this procedure. They will want to know how they are doing in the course. Laura may need to give them some general feedback on their student folders each week or so. One way to handle the final assessment is to assign grades on the basis of the best pages each student has written during each marking period. Students select three to ten of their best pages from their folder of completed work, clip them together, and put them in a separate folder they call their *portfolio*. The number of pages on which to base the assessment should depend on the students' age and skill level. Laura may also decide to insist on a certain number of pages as the minimum amount of writing she expects in the folder in order to assure that the students have enough pages to select from for their portfolio presented at the end of the marking period.

---

[7]Elizabeth F. Haynes, "Using Research in Preparing to Teach Writing," *English Journal*, 67, no.1 (1978), 87. See also Diederich, *Measuring Growth*, 22.

One advantage of this method of scoring papers is that it mirrors the way published writers are evaluated in the world outside of school. The merit of a writer is not determined by the average of one's total output, but by the best work one chooses to share with a wider public. Also, by avoiding defending a grade until the end of a marking period, Laura reduces the number of situations like the one presented here; and she can also show weaker students what she expects by asking them to look at the portfolios of their more accomplished peers to get an idea of what they should be doing.

The best thing about evaluating written work this way, however, is that when Laura has a conference with a student, she can talk about what a draft needs without also defending the grade she assigned it. She can concentrate on suggestions for improvement at the very time when the student is most receptive to instruction: right after having generated a first draft but before having exerted a great deal of effort to complete and edit a final version. In other words, Laura catches the students while they are teachable.

CHAPTER 2

UNDER SIEGE

SITUATION

"I need to go to the water fountain," Ernie announces. Gary shakes his head, "No."
"How come she got to go?" Ernie asks, ever alert to the injustice of Mr. Gustavson's decisions.

It is useful to see this vignette in the sequence in which one of the authors observed it while the audiotape rolled.

8:07   The teacher, Gary, enters the room.

8:09   The first two students walk in and sit down, as Gary goes through his attaché case and pulls out his grade book.

8:10   The bell rings, signaling the start of class. Four more students arrive; one sighs loudly as he swings himself into his seat. Terry, a quiet boy, settles into the front seat, pulls out his grammar book, and visibly tries hard to be "good." He looks up at the teacher expectantly. Others arrive and exchange glances and a few words.

8:12   Gary moves to start the class, although only half of the students have arrived. He doesn't smile. "Mr. José Diaz, get in your seat," he barks out to one of the three students standing by their desks talking. Two of them sit down rapidly.
        Gary writes on board "OS" and says, "Out of seat," and puts under it "JD," mumbling "José Diaz."

"What the . . . ?" grumbles José, watching his initials scratched onto the board.

Gary grimly writes "SOT," "speaking out of turn," and again the initials "JD."

8:14   Ernie shrugs at his friend José. "Jeez! Hey, Mr. Gustavson, why you do this?"

Gary, who is busy recording the latecomers in his grade book, glances up at Ernie. "Talking out of turn," he says, and puts his name under "SOT." "Raise your hand first."

Gary turns back to his attendance book as he mumbles, "Good, Regina came in." He smiles at her, his first eye contact with a member of the group. "Patricia?" He looks up, then checks her name. The students are engaging in whispered conversation. Terry loans Patricia a ball-point pen. It is clear that the talking of the other students does not bother Gary as much as Ernie's talking does. Gary seems not to notice the others, whose quiet exchanges do not strike him as confrontational.

8:16   "Can I go to the bathroom?" Maria asks. He nods. She leaves.

"Pick it up, if it's falling," Gary says to José, who reaches out from his desk to hold on to one of the bulletin board posters that has come loose. José ceremoniously gets up, takes a bow, and takes down the poster and lays it on top of a filing cabinet, swaggering back to his seat relishing his moment.

8:17   "I need to go to the water fountain," Ernie announces.

Gary shakes his head, "No."

"How come she got to go?" Ernie asks, ever alert to the injustice of Mr. Gustavson's decisions. He is now standing up and gesturing toward Maria's seat. "Ernie, take your seat." He continues to stand, barely holding in his frustration.

"Ernie, out of seat," Gary says, and puts his initials under "OOS" on the board.

A couple of other boys laugh and say "Oooh," derisively to Ernie.

By now Ernie is fuming, and the whole class is talking. Gary is trying to get the attendance book record straight and to keep the class quiet. His strategy clearly is not working. Ernie, furious, starts to protest.

"Ernie, speaking out of turn," and "SOT" goes up on the board again.

"Hey, why did you write my name down?"

"Because you're out of seat and speaking out of turn. Now, settle down so we can begin. You're holding the class up right now." Gary's tone is even and tightly controlled. He clearly expects his logic to prevail, but his distaste for his job is not disguised. Ernie, his rage barely contained, retorts with a loud and phony cough.

8:20   Ten minutes after the bell, Gary closes the grade book and stands in front of his desk. His change in tone signals the teaching has begun. "Uh, we're going to take another look at grammar, as we've done before. Our immediate goal is to prepare for the language proficiency test, which is Thursday of next week."

"Oh, *now* you tell us," Lana complains.

"I mentioned it to you earlier when I . . ."

"No, you didn't," Jerry interrupts. Other no's echo. "Wow!"

Gary pays no attention to the interruption and goes on, ". . . when I pointed out there were two reasons to study grammar, two ways to study grammar this year. One way is through your writing and your correction sheets, and the second way is through grammar exercises in preparation for the language proficiency test." Gary drones on, despite mumbled protests rising in the class. "Uh, if any of you have the work sheet from yesterday, will you give it to me now . . ." It is clear from this statement he does not really expect them to have their homework completed.

"It's in my locker."

"If you don't have it today, bring it tomorrow, or give it to somebody if you're going on the field trip. Yes?" Gary recognizes a hand.

"Can we bring it to you later?"

"Yes." Questions about the field trip follow. Gary responds with, "See Mrs. Pilson, she knows about it. Now back to the grammar."

Two or three students start to jostle each other, complain, and fuss. "Can I go to my locker for my paper?" Mary asks. Gary ignores her. The class continues to grumble among themselves.

Gary is back at the blackboard. "Speaking out of turn, we've got . . ." and he writes down initials of three students.

Then, without comment, he continues over loud coughs and sighs.

8:25   Sam answers his question correctly and asks enthusiastically, "Hey, do I get points for that?"

"No, you only get negative points for speaking out of turn."

"I wasn't speaking out of turn."

"Right now you are. Quiet, please." Gary is trying hard to be reasonable, but it's clear the entire class is siding with Sam. Derisive laughter spreads as Sam's initials go up. Clearly the game now is to get the initials of a classmate on a board now covered with initials.

8:30   Somehow, twenty minutes into the class session, Gary gets the class onto the right page of the workbook, and they settle down for a few solid minutes of work. The class is quiet; this is school as they have experienced it, and the fun of watching Ernie or José get skewered by Mr. Gustavson ebbs for a spell. As the class works, Ernie shoves the empty desk in front of him into the back of Terry, the quiet and obedient student in the front row. Terry complains loudly, and Ernie asks why Mr. Gustavson doesn't put Terry's name on the board. Gary ignores the question.

8:40   Gary, seated at his desk, calls on students around the room, from the right to the left, asking each in turn to read out answers to each of the workbook questions. The only break in the routine is when Samantha responds correctly, and after Gary compliments her she takes four exaggerated bows to the class. Then Gary asks the class what the signal for a proper noun is and waits for a hand to go up.

"He acts proper," Ernie blurts out.

"Ernie," says Gary as he goes back to the board adding a check for talking out of turn.

"You catch me talking?" Ernie is outraged again.

'You're right."

"You didn't catch nobody else."

"Just the people who were listening to you, Ernie."

"So you say I'm the only one who's talking?"

"No, I'm saying that you were doing it more than other people," Gary says helplessly.

"Hey, I open my mouth and said that stuff (the hand lotion Patricia had spilled on her desk) is fat . . ."

"That's enough."

"And everybody else is singing and stuff." Ernie reminds Mr. Gustavson that, at the time his initials went up on the board, there had been a low level of noise in the entire room. At this point an audible hum comes from at least three other students in sympathy with Ernie's plight.

"I catch you or I don't. You'll have to worry about *you*, Ernie." "Oooh," says Zach, jeering. His name gets a check as well. Several students laugh. The humming continues.

8:45   The students go back to their workbooks and relative quiet reigns for a few minutes.

Noticing a hand, Gary says, "Ernie?"

"How come you . . ."

Gesturing with his head at the initials on the board, Gary replies, "That's one point. Don't let it bother you. Let's get this done and do the job."

Patricia announces loudly, "I'm finished." She is ignored. Gary gives out two pencils to students who don't have them, and he writes "Pencil" on the board and puts down their initials. By this time, several students are talking, but Gary ignores them.

"May I go to the garbage?"

"Yes, you may," and Maria starts to amble slowly up to the wastebasket behind Gary's desk to throw away her Kleenex.

"Come up here, promptly," Gary barks. José laughs loudly at Maria.

"Out of turn, Diaz," and another check goes up beside his name.

"Ernie?"

"Don't put my name down no more."

"Don't talk anymore, Ernie."

"Yes, but he said . . ." Another check goes up by Ernie's name.

8:47   Lou, a large, quiet girl sitting in a back corner, very ceremoniously gets out of her seat and walks slowly up to the wastebasket in clear defiance of Gary's effort to get everyone to ask permission first. She makes eye contact with almost everyone in the room as she elegantly tosses a crumpled paper into the basket. It is clear she has won the group's admiration as no one reports her to Gary, whose head is bent over his teacher's edition of the workbook.

As the group goes on with their work, Zach leans over in his chair and starts to joke with Ernie. Others ask questions about the work. Gary puts Zach's name on the board and adds a seventh check to Ernie's name. "Zach, will you sit back over here, please." Gary points to a desk by the door, away from the other students.

Zach starts up to the wastebasket, "I'm just throwing this away . . ."

"No, now!" Gary shouts.

"It's hot over there, man!"

"New category: not following directions," Gary says as he writes "NFD," but turns back to the class before he puts Zach's name under it.

Ernie laughs loudly, telling Mr. Gustavson to put down Zach's name, and Ernie gets another check by his name.

Zach, still standing, rebels: "Hey, there's bugs over there, Mr. Gustavson. There's bugs." The whole class is laughing, admiring Zach's *chutzpah.*

"Are you going to sit over there or not?"

"There are fuckin' bugs over there."

"Uh, cursing," and Gary writes down another category with Zach's name under it. Zach slowly struts to the seat by the door, elaborately brushing off the desk and seat before he sits down. The game now is for each person to show as much defiance as possible without getting his or her name on the board.

8:50   Gary, clearly very tired of this class, drones on. "Now 'truth' is difficult because it's an abstract noun. It's not something you can point to, OK? The way you can other . . ."

Zach interrupts, "Hey, there's bugs over here, man."

"Just show me one, and I'll give you permission to move."

"I've already killed one in my hand." The class is laughing now, followed by a steady undercurrent of noise. Soon Gary is shouting above the hum of the class.

"Why are you yelling at us?" Patricia shouts.

"Patricia, quiet please. Patricia, you're still in the A range, but you may get lower if you keep talking. Any other questions on the exercise?"

He calls on Ernie, and Ernie identifies a common noun and a proper noun correctly. Ernie smiles and gets up for a tissue, just the way a couple of other students did earlier. Gary hadn't noticed them. Gary puts down Ernie's initials for "out of seat without permission."

Zach shouts again, "There's bugs over there, man."

"Show me one. OK?" He asks Zach, "Will you pick up your book and follow this, please."

"This place is bug infested, man," and the class giggles.

Gary, not smiling, gives up on Zach. He goes back to the workbook and reads aloud to the class. "Patricia, put it away, please." She is still working with a bottle of hand lotion. "Patricia, will you read that page, please." She reads dutifully, if flatly. Several students are talking together and swapping horseplay as she reads. Gary ignores this. "Recognize the uses of a noun," he drones. By this time several students are laughing at something José has said. "José, stop it or face a referral."

"Wow," Ernie is stunned.

Gary reads the next sentence. "'Robert De Niro is a talented actor.' What is the verb there?"

"Robert De Niro," Zach says, as he kneels up on his seat to act the part, snapping his fingers.

"No."

"It's the subject," Terry says loudly.

José yells, "Ain't he speaking out of turn?" clearly attempting to get Terry, who has been trying hard to be studious all morning, into trouble along with him. Terry shakes his head. "If he don't write that down . . ." José is furious. Gary puts down both initials under "SOT," and the whole class laughs. José yells up to Terry, "You were talking out of turn, you fat . . ."

"What you gonna lie for?" Ernie asks, and by this time José and Terry are almost at the point of blows. The class is taking up for José, whom they think is being picked on by Gary. The whole class is talking about José's plight. José shoves the desk in front of him forward, ramming Terry's desk from behind. Terry turns around to yell at him.

8:57   Talking above the general din, Gary goes on with the lesson, feigning an even temper: "Zach, let me review things for you. If you have the verb 'to be,' . . ." Ernie and José both have their hands up, but Gary pays no attention. Maria reminds Mr. Gustavson that they have their hands up. Her name does not go on the board for speaking out of turn. Clearly, Gary has given up catching folks who are talking out of turn.

8:58   José again rams the desk in front of him into Terry's back.

"Hey, he's pushing my chair. Did you see him pushing my chair?" Terry shouts. Gary looks at the desk and turns and erases one of the checks by Terry's name.

José yelps, "Hey, he erased it. Will you erase mine?"

Gary goes back to the lesson, and while he is engaged with the grammar lesson, Maria quietly goes up to the board and erases two checks beside José's name. No one says anything, not even Terry. Clearly, Mr. Gustavson is bigger prey than Terry, and others in the room start to whisper to her to erase their check marks. Zach, from his bug infested chair, starts complaining again about his desk by the door.

Maria opines, "This class is crazy."

9:00   The bell screams, to everyone's relief. Gary goes out the door after the students, never looking back at the initials on the board.

QUESTIONS TO CONSIDER

1. What is happening in this class?
2. What can Gary do to recover from the siege he is under and regain the upper hand?
3. Is this class hopeless?
4. When did Gary first lose control of the class? Is there anything he could have done at that point to improve the situation?
5. How would you set up a system of controls in a class like this one?

PERSPECTIVES

Gary and his students are adversaries, opponents. He and the class seem to care very little about each other as persons. Each side interacts only with the other's role as teacher or student. The break in this relationship probably occurred long before the day recorded above, if there ever was a relationship at all. Both sides are keenly aware of the other's weaknesses and how to exploit them, though the students, in this case, are the decided victors.

Gary is in a difficult situation. These students dislike school and probably feel disenfranchised by the institution. They seem uninterested in academic success in general, and are particularly bored by the basic elements of grammar. To amuse themselves, perhaps, or to make themselves feel they belong here, they become preoccupied with taking control of the class. So far, the room is theirs. But all is not lost.

Reading this case is like reading a list of missed opportunities. Two students arrive a couple of minutes before the first bell. This is a prime time for Gary to exchange a few words, to break out of his role and discover who these students are as people. "Good morning. Did you see the Bulls game last night?" He would do well to start each period standing at his door, greeting by name each student as he or she enters, and sharing even a brief exchange of words: "We missed you yesterday. Are you feeling all right?" "I like your shirt; is it new?" He needs to let them know he actually sees them, recognizes their individuality, and is glad they are there. Instead, he buries himself in his attaché case. His first words of the day are "Mr. José Diaz, get in your seat." The challenge begins.

Further depersonalizing their relationship is Gary's elaborate point system, the administration of which occupies the greatest part of the period. It is a colossal waste of time and energy, given that it does not even achieve its intended effect, order. It seems to create more discord than anything else. In this system there are no rewards for correct answers, good behavior, or completed work. The only way to get attention in Gary's class is to break a rule. The student is then rewarded with his or her initials in print and with points, the object of most contests. A student who is particularly adept at rule breaking can accrue many points and win the admiration of his or her classmates. At the end of the period, perhaps not surprisingly, Gary leaves the room without so much as a glance back at the board. It is of no use to him or his students.

The system fails both because it focuses attention on infractions and because it is inconsistently administered, if not downright fickle. It does not achieve its desired effect and it takes up too much time. The kids think it is a joke, so Gary winds up looking like a buffoon. Like a married couple who argue about who last took out the trash rather than what is really on their minds, Gary and his students use the system to keep each other's humanness safely at a distance. As with any system that does not work, he needs to get rid of it.

Ironically, Gary's priority—order—is the one thing that seems to elude him most. His zealous quest for order has driven him to this system, and he is willing to stop cold his lesson time and time again to dole out points and face the students' complaints of his system's injustice. What does this teach the students about what Gary thinks of the system in relation to the lessons of grammar? Gary is lost. He has an energetic and disgruntled group—a touchy situation, particularly when he is trying to teach a subject of little interest to any of them.

His first order of business ought to be to re-establish himself as a human being. It may be too late for him to do that with this class, but the following year he will do well to, as Carl Rogers asserts, "be himself, not deny himself." He should start to share with the class more of who he is and how he feels. As Rogers claims, a teacher needs to be "a person to his students, not a faceless embodiment of a curricular requirement."[1] As it stands, Gary is faceless to his students. He won't look at them, he never smiles, and even when he is angry he feigns an even temper. He is denying the most important functions a face performs.

Next, he will have to convince his students he recognizes *them* as human beings. He will need to listen when they voice legitimate concerns: Patricia's poignant and valid question, "Why are you yelling at us?"; Ernie's "Why you do this?"; and Maria's perception, "This class is crazy." Even Zach's concern about bugs deserves some attention, even if only a quick acknowledgment in the form of a joke or a genuine question of concern, "What kind of bugs, Zach? I'll report it today." The power of Zach's outburst will be greatly diminished if it does not rankle the teacher.

There are various ways Gary could begin to bring humanity back into the classroom. But first he should signal that a change is coming. He might erase the points from the board. Let them holler or moan or cheer, if they need to. He could surprise them further by positioning himself somewhere they are not used to seeing him, like at a student desk, on top of his own desk, or in the back of the room. He could change his manner—give them a smile, a soothing word, a candid question: "Do you want to do well on this test? I really would like to help you prepare for it, but I can't when the room is so disorderly." Maria and Patricia are sure to have answers. If it seems appropriate, he could tell them how this situation makes him feel: "I get really frustrated when everyone is talking or getting out of their seats. It's so hard to get anything done. How do you feel when the room gets this way?"

He also needs to change out of his combat fatigues, so to speak. He is too ready to do battle. Why should Sam get negative points for asking whether he gets points for his correct answer? He's asking, after all, because he did something right and got nothing for it. Why does Patricia get overlooked when she finishes ahead of everyone? If Zach thinks he sees bugs, why force him to stay there?

Gary needs to show these students he trusts them. Now all he shows is a prevalent distrust. He writes down the initials of pupils who borrow pencils, presumably so they won't keep them. He

---

[1] *Freedom to Learn for the 80s* (New York: Macmillan, 1993), 122.

demands that Zach show him the bugs. The whole point system itself is built on his lack of trust in their ability to behave without his cracking a whip. Gary is working so hard to get control that he can't see he has lost it.

He has a room filled with energy. He should stop trying to curtail it. For example, Zach mentions the bugs just as Gary is starting to talk about nouns. "Bugs" is a noun. Put it on the board. It also can be a proper noun, as in "Bugs Bunny." Put it on the board. *Let* them groan. What other nouns and proper nouns can they think of? Break the chalk into several pieces. Have them fill the left side of the board with proper nouns and the right side with nouns. Some may be foul: so be it. The ultimate goal is that they demonstrate that they know what a noun is. The power of foul words, too, could be greatly diminished if Gary were not to make a fuss. Then ask for verbs. Let the kids fill the right side of the board with verbs. After the verbs, generate a list of adverbs. Add a list of adjectives before the list of nouns. They could then take words from each list and make sentences. Gary could even take these sentences and type them up for the next day. That would be their parts-of-speech quiz. These kids want to get out of their seats and perform, get recognized, see their name and words in print. Let them do it, and they may stop demanding it.

Gary probably should change his lesson plan. For starters, it needs a specific beginning and also some closure; it now has neither. He drifts into it ten minutes after class starts, unbeknownst to most of the kids. Later, the bell sends them all their separate ways at the end of the period, not the end of the lesson. He also needs to tap into their interests. This seems like a competitive group. He could arbitrarily divide the class into two sections and give them team names, such as the Bug Smashers (and make Zach the coach) and the FDs (follow directions). If he insists on using the grammar book, it could be useful here. Better yet, they could use the sentences they wrote. They could do a variation of a game show everyone knows, like *Family Feud*, or one they can name and adapt. In the *Family Feud* variation, one member from each team comes forward. An item is read from the grammar book. The first one who has an answer slams her or his hand on the desk. If the answer is correct, the student gets a—*point!* If the answer is incorrect, the item goes to the other player. If there is still no correct answer, the question then goes to the next players from each team. Now Gary would be giving points for correct answers, instead of for breaking the class rules.

If he is hesitant at first to deal with the energy that competition almost always generates, he can divide the class into small groups or pairs. Each group or pair can be responsible for teaching one section.

If he is serious about changing the way his classroom operates, Gary must start over. It isn't as hard as it sounds, particularly because the kids are probably already eager for him to do it. In so many words, that's what they have been saying all along. They like to talk and voice their opinion. Human beings do. Gary would do well to take a full period, perhaps change the seating so they sit in a circle rather than the customary rows, and propose this problem in need of a solution:

1. We have a grammar test coming up. We have to take it. I'd like you to do well.
2. We are having trouble preparing.
3. What ideas do you have for helping each student get the best grade he or she can?
4. What reward would you like if the class does well?

It will take time. The class may distrust him at first, as they probably should. But if he addresses them by name, listens to them, hears their concerns, reacts to them rather than ignores them, responds to their positive rather than negative words and actions, allows them to devise ways of learning the material, and shows he trusts them, he will begin to earn their trust and respect in return. He and his students will become teammates, rather than opponents.

CHAPTER 3

GETTING THE
INTERPRETATION RIGHT

SITUATION

"So wait. So you're saying we can't see what we want to see in a poem? We have to see what Frost wanted us to see. Is that it?"

Carol begins her unit on poetry by having her middle-level class arrive at a working definition of poetry they "all can live with for the time being." They come up with this: "An expression of an emotion or idea or an observation using carefully chosen words."

At the end of the first period, she tells her class she has a mental image for the unit on poetry. "It's like we're all lying on a hillside together somewhere gazing up at a sky thick with clouds. One of you may see a bear, another may see an Indian chased by a flounder, while I may see the image of Zeus kissing the nape of Hera's neck. Does that mean that one of us is right and the others are wrong? Of course not. It simply means we all will see different things in the clouds. It's much the same with poetry."

At the start of the next meeting, she hands out copies of a Robert Frost poem and reads it aloud twice.

Stopping by Woods on a Snowy Evening

Whose woods these are I think I know.
His house is in the village though;
He will not see me stopping here
To watch his woods fill up with snow.

> My little horse must think it queer
> To stop without a farmhouse near
> Between the woods and frozen lake
> The darkest evening of the year.
>
> He gives his harness bells a shake
> To ask if there is some mistake.
> The only other sound's the sweep
> Of easy wind and downy flake.
>
> The woods are lovely, dark and deep,
> But I have promises to keep,
> And miles to go before I sleep,
> And miles to go before I sleep.[1]

Carol opens the discussion. "Let's start with the obvious. What's going on in this poem? Where is the speaker and what is he doing? Josh?"

Josh replies, "This guy is in a sleigh on a snowy night and he has gone to an area where he's never been before. He sees a house and he thinks he knows who lives there. So, then, he realizes it's getting late and he decides he better start home because it's a long ride."

Carol smiles. This is a start. "All right. Now, let's dig a little deeper, Josh. Look at the last two lines. Why do you think Frost repeated them?"

Josh looks around the room for some support. When it becomes obvious none is forthcoming, he slouches in his desk. "Guess he couldn't think of anything else."

Carol says, "Well, I happen to know Robert Frost was a poet who, as our definition of poetry suggests, was very careful about every word he put into his poems. Gail, why do you think he would repeat the same line twice?"

Gail looks up from the creased note she has been reading, "Um. To make sure we got it?"

Carol moves toward Gail, "Good. I think so, too. What is it, do you think, he wanted us to get?"

Josh's hand shoots up, "Oh! That it's late and he has a long ride before he can sleep."

"Well, what do you think he means by 'sleep'?" Carol now moves toward Josh.

"Sleep. Like put on your pajamas, snore, dream." Basking in the snickers of his classmates, he adds, "He can't do that until he gets home."

---

[1]From *The Poetry of Robert Frost*, edited by Edward Connery Lathem, Copyright 1923, Copyright 1969 by Holt, Rinehart and Winston, Copyright 1951 by Robert Frost. Reprinted by permission of Henry Holt and Company, Inc.

"Well, 'sleep' is a word that can be understood in different ways," Carol offers. "There's the literal meaning, which is the way you're seeing it. But there are also the figurative meanings, and there are many. Cory, what else do you think Frost might have meant by the word 'sleep'?"

Cory sets her head on her fist and thinks. "Relax, maybe?"

Carol moves to the front of the room. "Okay. But I think we're still on the literal level. Um. Sleep, sleep, sleep. Let's put on the board all the words we associate with sleep."

"Bed!" "Sheets!" "Pillows!" "Boredom!"

"Good. More?" Carol is writing fast.

The volley diminishes. "Um. Relaxing." "Dreams." "Nightmares." "Sex."

"Wait a minute," Carol turns to them. "Does anyone know what the French call 'sleep'? No? *Petite morte*. Who knows what that means?"

Cory answers without raising her hand. "Little death."

"Yes. So let's think a minute about what this poem might be saying if Frost were using the word 'sleep' in a figurative sense, to mean death. Yes, Josh?"

"Was Frost French?"

"He was American."

"Well, I don't think he meant death at all, then." Josh says. "I think he meant he had a long ride before he could sleep, snore, dream. I identify with the poem on that level. I like it that way."

Carol says, "That's good, Josh. I'm glad. But suppose we also explore what *Frost* might have had in mind?"

"Why? He's dead, isn't he? We'll never know anyway."

Gail closes her history book, having finished the worksheet due next period. "Besides, shouldn't we all look at it however we want? Like the clouds?" Gail nails Carol to her own metaphor.

"Perhaps the clouds was a poor analogy. Clouds are natural formations, they just happen. Poetry is the exact opposite, really. Art has a human hand that shapes it into a very specific form. Perhaps I led you astray with that analogy."

Josh is testy now. "So wait. So you're saying we *can't* see what we want to see in a poem? We have to see what Frost wanted us to see. Is that it?"

"No," Carol says, "of course not."

"Then what are you saying?" Gail asks.

Carol looks anxiously at her watch, hoping the bell will end her quandary.

QUESTIONS TO CONSIDER

1. What should Carol do next?

2. How can she help the students appreciate the resonances in this poem without their rebelling and charging her with obscure symbol hunting or asking why Frost didn't just say what he meant?

3. What metaphor might she have used instead of the cloud metaphor to have avoided the hole she dug for herself?

4. How could Carol have helped the students connect this poem with their own experience?

5. How would you role play a different dialogue between Carol and the class?

PERSPECTIVES

Carol is wise to admit that her cloud metaphor doesn't work. Interpreting a poem is not like taking a Rorschach test, where the goal is only to find out what is in the reader's mind. Nor is it like uncracking a code, where the goal is to arrive at one clear, unambiguous message. The best poems condense a general meaning into a literal image; they use figurative language to economically present more than one possibility.

James Moffett's metaphor might be more apt for Carol's students. Consider a poem as music, where literal meaning compares "to melody, in which one note at a time is struck sequentially, and figurative meaning to chords, in which several related notes are struck simultaneously."[2] In a chord, several things are referred to at once. When a writer needs to put something in clear, precise, referential language, such as the directions for a fire drill or a list of antidotes on a bottle of poisonous substance, literal language is necessary. However, when one's goal is to express several possible meanings at once, deliberately ambiguous language is appropriate to strike a chord in the reader.

True, one cannot read a poem well if the literal meaning is violated; one has to take account of what the words say on the surface level. At the same time, however, a reader needs to be sensitive to the resonance of multiple meanings that lie in the "chords" of poetic language. Most students acquire such sensitivity only slowly

---

[2]James Moffett, *Detecting Growth in Language* (Portsmouth, N.H.: Boynton/Cook, 1992), 27.

over time. Just as a chord is a "complex of potential melodies,"[3] so figurative language is economical and embodies several possible meanings.

Carol's students are probably new to this kind of reading. How can she introduce them to it without alienating them from a process that probably feels arcane? One way might be for her to think about her students' reading process in terms of transactional theory.[4] Carol's goal appears to be based on two conflicting assumptions: (1) that a text can be interpreted differently by each reader, and (2) that the text is a fixed thing, something that the author determines should leave the same imprint on all its readers: the commonly accepted interpretation. If she saw the reading process instead as an exchange—a transaction— where the reader and text shape each other, she might be more will-ing to let the students negotiate their own meaning.

Dillard's metaphor for the reading process might help Carol think about her problem. Dillard sees the relationship between the reader and the text as that of a river and its banks. Each affects the other.[5] Rosenblatt argues that a poem is what happens in a reader's mind when its words begin to function symbolically, resonating feel-ings, images, and concepts. Rosenblatt sees

> the reading act as an event involving a particular individual and a particular text, happening at a particular time, under particular cir-cumstances, in a particular social and cultural setting, and as part of the ongoing life of the individual and the group.[6]

The meaning of Frost's poem does not enter the minds of the students the same way it comes to Carol. What each reader brings to a poem shapes its meaning for them.

Viewing the reading process this way does not mean Carol must abdicate her attempt to help students engage in the text at a deeper level; she merely needs to give them longer to negotiate its meaning on their own.

The first thing Carol will do if she accepts Rosenblatt's view is to ask the class at the start of the next period simply to write briefly and

---

[3]Moffett, *Detecting Growth*, 27.

[4]Louise Rosenblatt, "The Literary Transaction: Evocation and Response," in Kathleen Holland, Rachael Hungerford, and Shirley Ernst, *Journeying* (Portsmouth, N.H.: Heinemann, 1993), argues that reading is a transaction, a mutually shaping exchange between a reader and a text. See also her classic, *Literature as Exploration* (New York: Modern Language Association of America, 1983, originally published in 1938).

[5]Annie Dillard, *Living by Fiction* (New York: Harper & Row, 1982),15.

[6]Louise Rosenblatt, "Viewpoints: Transaction versus Interaction—A Terminological Rescue Operation," *Research in the Teaching of English* 29 (1985), 96–107.

quickly in response to Frost's poem. Did they like it? What picture or image struck them the most? What feeling or mood does the poem evoke? Do they sense any tension in this poem, and, if so, where? These questions are meant to evoke an aesthetic response, one that focuses on the qualitative effect of the poem on each reader. Then Carol will have the students meet in small groups and read to each other what they have written. She will ask each group to appoint a reporter to write a summary of the common elements and the differences in their responses. After the groups meet, each reporter reads his or her summary for the class as the teacher notes in two lists on the chalkboard similar responses and different ones. At that time she reads her own responses to the questions she has asked the students. This is her first attempt to nudge them toward a more symbolic reading of the text.

Small Group Text Rendering

A text-rendering session might help students who either refuse to struggle to interpret a text or who are passive and silenced in the face of a teacher's interpretation.[7] To set up a text-rendering session, Carol divides the class into small groups of three or four and shows them a chart with the following directions on it:

1. Read the poem aloud, each person reading a part.

2. Do not talk about the poem. Instead, have a conversation with each other using only the words of the poem. The phrases or words can be in any order. Experiment by varying your tone of voice, gestures, and emphasis.

3. Do a couple of different readings of all or part of the poem; compose and recompose it as a group. (In jazz terms, you are going to be "jamming" on the poem.)

4. Stop and write briefly and quickly whatever you are thinking at this point about the poem. Write anything you want to say about the poem.

5. Read your writings to each other.

6. Choose a part or all of your adaptation of the poem to present as a group performance of the poem, and rehearse it. The phrases may be in any order that pleases you.

7. As a group, present your adaptation of the poem for the whole class.

---

[7]This approach has been used effectively by other teachers, such as Susan Lytle, Elaine Avadon, and Peter Elbow.

After each of the groups has presented its rendering, Carol can ask everyone to write what he or she thinks Frost was saying in this poem. How does the speaker in the poem feel about the woods? At this point she is aiming for an *efferent* response, to use Rosenblatt's term. Carol is moving away from the fuller personal response to a narrower focus on what the poet actually wrote. See Chapter 9, "The Book They Have Read Before" for more on Rosenblatt's distinctions. Although only a few of the students may have reached the interpretation Carol would prefer, all of them will have had an experience with this poem they can internalize, and the rebels against symbol-hunting will be kept at bay.

At this point, Carol can lecture on the common interpretation of this poem as implying the lure of death and read Keats's "Ode to a Nightingale" in this same context. As she asks the students to do their first freewrite on Keats's poem in preparation for another text rendering, she asks them why they think she is linking the two poems together. She will have had an opportunity to introduce the more common interpretation of the Frost poem without insisting that the students accept it. Since her voice is always going to be the one with the greatest authority in the classroom, she need not worry if some of the students prefer their own interpretations at this age. They may go away puzzling over her strange reading of the poem, which could be the beginning of a new insight.

CHAPTER 4

THE TOUGH GRADER

SITUATION

"Well, what is an A paper then? Tell me, and I'll do one for you."

Steve's first semester as an English teacher is about to end. He was very lucky that the junior honors teacher had to take a maternity leave that fall because this meant he was assigned to her class at the beginning of the term. Thus, unlike most first-year teachers, he has been blessed with an excellent group of students, and he has thoroughly enjoyed his interactions with them. He feels proud he is establishing a reputation for himself in a department and school recognized for its high academic standards. He smiles to recall the conversation he accidentally overheard between two of his students:

"I have heard Mr. Johnson looks up every footnote to be sure you have the right page!"

"He does; he's also read every book or journal you quote from. You can't be too careful."

Steve knows there is no way he can be that attentive to detail or that omniscient, but he is very happy he has that reputation. These are able kids, all of them aimed toward some of the nation's best colleges and universities, and they deserve the most bracing challenges he can throw at them.

His students have turned in their term papers, projects they have been working on since the first week of the semester. It is meant to be the culmination of the work they have studied that semester, including methods of research, research paper format, organized writing, and an in-depth look at an aspect of Shakespeare's work. The project counts for two thirds of their semester grade.

He is pleased with most of the papers. The work is thorough, carefully presented, and well-informed. He gave out Bs and B-plusses to over half of his students. There are quite a few Cs but just one A. That goes to Andrew Banks, who produced a music video to accompany his paper. Steve has conducted private conferences with each student, discussing the paper and explaining the grade. All conferences went well.

Except one. His most ambitious student, Marta, sat stone silent at the conference, her lips pursed, her eyes averted, her foot bobbing to a blur. When Steve asked if she had any questions or comments, Marta shook her head and left.

But today after school Marta arrives at Steve's door, armed. From her left hip pocket, she produces a note from her parents containing a detailed explanation of why they would give her paper an A. From her right hip pocket she pulls out a letter from her Uncle George, a college professor, who declares that Marta's paper rivals those of most of his pre-med students. On her own behalf, she has prepared a speech, the gist of which is that this is the best paper she has ever written. Everyone thinks so except you, so what's your problem?

"I agree," Steve replies. He sits behind his desk and motions for Marta to take a seat opposite. Marta does not move. "That is a very fine paper indeed. And that's why I gave it a B-plus, the second highest grade I gave out on this project, by the way."

"So, wait. Should I have done a video?"

"No, no, no. That's not what this is about."

"Well, what is an A paper then? Tell me, and I'll do one for you."

Steve laughs, "Listen, Marta . . ."

Marta shakes her head and her eyes go narrow. "Should I have written more?"

"Depends on what it is more of."

"OK. More isn't it. How about fewer references? Or more references?"

"Marta, your use of references was excellent . . ."

"OK. Maybe we're narrowing it down. Should it have been longer? Shorter? Wider?"

"Marta, look. I know it seems like a simple question to you, like I could offer you a blueprint or a recipe. But I don't have those things. I have a—a what? a notion, a model in my mind, I guess, against which I compare my students' papers. But I can't put it into the precise terms you are asking for. I just can't. Believe me, I have tried."

The next day, Steve receives a call from Marta's father. When Steve runs that same speech past him, the father blares back from the receiver, "Then how in heaven's name did you find your way to the teacher's desk in an honors classroom? You'll not hear the end of this, young man!"

QUESTIONS TO CONSIDER

1. How is Steve going to maintain his reputation as a strong teacher with high standards for honors students and still deal with Marta and her father?

2. Should Steve back down on the grade? What would be the short- and long-term consequences of doing this?

3. What is the next thing he should do? Should he arrange for a conference with both Marta and her father to go over the paper together?

4. How can he make the model of an A paper in his mind any clearer to Marta and his other students, or can he?

5. Should he try to get support from the department chair or other teachers?

6. What other options does he have?

PERSPECTIVES

Steve has worked hard to prove himself worthy of teaching an honors class, and he has a right to be proud of the good work his students have produced. His only problems are his grading criteria and his difficulty in explaining them to Marta and her father. The criteria for evaluating any paper, and especially a paper that weighs so heavily in a semester grade, should not be a mystery to the students.

As we suggest in Chapter 1, "Defending a Grade," having a set of sample student papers that merit an A grade, would be useful, but as a new teacher with his first honors class, he will have to ask one of his colleagues for such a set of sample papers. With these, he could explicitly compare Marta's paper with one written by an anonymous student in another class and thereby avoid the direct comparison of two students who know each other.

Steve would do well to find out how his grades compare to the distribution of grades in other honors classes in his department. This information is usually available from the central office, if not from other members of the department. Any new teacher should try to have his own grade distribution at least roughly resemble that of other classes like his. It is quite possible Steve is excessively tough in giving out only a single A, even if he plans to give out more as the final semester grade. If Steve's distribution is out of line with the rest of the department, then Marta and her father have a valid point (but not a *conclusive* point).

He can also find out if there is an appeals procedure within the department for a student who feels he or she has been treated unfairly. If there is no established procedure, Steve can tell Marta he will ask two of his colleagues to read Marta's paper and grade it as they normally would a paper in an honors class. If they both agree it merits an A, then Steve will change the grade.

Another option is to leave the grade on this paper as a B-plus and make it very clear to Marta that his policy is to give almost no As on papers, but that she has a very good chance of making an A in the course if her daily participation or whatever else goes into the grade remains at the level it is now. That way Steve can save face by not simply backing down under pressure (never a good precedent to set), and yet he can hope to disarm Marta. Then, before he settles on final grades for the course, he will need to be sure his grade distribution is in line with that of other honors courses.

A fifth option is to do a "read around." This is not something Steve should do as a response to Marta's complaint, but rather a procedure that will help all of his students gain a perspective on how their own work looks in comparison with the papers of other students. In a read around, every student paper is read by every other student. It is important that no one feels that he or she has been judged by his or her peers as a bad writer. Thus, a read around works best if students do not know each other's topics and if the papers can be produced on computers or typewriters. Ideally, the students should read all the papers blind, without knowing who wrote which paper, but this is not always possible. Here are the steps Steve could follow:

1. Steve assigns the same topic to the entire class, and students are not to collaborate in prewriting activities. Instead, they engage in strategies such as brainstorming, webbing, or sketching on their own. Then they write individually and proofread their own papers.

2. Steve collects the papers, removes the cover sheets and photocopies the first page of each with the author's name blocked, so the papers can be read anonymously. He then randomly orders the papers and assigns each a number.

3. He gives the students a list of no more than five criteria to use to evaluate the papers. These could refer to such qualities as focus, supporting details, organization, word choice, and mechanics. This would be a good time to review and illustrate with examples each of these features.

4. The students meet in groups of four, and Steve gives each group four randomly selected papers. If any students get their own paper, they read it just as they would any other paper and do not let anyone know whose it is.

5. Each group reads all four papers and then discusses them to decide together which is the best of the four, using the criteria for evaluation that have been presented. The process of reaching consensus provides a good learning opportunity as they focus on what makes a paper good. They list the best paper's assigned number on a separate piece of paper. A more complicated, but more informative, procedure is to rank all of the papers, assigning four points for the best, three for the second best, and so on.

6. When the four papers have been discussed, the group passes them on to another group, and then reads another packet of papers passed to them.

7. When all of the groups have read all of the papers, a spokesperson for each group reads off their list of winners, and those numbers are tallied on the board beside the numbers Steve assigned to each paper.

8. The paper with the most points wins. If the winning writer chooses, he or she may read his paper to the class. The class can then tell that writer why they selected his or her paper. Those whose papers did not get the highest score will not be identified in any way, but all the students will have the advantage of seeing the range of papers in the class. They will also have a better sense of what qualities go into a good paper.

The advantage of this procedure is that all students have an opportunity to develop a general idea as to how their own paper ranks with all the other papers, and yet they can see for themselves the qualities of the paper that merits the top grade in the class.

CHAPTER 5

THE DISAFFECTED TEACHER

SITUATION

Once, in frustration, she looked at her students and even wondered aloud, "Why do you bother to come here every day? I don't understand you. I don't understand anything about you."

Erin sits in the rear of her darkened classroom watching her senior low-level students watching *Glory*.[1] A girl rises from her seat and throws several wads of paper across the room; they hit a boy in the head, a boy at whom that girl frequently aims both real and verbal missiles. Several other kids return the volley. Erin keeps her eyes on the screen. By now she has stopped being irritated by their lack of attention, or appalled by the way they cheer and laugh at the violence, or how they scoff at any displays of emotion, and chatter during the talky parts. She is just grateful for the 122 minutes of film she can spread over the next four days, four days she can spend in the back of her darkened room, rather than in front.

Erin graduated from college *cum laude*. She was captain of a highly successful debate team, made a name for herself on campus for her portrayal of Hedda Gabler, and frequently contributed to *Leaves of Grass*, the annual literary magazine. She even had one of her own short stories published in *Ploughshares* before she was twenty-one. She loves literature, both classical and contemporary. She has always associated with people with whom she could spend hours

---

[1] Columbia Tristar Home Video, VHS 70283 (Burbank, Cal.: Sony Pictures Entertainment, 1990).

discussing everything from Strindberg to Toni Morrison, Woody Allen to Kurasawa.

She landed a student teaching position at Edison High, which was nationally known for sending ninety-two percent of its graduating seniors to college. Her master teacher, Helen Gardner, then in her twentieth year as an English teacher, taught two senior honors and two Advanced Placement courses. Erin was thrilled. She got to teach Chekhov, Faulkner, Ibsen, and Kafka. She even threw in a little Alice Walker and John Updike. Helen was so excited by her students' reaction to these authors that she promised to incorporate them into future classes and use the materials Erin had developed.

That class energized Erin. She loved going to work each morning, knowing the kids would commit themselves wholeheartedly into every challenge she threw into their path. She told her husband, Rob, she couldn't believe she would one day be paid for doing what she loves to do—reading, talking, and sharing ideas. She applied for a job at that school, but there were no openings. However, within four weeks of receiving her master's, she was offered a job at a school in the town where she and Rob lived and Rob worked. She was ready, she thought, for any challenge.

She was assigned three one-level classes in which no student was reading above the fourth-grade level, and two middle-level classes which, because of cutbacks in spending, were bloated to thirty and thirty-two students.

On the first day, she tried to talk to the students, as she had with Helen's classes, about all the exciting things they would encounter in this course.

"Like what?" a hoarse voice demanded.

She told them about the wonderful books, all the writing, and her favorite part, the discussions. Her enthusiasm was met with silence, rolled eyes, and some of the most elaborate and vociferous yawns she had ever heard.

"OK," Rob told her that night. "So they're not Edison kids. So what? Don't try to make them something they're not."

At the moment, his words comforted her, but as the kids grew more and more antagonistic, challenging her verbally and, at times, physically, she grew increasingly resentful that they were not, in fact, Edison kids and, she had to admit, she couldn't understand why they didn't want to be. "Let me mold you," she wanted to say. "Trust me. Allow me. You have no idea what I can do for you!"

But no matter how hard she tried, how many different topics she brought in or how many techniques she experimented with, she couldn't engage them in discussions of anything beyond violence or the trashy gossip or vulgar jokes about other students that happened to be going around. They rarely produced any homework and clearly were not doing the assigned readings. Once, in frustration, she looked at her students and even wondered aloud, "Why do you even bother to come here every day? I don't understand you. I don't understand anything about you."

"'Cause we *got* to come," was the response. "'Sides, this is where everybody is at."

She knew nothing about them, it was true, and that's what hurt. They had not been where she had been, were not headed for what she had in mind for them or for herself. By second semester, she was talking to Rob about moving or applying to different districts, even looking into a different line of work. She knew it wasn't healthy to wake up every morning and dread what she had to do for the next seven hours.

Then one day everything began to change. It was the day after a sympathetic colleague had handed her a workbook filled with very short stories to read and simple questions to answer about them. She duplicated three sheets and handed them out the next day. She was surprised by how willingly the kids accepted the sheets, and how quietly they worked on them. She had been afraid they would find the sheets silly, repetitious, boring, which they were. But the kids seemed to crave them. They wanted more. The next day she reproduced a stack of eight different sheets. They worked independently and turned them in when they were done. She graded them and handed them back in silence. Life had suddenly become easier. The fewer interactions with them she had, the more tolerable the day. She was getting through. This was not the sort of teacher she wanted to be, not the sort of teacher she dreamed of being. But the kids really did *like* the sheets and maybe they were getting something out of them, something she couldn't understand. Was that so bad? Was she really so awful?

So she sits now in her darkened room, watching them watch *Glory*, thinking maybe she should have them write a reaction piece when the film is over on Thursday, but then she would have to face the fact that no matter what kind of spin she put on it, she would only get five papers at the most and they would be hastily prepared, perfunctory pieces she'd resent. So while one of the boys rewinds the tape to replay their favorite battle scenes, she leafs through the workbook for three sheets that will keep them busy and quiet after the film is over.

QUESTIONS TO CONSIDER

1. How did Erin get to this point?
2. How can she create the classroom she envisions? Or *can* she, in her present situation?
3. How do you feel about the way she has adapted to her students?

PERSPECTIVES

Erin has a classic case of "burn-out." She's not living her ideals and is willing to buy her own peace with the coin of a curriculum she does not value. Her own achievements have led her to expect a better lot. It's as if she were all set to teach, and the wrong students came through the door. She longs for teenagers who are worthy of her considerable gifts as a literary specialist. The worksheets she has chosen to fill her students' days will keep them forever at bay, and she will not have to confront her own frustrations at the lives the students are leading and the limits of their vision. Moreover, the students' expectations are fulfilled. This is school as usual—routine, predictable, and dull.

Erin has at least five choices. For one, she can continue with the worksheets and films. This has the advantage of keeping the students from confronting her, giving both her and the students the sense that they are at least *doing* something. The cost is great. First, there is the stultification of student intellectual growth. Just because they are reading at fourth-grade level does not necessarily mean their minds are at that level. Just because they don't identify with her enthusiasm for the literature she loves does not mean they have no interests. Erin doesn't know what these students are capable of because she hasn't yet connected with them at a deep enough level for their potential to show. If she continues with the worksheets, she will never know.

There is a danger to herself as well. If Erin continues to teach in a way she knows is not appropriate or challenging, something will happen to her. She will wake up to find her life as savorless and dull as the assignments she has been giving the students. There is nothing more psychologically damaging than to keep on doing something you do not believe in.

Second, she can ignore Rob's advice and push to make the kids into Edison students, continually laying on them the challenging literature the Edison classes had found so interesting. This might work if she kept the reading assignments short, nudged them slowly, and did not give up during the first few weeks when the discussion bombed. However, this strategy does not address the fact that the students cannot read the literature Erin would choose, and this fact alone will increase their hostility toward her.

She can also go to a counselor herself and talk long and hard to try to understand why the low level of the students is so demoralizing to her. After all, the world is full of very able teachers who spend their entire professional lives working with learning disabled or even severely retarded individuals and who do not feel their professional talents are wasted. Somewhere in Erin's past she got the message that good teachers taught smart kids. The truth is, of course, that what makes a teacher good is not who walks through the classroom door but what the teacher does after they get there. Students learn because of the quality of interaction with the teacher and the challenges of the curriculum. So part of the problem is inside Erin herself, and the first thing she needs to address is her attitude toward the class. Without some soul searching, Erin is unlikely to change her attitude toward her one-level classes, and without that, no other changes will make much difference. In this soul searching, she will need to face the question of whether or not this is the career for her.

As well, she can try to get to know the students better, so that she can select literature and writing topics that fit their interests. Donald Graves[2] suggests teachers make a list from memory of all of their students and then go through the list and jot down as many things as they can about each student's interests, favorite activities, friends, topics of conversation, etc. What all teachers find out when they do this is that they know a great deal about some students and very little about others. There are usually some whose names do not even come to mind. The teachers' next task is deliberately to try to learn as much as possible about the students with blanks after their names. The very process of finding out will help them connect with these students. Teachers then repeat this exercise the next week to find out how much better they are doing.

Finally, Erin can change her curriculum, finding literature that will connect in some way with both the reading level and the interests of the class. (This suggestion may have to wait until another term.) She would do well to have students work more often in pairs, writing responses to a set of personal questions, such as: Did you like

---

[2]Donald Graves, *Writing: Teachers and Children at Work.* (Portsmouth, N.H.: Heinemann, 1983), 22–28.

this story or this book? Would you recommend it to a friend? Which part was the most interesting? Would you have ended it differently?

After each pair of students has answered the set of questions, the groups share their responses. The large-class discussion is energized by this prior exchange in pairs. If the students continue to have values at variance with Erin's, at least they have had an opportunity to hear how their peers feel. (See Chapter 13, "Diversity of Heritage," page 120, and Chapter 16, "Untracking," page 138, for references to lists of ethnic or adolescent literature that may appeal to Erin's students.)

CHAPTER 6

THE LESSON THAT FLOPS

SITUATION

The kids stare. One of them whispers, "What's he doing?" Carl swallows the lump in his throat. Pauses. Stares back at them. "Who can tell me what chanting is?" Silence.

Carl has a great idea. The kids will love this. They have been reading Golding's *Lord of the Flies* and making it quite clear that they find the descriptions too long and, as one student has said, "too descriptive." They want action.

Today Carl has decided he wants to get into a discussion about the primitive effect chanting can have on a group of people. They will talk about its power to galvanize, unify, even mesmerize a group. He comes to work with a tape of jungle sounds he has found at the library. He will have it on as the class arrives and play it through the period. He scrawls across his blackboard the words, "Kill the beast, cut his throat, spill his blood." He will have them begin by chanting the phrase, softly at first, then louder and louder. He wonders what he will do if it gets *too* loud. He runs to the next room and warns Bill, his neighbor, that it could get a bit wild in a few minutes. Bill smiles, "I'll look forward to it."

As Carl envisions the class chanting, the idea begins to build in his mind. A quick look at the clock tells him he still has three minutes before the bell, just enough time to arrange the tablet arm chairs in a circle. If only he could find a way to create the illusion of a fire in the middle.

The kids arrive. The first girls stand in the doorway and roll their eyes. "So, like, where are we s'posed to sit?"

Next, a group of four boys arrive. "Aw man, no! What is this supposed to be?"

Undaunted, Carl turns up the volume on the tape and takes attendance. Then he caps his pen and stares at them a moment. Quietly, nearly imperceptibly at first, he begins to chant. "Kill the beast, cut his throat, spill his blood!" He pounds out a rhythm on his podium. "Come on. Everybody. Kill the beast . . ."

The kids stare. One of them whispers, "What's he doing?" Carl swallows the lump in his throat. Pauses. Stares back at them. "Who can tell me what chanting is?" Silence. "What is chanting?" Silence. Shuffling in the seats. "Ever hear the word?"

Ann-Marie raises her hand slowly, almost unintentionally. "Like, words, that—I mean, saying words—uh. Forget it."

"No," Carl says, leaning toward Ann-Marie expectantly. "Say what you were going to say."

"Never mind," Ann-Marie says.

Silence.

Carl walks behind the circle. Most of the kids stare at their legs, like the spokes of the big wheel in the room. "What is it like—um. Have any of you ever been somewhere where a lot of people have been chanting? Anyone?"

They slouch. A few open other homework.

"Like a football game, maybe?" Carl says. "Nobody?" He is talking too loudly now and he knows it, probably smiling too broadly too. Sweat, like an insect, crawls down his spine. He searches his mind for an example to get them started, but his mind is blank. After a few moments—he really has no idea how long—he becomes aware he is staring at them as blankly as they are staring at him. "What do—Let me rephrase that. What effect does the boys' chanting have on them?"

"What is he talking about?" someone mumbles.

"Do you think maybe it would make them feel unified? Alexander?"

"Yeah, I guess."

"Yes, I do too, Alexander. Very good. It probably would make them feel unified. What else?"

Becky lets out a howling yawn and everyone laughs.

"That sounded like an animal," Carl says. "I mean no offense, but didn't it?" Carl laughs, but the laughter in the room stops. "Do you think it's possible that, I don't know, something awakens in us, some animal part of us, awakens when we chant? Is it possible there is a beast in us? Kim?"

"Yeah, I guess."

Silence.

Now Carl himself is wondering what he is talking about. He stares at the center of the circle where the fire might have been. If only there had been a fire.

QUESTIONS TO CONSIDER

1. Why isn't Carl's drama working?

2. Why are the students so reluctant to participate?

3. Where is the source of the problem—his idea for the lesson or the way he is conducting it?

4. Is there any way he can get the students to "buy in" at this point in the lesson?

PERSPECTIVES

The most brilliant teaching idea in the world is only as good as its execution. Carl has underestimated his class's commitment to expected routines. They aren't buying for a minute his imaginary world, and until they accept the "what if" world he is struggling to set up, his chanting will not build to the emotional climax he envisions.

It's too late in this lesson to continue with his plan. Carl is not going to be able to ignite that metaphorical fire, so it's time to give that up. He has put a spotlight on the kids; they are on stage before they have had time to don their roles, and their defenses are up to hide their embarrassment. He needs to let them shrink back into the wings while he helps build their belief.

Here are ways Carl might have begun this lesson more fruitfully. He might have turned on the jungle music and read aloud to set a mood; he might then lead a guided imagery and have the students write to stimulate their own imaginations; or he might have them all work in triads simultaneously and without an audience to create a *tableau vivant*, a picture created in gesture and body position but without dialogue, that captures the feelings of the lost boys on Golding's island.

Carl's simplest tack is to read aloud from the novel over the recorded sounds of the jungle. Since the descriptive parts are not his students' favorites, he should skip to the next section of the book that shows action or presents dialogue. After he reads for a while, he might ask volunteers to assume roles in a dialogue he has started to read. Each participant can read not only what the character says, but also the "he said" tags. Carl can explain that this is in the tradition of Readers' Theater.

Another way to go, a bit riskier given the coolness the class exhibited in response to his earlier sortie, is to ask the students to close their eyes and imagine they are one of the boys on Golding's island. They may choose whichever character they wish. Slowly Carl can feed in such prompts as: Where are you seated? What time of day is it? Listen to the jungle sounds. What animals do you think are making these noises? How are you dressed? What mood are you in? What do you most fear as you sit here in this place? Now imagine a fire in the center of this room. Keep your eyes closed, but move closer to the fire in your mind. Feel the warmth on your skin. Watch the tongues of flame blaze up. Think about how your life is different here on this island from your life back home. Now the fire is dying down. Go to the place where you usually spend the night, and, in your mind, lie down to rest. What are you thinking as you drift off to sleep? Open your eyes. Get out a piece of paper and write down what you have been thinking and feeling as you drift off to sleep. (See Chapter 1, "Defending a Grade," for more suggestions on guided imagery.)

Carl needs to assure the students that what they write is private; they may choose not to share it. He should ask them to let the sounds of the jungle wash over them as they write. How would they feel if they were part of the group stranded in that place, not knowing if they would ever be rescued?

After everyone has had time to write, he might have them meet in triads to talk about the experience. If any choose to read what they have written, they may do so. Again, the goal is to not put anyone in the limelight until he or she is ready.

A third option might follow the other two on another day. This time, Carl asks the class to again assume the roles of one of the characters in *Lord of the Flies* and meet together in triads to pantomime building a fire. Each group of three may go to any corner or place in the room they like, and no one is to watch any other group. At this point, Carl can cruise from group to group, making suggestions only if asked. He should expect some off-task nonsense, as it will take a while for the group to feel comfortable enough to be serious. He can remind them that the hardest task for actors is to actually believe in their roles, and he should let them know that when they giggle and fall out of role they make it very hard for the others in their group. As they work together to build their fires, he can remind them to use their bodies to convey their feelings, first, toward the fire they are building, and then, toward each other, and finally, toward their predicament.

Then Carl can stop them and have them talk as a class about the moods these groups of boys might have as they worked together on their fires. How could they show with their postures and their facial expressions that this fire was not just any fire, but rather a signal in the night to a passing ship that they are abandoned and alone? How would they feel if this fire were their only hope of being rescued? Then Carl could send them back to their groups and give them the task of using their three bodies to symbolize their feelings, and then freezing their bodies into a group picture that would project those feelings. In other words, they would without words project the mood of their scene as if it were a framed picture by an artist. They would simply assume a pose they decide best projects their feelings, but they would not act out a scene nor do any speaking. They would become a *tableau vivant*, a "living" picture. Only at this point would Carl ask for volunteers to take the spotlight. When it looked as if most of the groups were ready, he would stop and ask for one group to volunteer to assume their poses so that all the other groups could look at them and discuss the mood they are projecting.

After all of these non-threatening activities, Carl's students *still may not be ready* for the chanting. Their resistance may be rooted in their having to assume the role, not of admirable primitives, but of a mob gone mad. The shock of recognition that comes to most readers of *Lord of the Flies* is that if this depravity could emerge in these middle-class schoolboys, "there, but for the grace of God, go I." Perhaps Carl's teenagers are not ready to accept such a traumatic possibility about themselves, and shoving them into the role of chanting cannibals is making them villains in their own eyes. It is as if he started out a rehearsal of Dubois' *The Seven Last Words of Christ* with the sharp shouts of the crowd mocking Jesus before Pilate, "He is death guilty; He is death guilty; Take Him, Take Him, Let us crucify Him!" Most choruses have to warm up to that part of the oratorio. Even if the students can identify with the mob psychology of Golding's gang of primitives, they may not want to play up that part of themselves in a performance.

CHAPTER 7

THE PAPER LOAD

SITUATION

I had always thought I'd turn essays back within two days! I don't know what has happened. I guess I'm just a hopelessly slow reader."

The summer before she began her teaching career, Scottie Rogers pored over the 176-page *English Department Guidelines and Expectations*. Under the heading "Writing Requirements," she discovered that the department required students to produce some type of writing each week. That sounded reasonable to her because she firmly believed that practice was one of the most effective teachers of writing.

She worked out her first-semester schedule, which included six novels, two plays, and a unit on poetry, and essays that would be turned in each Friday—eighteen in all. The night before school opened, she looked over her plan one more time. It looked good, very good. As a lover of hard, productive work, she was sure she would have found this schedule stimulating when she was a student.

Now it is December, and she is about to begin a two week winter holiday. Her parents had talked last July about her coming to visit them in Boston, but now she isn't so sure she can do it. And if she were to go at all, it would have to be for no more than a weekend. And she would have papers to read, comment on, and edit while she was there.

"Why?" her mother wants to know when she calls.

"Oh, Mother," Scottie sighs, "I have so much work to do. I have a stack of essays to read, some of them three weeks old. I had always thought I'd turn essays back within two days! I don't know what has happened. I guess I'm just a hopelessly slow reader."

"How many students do you have?" asks her mother, a retired history teacher.

"112."

"Sweetie, you get 112 essays a week? You have to slow down. How do you stand it?"

"I love the kids' essays. A lot of them are really good, and they keep me going. But it's the ones with all the spelling and comma errors that slow me down. I sometimes spend up to a half hour on a really bad one. Some of them have multiple errors in every sentence!"

QUESTIONS TO CONSIDER

1. Is Scottie being too hard on herself?

2. Is her commitment to reading each student's weekly essay commendable? If so, is there any way she might simplify her responses to the papers?

3. What other ways might she arrange for feedback on student papers?

4. How else might Scottie get students to learn how to write better papers?

PERSPECTIVES

Scottie's commitment to the improvement of her students' writing is commendable, but she is locked into a single, unworkable method of achieving this goal—reading, commenting on, and editing each of her students' papers herself. Unless she is requiring that students revise and edit their own papers based on her suggestions, they will probably not internalize the revising and editing skills she wants them to develop.

The students themselves need to learn how to revise and edit their own work. But in order for this to happen, something has to give in her program. Alternatives Scottie needs to consider are (1) insisting that careless errors be corrected before she reads the papers; (2) reducing either the amount of literature students read or the number of writing assignments they complete, to enable her to devote some class time for students to revise and edit their own papers; (3) holding mini-conferences during class with each student;

and (4) giving editing quizzes. The students obviously need mentoring to learn how to improve their drafts; as it stands now, Scottie is the one doing most of the work. She needs to change that.

She can start by simply refusing to read any papers that appear not to have been edited or sent through a computer spell-checker.[1] She might set up a checklist for students to use in editing their own papers, and if she finds as many as three mistakes that she feels the students can correct on their own using this checklist, she gives the paper back for corrections.

Unless some class time is spent getting feedback from peers and the teacher and revising the content of a piece in response to that feedback, students may well spend the entire semester simply continuing to produce papers with the same limitations. Scottie could decide to have one paper due every *other* week instead of every week. The departmental guidelines she is following do not stipulate that each piece of writing each week needs to be on a new topic. Some could be revised versions of papers written the week before. She would cut her paper load in half, and students would have time to spend at least one class period in triads reading first drafts aloud to two peers. The focus of the triads should simply be to give feedback on the content of each piece. If each writer reads his or her own draft, the listeners will not be able to see the papers and so won't be distracted by mere editing issues; instead they can help the writer think about what needs to be done globally to make this draft better—what would make it clearer, more appropriately elaborated, better organized, etc. One way to structure the responses is to have each listener respond to these three prompts, which can be put onto a chart:

> You seem to be saying . . .
>
> The one picture or idea that stands out is . . .
>
> One thing I would like to know more about is . . .[2]

The feedback is likely to spur an elaborate and even defensive response by the writer. However, sometimes students have more commitment to setting the record straight *in writing* if they are *not* allowed

---

[1] If students have difficulty distinguishing homonyms, suggest they use the computer software program *Ghostwriter* (St. Paul, Minn.: Minnesota Educational Computing Corporation).

[2] Peter Elbow, *Writing with Power* (New York: Oxford University Press, 1981.) See particularly Chapter 23, "A Catalogue of Reader-Based Questions," for a set of non-judgmental ways peers can show writers how their words have affected them. See also Elbow's classic *Writing Without Teachers* (New York: Oxford University Press, 1973).

to talk first. Since it is possible for an oral response to dissipate the energy the writer needs for later revision, Scottie might decide to set a rule that the writers cannot tell the group how they feel about the feedback, but are allowed only to take a few notes. Then, after all three writers have shared their drafts, they can spend any remaining minutes of the class period sketching out the additional material or revisions they will need to incorporate to improve their drafts.

Scottie can also meet with students for mini-conferences, focusing initially on questions or problems the writers are having concerning the content of the piece, and not primarily on editing matters. This can be done on the same day as the groups are meeting in triads to give feedback on content. Scottie would need to have read (but not to have edited) the drafts the night before to be ready for the conferences. She takes one student at a time and asks him or her questions that are likely to elicit elaboration and rethinking of the entire thrust or organization of a draft. She will need to keep the response to each individual student short—ideally, focusing on just one type of problem with each mini-conference—so she can give each of the students individual suggestions during a single class period.

As students confer with her, they may also pick up ways to respond to each other's drafts when they are meeting with their triads. Scottie's social interaction with students is likely to be internalized, influencing the way they think about their own and their peers' drafts.[3]

If most of the papers Scottie has read need to be revised in similar ways, she can start the class with a mini-lecture about a common problem evident in most of their drafts. Her temptation, since she is somewhat of a perfectionist, will be to cover everything. (After all, that is the way she has been reading and correcting the students' papers all term.) She will have to discipline herself to focus on just one or two major representative problems and let the rest go for the time being.

If Scottie can spare another class period during the two weeks during which the class is working on drafting and revising a single essay, she may again hold mini-conferences with each of the students and respond to their second drafts, while the rest of the class meet in their triads. But this time the students in triads read each other's drafts silently and suggest changes—both for revision of content and of style, usage, and mechanics.

---

[3]Lev Vygotsky theorizes that thinking is the internalization of social interaction; his claim has been extended to the process of writing, which is the manifestation of thought. See K. Bruffe, "Collaborative Learning and 'the Conversation of Mankind,'" *College English* 46 (1974), 635–652.

The day before the final drafts are to be handed in to her, she can have the students bring in their next-to-last drafts and go over them with a partner for a final proofreading for spelling or punctuation errors or typos. She can start this class period with a mini-lecture on a common editing concern. For example, she may show students how to find sentence fragments, and then have them read their partners' papers, beginning with the last sentence, and working backwards up to the first sentence. That way, the fragments are more likely to catch their attention. (See Chapter 8, "The Mandated Language Proficiency Test," pages 74–76, for more suggestions for mini-lectures on editing matters.)

Additionally, from time to time, Scottie might give the class an editing test. She can have students write a single paragraph of their own, such as a brief summary of a piece of literature they have read, and she can grade this paragraph only for mechanics that are on the chart of items to look for in proofreading. She can wield her red pen authoritatively at this point without the risk of inhibiting the flow of language she wants to foster in other writing assignments. Students will know from the beginning that this is an editing test, and each error will lower their grade. Scottie may choose a paragraph to read aloud for this editing test, just to separate the focus on form from the act of writing, which, for most students, is best done in the first draft as free from editing concerns as possible.

One final option that will save her time in marking papers would be to assign grades only to a portfolio of work, as recommended in Chapter 1, "Defending a Grade." Scottie needs to remember that every time she edits a paper, marking all the errors, she is taking away a learning opportunity for her students.[4]

---

[4]For more suggestions on ways to help students learn to revise and edit their own papers, see Gene Stanford, *How to Handle the Paper Load* (Urbana, Ill.: National Council of Teachers of English, 1979).

PART II

FOCUS ON
THE CURRICULUM

CHAPTER 8

THE MANDATED LANGUAGE PROFICIENCY TEST

SITUATION

"I don't really care about no stupid noun-this or adjective-that," Angel says, "long as you know what I'm sayin'. Like, if I'm like, 'Hey, I be tired o' seein' your bald-headed self all up in my face for no reason,'—are you gonna try an' tell me you don't know what I mean? **Please!"**

In college, Paul Grossman learned not to teach grammar in isolation. He had read everyone from James Moffett to George Hillocks on the subject. Most of what he read told him the same thing: grammar exercise books teach little more than how to do grammar exercises.[1] There is only slight carry-over from the exercises to student writing. And this made sense to Paul. He has always considered himself a reasonably articulate and correct writer, and yet he was a terrible student of grammar in secondary school. Even today, if you ask him what a predicate nominative is, he'll make a dash for the grammar book.

Now he is in his first year at Prairie Hill High School, his own alma mater. He "teaches grammar" to low-level freshmen by having the kids read a lot, write and rewrite often, and engage in frequent

---

[1]George Hillocks, Jr. and Michael Smith, "Grammar and Usage," in *Handbook of Research on Teaching the English Language Arts*, edited by James Flood, Julie M. Jensen, Diane Lapp, and James R. Squire. (New York: Macmillan, 1991), 591–603.

discussions on topics of interest to them. His students are constantly using and experimenting with words. Following Tom Romano's advice in *Clearing The Way*,[2] Paul does not correct the mechanical errors in his students' papers until the final stages of writing. He's found, just like his college readings told him he would, that their writing, uninhibited by fears of making a mistake, is fresh and intimate, often even eloquent, whether they are writing about personal experience or about the literature they are reading.

It is now February, and his class is halfway through *To Kill A Mockingbird*. The trial of Tom Robinson is just about to begin. However, in one week, Paul will have to administer the board-mandated language proficiency exam. This one-hundred-item grammar test is given every year. Each grade- and ability-level has its own exam, and students are graded on a curve with all other students at their level. Preparation time varies from teacher to teacher. He has heard of some teachers who spend as much as six weeks on grammar alone in advance of the exam, and of others who do no preparation at all. He feels both extremes cheat the kids. He doesn't dare not prepare his students for this exam. His own plan had been to give his students a quick one-week review, but now that the week has come, he hates to tear their riveted attention away from Tom Robinson's fate. But there is also Paul's own fate; he catches a vision of himself standing in the department office watching his students' dismal scores go through the scanner.

"You don't need to bring your novels tomorrow," he tells his class. "We're going to put them away for about a week so we can do"—(Lord, his voice even catches on the word; if only there were a euphemism)—"gra- grammar."

Angel is first; she's always first to speak her mind, and her mind "plain and straight" is all she ever speaks. "I don't really care about no stupid noun-this or adjective-that," Angel says, "long as you know what I'm sayin'. Like, if I'm like, 'Hey, I be tired o' seein' your bald-headed self all up in my face for no reason,'—are you gonna try an' tell me you don't know what I mean? *Please!*"

As Paul runs his hand over his bare temples, Louis joins her, "Long as we got some communication going on, what's it matter if I got proper speech or not?"

"And how come," Angel is out of her seat now, filibustering—a word she may not know, but a technique she has down pat—"How come, listen to me now, how come they got to call it 'proper speech'

---

[2](Portsmouth, N.H.: Heinemann, 1987.)

anyway? Who made that up? Like what I be saying's not good enough? Shoot!"

Nisha, who likes to stand at whatever pole happens to be opposite to Angel at any given moment says, "But thing is, my momma, she says if you want a good job you can't be goin' into no job interview talkin' like 'I be this' or 'I be that.' Says we got to be bilingual."

The class emits "ooh's" and "ah's" in mock approval of her well-chosen word. She stands and curtsies quickly, then sits, laughing.

Angel moves toward Nisha and jabs her own hips with her fists. "It isn't like I can't turn it off and on. I learn this grammar shit (sorry, Mr. Grossman) every year of my life and I get As—thank-you-very-much—on the tests, then I forget it all till next year, so it works out."

"Like you really get As," Nisha snaps.

"I do! And I don't got to prove it to you or nobody, 'cause I know I do."

Paul decides the conversation, though originally productive, has, as usual, taken a personal turn, so he tries to break it off. He makes an attempt to explain his rationale for teaching them grammar in the context of their writing while, at the same time, being careful not to set them up for failure in the coming years. He is acutely aware that fifty-two weeks from this day they will probably be doing grammar again, and it is as likely as not they will be doing it with a teacher who loves the minutia of grammar as much as he hates it. He finds himself talking theory on a plain that seems to make absolutely no sense to most of them. But Nisha, who appears to have followed his diatribe, finally says, "Is that what you really think?"

Paul nods.

She asks, "But what if you're wrong?"

Mercifully, the bell rings and off they go, most of them leaving behind the grammar books he had laid out on the writing arms of their chairs before class.

The next day, Paul has written the words "Parts of Speech" on the board, but before he can say anything, Leo mentions a news story he had just read about a black man who had been arrested for allegedly robbing a white-owned liquor store. Leo says, "So, Mr. Grossman, it's like Tom Robinson, isn't it?" Then in a paraphrase of a passage from *Mockingbird* that Paul recently had written on the board, adds, "That man was guilty the minute the old white dude opened his mouth and shouted 'help'."

Angel rises and has a few things to say about the American judicial system, but when Paul urges her to "hang onto that thought till next week," she snaps, "Well, shoot then. Can I go to the bathroom?"

"Not right now, Angel, we're going to do grammar," Paul says. Then to the class: "Turn please to page six. Parts of speech. There are eight. Let's see if we can name them. But wait! Try to do it without looking at the book."

"Verb!"

"Adverb!"

"That's right. What else?"

"Noun."

"Adnoun."

"Well, adjective. What else?"

"Invention," Chloe yells.

"No. But close." Paul moves toward her. "Try again."

"Infection. Interfection! No. *Intervene!*"

Paul pauses. The term has now slipped his own mind. He glances at the book on a nearby desk. "Interjection."

"Can I *go* to the bathroom? 'Cause if I can't, I'm going anyway!"

"Not now," Paul snaps at Angel, one of his favorite students, in a tone more sharp than either he or his class is accustomed to hearing from him. Their backs go up. Suddenly Nisha wants to know why Angel can't go if she's *got* to go. And come to think of it, she's got to go herself—now. Then Stephanie, too.

Paul crosses his arms and leans against the chalk rail, stares at them a few moments, then says, "Guys, I don't even recognize you. What's happening here?"

"Us?" Nisha says, "What about you? You don't look so much like your own damn self neither."

"We have one week until the exam," Paul says. "Let's do what we have to do, then go on back to Tom Robinson."

The three girls start to walk out, saying they plan to take his advice and do what they got to do. He halts them with a shout, a horrible sound, abrupt, even mean. They shout back. And now others want to go, too.

Paul throws his arms in the air. "What's happening to us?"

Angel says, "We're all crazy. Everybody in here's crazy and stupid, that's why they got us all in one room, ever think of that? We don't know *shit*, never *will* know shit, so they put us in a room and forget about us. And don't even *try* and tell me it ain't true, Mr. *Gross Man*, Mr. White and Totally Gross Man."

That night Paul goes home, feeling exactly the way Angel described him, like a totally gross white man. He wonders: What if he *is* wrong, as Nisha suggested? What if he is just playing out his own political agenda at their expense? Are *they* anxious about the exam? What if they are angry because he did not prepare them? Should he have set aside, if not six weeks, at least three? He worries about whether he will win them back when the test is over. He tries to imagine how he and they will get through the next four days.

QUESTIONS TO CONSIDER

1. What is the source of the students' anger?
2. How should Paul respond to it? How should he respond to their insecurity?
3. Why did they turn on him so suddenly?
4. Should Paul continue with the grammar?
5. Should he have started sooner?
6. Should he have omitted the grammar review entirely?
7. Was he wrong to explain his own philosophy in the matter?

PERSPECTIVES

Paul is as frustrated and as insecure as his students are about the upcoming grammar exam. Because he does not believe in teaching grammar in isolation, any justification he can come up with rings hollow. The students are not used to having their teacher lay on them requirements he cannot justify, and this is behind their rebellious attitude.

Paul, as a first-year teacher, is not going to overturn the long tradition of administering the language proficiency exam every April. How is he going to help his students understand why he is doing this? He has to level with them somehow that it is important that they figure out how to do well on this exam. What he probably should *not* tell them is that his performance as a teacher will largely be evaluated on his students' scores on this single exam.

If he looks through the test, he will be even more demoralized. He pauses at this typical item on the one-hundred-item exam.

> "The girls were playing quietly with the paper dolls, and suddenly Martha _____ to scream at the top of her lungs.
> a. start
> b. starts
> c. started
> d. is starting"

The test maker probably intended this as a test of the rule that one should never change tense in the middle of a piece. However, this could well be the transition sentence in a story from the past tense into the historical present tense. A sophisticated writer might well make just such a transition in the middle of a sentence to emphasize the immediacy of the moment of the scream. So what to do to prepare students for such an exam?

It is too late to ease them gently into this test. There is nothing to do now in the next week but to help the students cram a bit. If Paul decides to use work sheets or workbooks for the review, it would be more energizing if he had the students work in pairs or triads so they could explain their reasoning to their partners. Then only those exercises that are causing trouble would need to be discussed with the whole class.

Paul would do well to talk with the students about what "language proficiency" is. Every time students speak or write they are demonstrating their proficiency in language. What the test measures is how well they can recognize such proficiency in sentences written by others. In other words, the language proficiency exam is mainly a test of three quite different types of skills: (1) mechanics of written language—punctuation, capitalization, and spelling, which the students have demonstrated in each piece of writing they have done all term, but need to recognize that they know when presented to them in a different format on a test; (2) usage— which always reflects the student's heritage language and is extremely difficult to change; and (3) parts of speech and the structure or syntax of sentences.

Paul needs to keep his review for the exam as simple as possible, and to avoid the arcane language into which many grammar books put this information. What follows are suggestions for how to do this. Although this material is readily available in other texts, we are presenting it here to illustrate how little needs to be taught directly to prepare students for a language proficiency exam.

Paul can start first with mechanics, with the goal of showing the students that they already know most of this, as they have shown in their writing. He can start by having the class look at a workbook page on a convention such as capitalization. After looking at two or three examples, he can pass out their folders of their own written work and have each student find a sentence that demonstrates knowledge of, for example, how to capitalize the names of persons, states, or cities. Then he reviews a few of the tricky conventions, such as capitalizing "the North" or "the South" when referring to a region of the country, such as the setting of *Mockingbird*. Then he gives a brief quiz, ideally one where almost all the students get everything right.

Students can go on to periods, question marks, and exclamation points, again finding examples in their own work of conventionally correct use. They can also look for examples in *Mockingbird*. One of Paul's goals is to build the students' confidence that parts of the exam will be very easy for them because they already follow the conventions in their own work. This might be a good time to define "comma splice," if the language proficiency exam demands that this be recognized by label as an error. Simply have a student find two short sentences in *Mockingbird* or another text, put those sentences on the board, substitute a comma for the period, and thus define "comma splice."

If his students need to review the uses of the comma, which language proficiency tests usually include, Paul can start with a simple reminder that writers use commas to make their meaning clear. He might want to simplify the guidelines (not rules) for using commas by reducing them to these five:

1. Items in a series—for instance, "red, white, and blue"—are separated by commas.

   (Be sure the convention selected for the optional comma between "white" and "and" reflects the option chosen by the exam writer.)

2. Commas after introductory material in a sentence

   Make a chart of subordinating conjunctions, and tell the students that when a sentence begins with one of these words, it *usually* has a comma after the phrase or clause it introduces. Common subordinating conjunctions are:

after	despite the fact that	unless
although	if	until
as	in order that	when
as if	since	whenever
as though	so that	whether
because	though	while
before		

   Some single introductory words, like "however," "well," "therefore," and "thus" are also followed by a comma. So are introductory phrases like "They said." (If "they said" appears in the middle of a sentence, it has a comma before and after it, according to the next guideline.)

3. Commas on both sides of interrupting material in a sentence

   Interrupting material includes, for instance, the name of a person addressed, as in, "Tell me, Josephina, where have you been?" Often, interrupting material can be identified as material that can be taken out of the sentence without significantly changing the meaning, as in, "You know, **of course**, that there is no commuter train near that address."

   The use of commas in non-restrictive constructions can be introduced as an instance of this guideline without using the terms "restrictive" and "non-restrictive," which often confuse young language learners. Instead, simply ask the students to decide if material is interrupting or not. If it can be removed with no loss to the essential meaning of the sentence, it is interrupting and needs commas before and after it to set it off. Then give them a sentence like the following and ask if they think the statement is true.

Women soldiers who cannot shoot straight have no business serving in the front lines in a battle.

Do they still agree when commas are placed before "who" and after "straight"?

4. When two groups of words that could otherwise stand alone as sentences are connected by the conjunctions "and," "but," "or," "nor," or "for," there is a comma before the "and," for example:

She went to the movie, but she didn't like it.
Joe saw the same film, and he raved about it.

5. Commas used any other time they are needed to clarify meaning

Inside, the children were sleeping.
In the summer, time seems to fly.

Students can again go back to their folders of written work, look for all the places they used commas, and list the reasons for each. They can also look for places where they omitted a comma but need one. Working in pairs, they might generate sentences that illustrate sentences where the commas change the meaning, as in the sentence above about women soldiers. Paul might set up teams and give points for the team that generates the greatest number of such sentences.

Preparation for the usage questions on the language proficiency exam can best be done orally. Students need to understand that they will be tested on *formal* usage, that of educated persons in academic and professional settings. If possible, bring in an audiotape with examples of standard speech and informal or dialect speech and have the students identify which is which. Suggest that students whisper the sentences aloud as they take the test to help them decide which words sound most correct in formal speech.

If the students have difficulty recognizing standard verb usage, give them a list irregular verbs simply to drill on and memorize. Avoid terms like "simple past tense" or "past participle," which they do not need to know unless they are learning the grammar of a foreign language. Have them drill instead on the verb inflections by using markers for time in this format:

| Today I **begin** | Yesterday I **began** | I have **begun** |
| Today I **break** | Yesterday I **broke** | I have **broken** |

So much for a quick review of mechanics and usage. Now, how is Paul going to help his students learn enough grammar to be able to analyze the syntax or structure of sentences? At this point, Paul cannot worry about whether or not students ever *need* to know this subject. He is obliged by the curriculum to help them prepare for the exam.

Perhaps the fastest way to learn to recognize parts of speech is to combine the feature analysis and descriptive techniques of the structural grammarians. This avoids the limitations of the traditional and hackneyed definition of a noun as a "person, place, or thing," which does not account for words like "beauty" or, in the following sentence, "yellow."

Yellow is my favorite color.

Structural grammarians distinguish nouns as those parts of speech that have a plural and a possessive as well as a singular form.

Those peonies are **beauties.**
The **yellows** of the daffodils and tulips are dazzling.

Another way to recognize a noun is to show that it can fill in the blank in the following sentence.

One _____ is here.

Proper nouns are the names of persons or places and do not normally have the same structural features as common nouns, but they function in sentences the same way common nouns do.

Adjectives are words that describe something or somebody and can fit into the following sentence.

One _____ man is very _____.

Verbs are words that can show past tense, usually by adding an "-ed" ending.

Adverbs are words that tell how or in what manner actions are performed. They often end in "-ly," for example, "happily."

After that brief introduction give each a copy of a few pages of a *Mad Libs* pad,[3] and have them play together for homework. *Mad Libs* are stories written with key words omitted, but clued by parts of speech designations; players fill in the blanks with the designated part of speech before they hear the story. Students who play the game quickly internalize examples of each of the parts of speech and learn to recognize them fairly well; this should help on the upcoming language proficiency exam. In addition, the zany inappropriateness of the sentences students produce will bring howls of laughter.

---

[3]Price Stern Sloan Publishers, Inc., 11150 Olympic Boulevard, Los Angeles, CA 90064.

An effective and creative way to review prepositions is to put two or three on the board and ask the class to contribute some more. When the chalkboard is filled, ask the students to write a prepositional phrase poem. The only requirement is that each phrase begin with a preposition. After they have written several phrases, they may, but need not, add a noun and a verb. What usually happens is that, after a few minutes of writing, students start reading their pieces to each other. Have volunteers read theirs to the whole class. Although the assignment feels strange, the sentences produced tend to be interesting. They appeal because of their novel, often periodic structure; their length, which tends to be greater than most student constructions; and their rhythm, which is reminiscent of "Over the river and through the woods, to Grandmother's house we go." Here's an example:

The Journey

Across the river,
Around the bend
Between the valleys,
Beside the banks,

Beneath the blue sky,
Beyond the green hill,
Down in the prairie
Toward the blue sea.[4]

After appreciating the genuine quality and range of subjects and moods such efforts usually produce, Paul can point out that if students are asked to find the subject or predicate of a sentence on the language proficiency exam, they first need to cross out, at least in their minds, all the prepositional phrases. This will help them determine the standard English inflection of the verb, as in the sentence, "One of the trees *was* severely damaged in the storm."

As Paul gains experience and marches toward tenure in the school, he can start raising questions about the appropriateness of the language proficiency exam and suggest alternatives that are more in keeping with the movement across the nation toward performance-based assessments, such as portfolios. (See Chapter 1, "Defending a Grade"; Chapter 11, "The Writing Competency Test"; and Appendix B for more on portfolio assessment.) He might also suggest changes in the curriculum to emphasize writing rather than grammar in isolation.

---

[4]Anneliese Arenas-Bowman, teacher at Kanoon Magnet School in Chicago, written as part of *Monday Magic Abracadabra*, published by the Chicago Area Writing Project, 1992.

CHAPTER 9

THE BOOK THEY HAVE READ BEFORE

SITUATION

*"It was this **same** book, dammit! This is what I hate about this school!"*

Nancy has carefully planned a five-week unit on *The Diary of Anne Frank* for her freshman low-level class. She spent the first week capsulizing Hitler's rise to power, showing the films *Night and Fog*[1] and *Friedrich*,[2] and discussing prejudice and anti-Semitism in our world today. At the start of the second week, she described the way the Nazi's systematically reduced, one by one, the rights of Jewish citizens, to the point where Otto Frank felt he had no choice but to put his family in hiding.

The students have been intensely focused on this study, eager for each day's new lesson, often arriving with questions of their own. Nancy has felt proud of the introduction she has made. However, today, when she passes out the text, the room is filled with groans.

"No way I'm reading this old thing again!" shouts Robert.

---

[1]Classic film, directed by Alain Resnais, juxtaposing scenes of historical film footage with still photos of tranquil scenes of former Nazi extermination camps taken a decade later. (Social Studies School Service, P.O. Box 802, 10200 Jefferson Blvd., Culver City, Cal., 90232, 1955).

[2]Based on Hans Peter Richter's novel of the same name, it tells of two boys in Germany during the Nazi era. Produced by Mary Johnson and John McGannon (Facing History and Ourselves, 1986).

Nancy asks, "Have you really read this book?"

"Last year!"

A quick survey of the class reveals that somewhere between seventy and eighty percent of the students have "studied" the book in junior high school. Others say they have seen the movie and don't need to read the book. Pedro slaps his hand down on the book and slides it off his desk onto the floor.

"Are you sure it was this version?" Nancy asks. "You're sure it wasn't an abbreviated text?"

"It was this *same* book, dammit! This is what I hate about this school!" Robert says, rising out of his seat and returning the text to his teacher's desk. Others do the same.

"Wait a minute!" Nancy commands. "But how *well* did you read it?"

"I read it," Susan says. "That's good enough."

"What do you remember about the Frank family?" Nancy asks.

Susan rolls her eyes, draws in a good chest-full of air and begins: "This girl is, like, this big-mouth in school, and she likes boys, but then her father says they have to pack only the things they can carry and hide in this attic. And they wore all their clothes even though it was hot."

Jeremy picks it up: "There's this other family there, and the lady is real obnoxious, and the man is fat. They have a son named Peter, and Anne gets this crush on him, so . . ."

Gretchen sits up. "She writes real personal stuff about her dad and mom and even about her own *period!*"

"All right," Nancy concedes. "You know the book."

They seem to have enjoyed the book the first time, and Nancy resents being deprived of the opportunity of introducing them to it. She is frustrated at their refusal to want to read it again. And she is angry there was not better communication between the feeder schools and the secondary school. What was the point of that series of articulation meetings last spring if it wasn't to avoid a fiasco like this one?

She leans over her desk and presses her knuckles down onto the stack of books. "The fact of the matter is, my friends, I am required by the English department to teach this book to you this year. And that's what I am going to do. This is one of those cases where you have no choice in the matter."

Groans, shouts.

"There's no way," Robert stands to speak for them all, "no way I'm reading it. I never read no book twice and I'm not about to start with no *Anne Frank*."

QUESTIONS TO CONSIDER

1. Is there anything Nancy can do to get these students interested in rereading this book?
2. What alternatives does she have, given that this book has been required by the curriculum?
3. What other questions might Nancy have asked to serve as a review of the text?
4. How could Nancy have connected this discussion with the previous week's discussion of the problems facing the Jews in Nazi Germany?

PERSPECTIVES

Let's face it: Nancy is angry. She has spent considerable effort preparing to teach this book, and this class of low-level students has thrown a road block in her way. How is she going to get them to realize they can learn something by rereading a book? How can she challenge them to go back and learn more significant facts about the book than the details they remember?

The Aesthetic Stance

She began by challenging them with a question to find out how much they remembered from their reading and, probably, also to find out if they were telling the truth. She wanted to find out what they knew about the book. Nancy wanted to find out what they remembered as *efferent* readers, to use Louise Rosenblatt's term.[3] . . . When reading in an efferent stance, the readers' focus is on the information they take away from the text.

She might have done better to try to evoke their *aesthetic* responses. When the stance of the readers is aesthetic, they are approaching a text in a frame of mind that attends not only to what the text says, but also to the feelings they have while reading it, the associations or memories it brings up, and the stream of images that pass through their mind. In an aesthetic stance, the readers pay attention to the lived-through experience of the literary work, that is to the world created while reading and the emotions or associations resulting from the experience. Students who are reading aes-

---

[3]Louise Rosenblatt, *The Reader, the Text, and the Poem: The Transactional Theory of Literary Work*. (Carbondale, Ill.: Southern Illinois University Press, 1978.)

thetically respond with judgments, preferences, or descriptions that are elaborated by a selection of story events or characters. Aesthetic responses typically begin with statements such as: "I thought it was good when . . ." "I enjoyed it when . . ." or "It was funny when . . ."

Although Nancy asked a question that was designed to evoke an efferent response—"What do you remember about the Frank family?"—her students showed her they were ready to respond aesthetically. For example, Jerermy said, "The lady is real obnoxious, and the man is fat."

An efferent stance, as Rosenblatt defines it, is characterized at its simplest level by a verbatim retelling: "This book was about . . ." A more sophisticated response—the one Nancy probably hoped her students would be able to produce after her five-week unit was completed—is an analysis of the elements of a book according to an outside structure: what was learned about the holocaust, the ways a diary account is like or unlike a novel, literary elements that can be discerned and evaluated, categories of experience or literature this book represents, and so on.

A recent study has shown that the aesthetic stance is associated with significantly higher levels of personal understanding than the efferent stance.[4] Students who focus during the reading process on the experience they are having as readers are more likely to get meaning from a text than those who focus on what they are learning. When students find connections in a text with their own lives, they understand it better. Since personal connections have been shown to be the most solid foundation for reading with understanding, Nancy might have done better to begin with questions deliberately aimed at an aesthetic response, such as "Did you like the book?" "Which was your favorite part?" "How did you feel when you read about . . ." Although Nancy is frustrated by the reactions she is getting from her students, they *have* related to the diary in ways that were meaningful in terms of their own lives. Forgetting for a moment that the class's goal is to get the teacher to drop that particular book as assigned reading, their responses do show they have made a personal connection. Gretchen, for example, remembers Anne's writing about her menstrual period. Nancy's challenge is to find ways to help students go beyond this personal connection they have made with *Anne Frank* to the larger historical context she has presented the week before. She'll do it best if she can expand on,

---

[4]Joyce E. Many, "Age-Level Differences in Children's Use of an Aesthetic Stance When Responding to Literature," (Ph.D. diss., Louisiana State University, Baton Rouge, La., 1989).

rather than deny, the personal connections the students have already made as they have read aesthetically.

Readers' Theater

Nancy needs to buy time. She doesn't have any alternate plans in her jacket pocket to pull herself out of this bind. One way to start is to concede that most of the class seem to remember some important moments in this book.

Let's posit the following scenario. After the class has rebelled, Nancy asks all of the class to write briefly. Those who have read the book jot down what they remember most about the book and how they felt about Anne Frank, her family, and their plight. Those who have not read the book write about what they would do if they heard they were to be taken away to a concentration camp and maybe even killed because of their religion:

- How would you feel if you were forced to leave your home?
- If you felt you could not get out of the country, how would you hide?
- What kind of building would be safest?
- How would you get the supplies you needed?
- How would you keep from being discovered?

Then she has the students divide into small groups to read to each other what they have written. Those who have read the book before will meet together to form small groups, and those who have not read it will form other groups.

Nancy then assigns those who have not read the book before to read carefully the first twenty pages of *Anne Frank*. She tells the rest of the class that their assignment that night is to prepare for a Readers' Theater presentation the next day. Their job is to scan a chapter they have read before and to find the parts that best capture the spirit of this diary. They will need selections that will play well dramatically. By this time the attitudes of the students may be less rebellious. Then Nancy hands back the books that the class had at first rejected.

Nancy will need to explain what Readers' Theater is. It is simply a group rendition by two or more oral interpreters, with or without a narrator. It is not a fully dramatized scene. The participants don't actually act out the parts as in a play, but they suggest the action with gesture, voice, and facial expressions. Stylized, understated body movements are effective. Because the action is symbolized, the audience needs to use its imagination to fill in the details. Any text will do because it does not have to be written in dialogue as a play script does. Sometimes it is effective to pantomime a scene while a narrator reads the words. When dialogue is presented, the words "he said" and "she said" can either be omitted or read by each player right along with his or her lines. Some readers can assume more than one role.

The next day, Nancy can hold a discussion with the whole class about the first twenty pages of the *Diary* that, by this time, all of them will have read. She will add any background information she feels they need to understand the text. Those who have not read the *Diary* before will be given the questions that Nancy has previously prepared (when she planned to teach *Anne Frank* to the whole class) to discuss and answer in small groups.

Then all the students will meet with the same small groups they met with the day before. The task for those who have read the book before will be to decide on a selection of no more than one and a half pages that capture a significant center of this book. They may choose several short selections from different parts of the book or just one longer passage.

Nancy then gives students directions for a Readers' Theater presentation, either on a photocopied handout, on a wall chart, or on an overhead transparency. Here is a list she could use:

1. Decide on a "cutting" of no more than one and a half pages total. The sentences or paragraphs you choose do not have to be next to one another in the text, and may be from different pages, but be sure they fit together smoothly. Add transition sentences, if needed.

2. Decide on one idea or mood that seems central to the piece.

3. Decide who will speak which lines. Figure out a way for each member of your group to participate. You may want to read some lines as a chorus.

4. Figure out a way to suggest the setting.

5. Work to alter the script to make the images stronger, the impact more intense, or the ending more dramatic.

6. Be sure all of you see the action in the same way. Decide together what the setting looks like.

7. Rehearse and change the script where appropriate.

8. Treat one line as a refrain to be read in unison if that would add to the impact.

9. Make a copy of the script for each member of your group and read it over several times until you can do it without hesitation.

Practice varying the timing or emphasis until you get the best effect.

10. Rehearse again, this time with simple gestures, if appropriate; then perform your script for the class.

While the groups are preparing their scripts, Nancy goes from group to group encouraging them to experiment with different renderings. She does not need to be a drama coach to do this. Her goal is not a polished dramatic performance but an understanding of the book. She wants the students to internalize the text so they can present one simple and clear image, mood, and focus.

They may need help rewriting their scripts so they will remain faithful to the text but, at the same time, reveal character and build to a climax. As students rehearse, they often memorize parts of their script, but this is not a requirement. The goal is to come to understand a text better through repeated rereading.

She can also meet from time to time with those who are reading the *Diary* for the first time, discussing issues that have come up for the readers and providing any necessary background information. They will take quizzes she has prepared and, after they have read and discussed the whole book, they will write as a group a collaborative essay on the most important thing they have learned from *The Diary of Anne Frank*.

Alternate Texts

While the students are devoting several class sessions to preparing, rehearsing, and then presenting their Readers' Theater scripts, Nancy can rethink her goals for the unit on *Anne Frank*, listing all the things she hopes the students would learn from a study of that book. Next she looks for other texts that would help students achieve the same understandings. It is probably too late to order a class set of a new text, but she might go to any local or school libraries she has access to and look up in the Subject Guide of *Books in Print* under Anne Frank, using the librarian's help. She can call the Holocaust Memorial Museum in Washington, D.C. (Ph: 202-448-0400) to request a copy of their *Annotated Bibliography*, which lists history, biography, fiction, and memoirs suitable for high school students.

After the Readers' Theater presentations, Nancy gives students who have previously read *Anne Frank* the option to read it again and discuss it just as the first-time readers will be doing. Both the second-time readers and the first-time readers will have discussion questions to guide them, and they will take quizzes and together write a collaborative essay.

If Nancy can get at least two copies of texts to replace the *Diary* text, two different groups can read the same book, sharing the copy among their small-group members. Because of the problem of taking turns carrying the book home to read, Nancy may need to allow some class time for students to read their books aloud to each other.

After they have all read the first half of an alternate text, they may choose to divide up the remaining pages among themselves. Then all of them scan the rest of the book, but one person will be responsible for each section of the remaining pages. He or she will read that part carefully and summarize it for the rest of the group. Then they can discuss it in their small groups, and, finally, prepare a quiz for the other group that has read the same book. Then the two groups turn in their quizzes to Nancy to revise and amend. (Nancy will need to do some quick reading to keep up with all the books the class is now reading.) After she returns the quizzes to the small groups, each group exchanges its quiz with the other group who read the same book, and they take each other's tests. (See Chapter 16, "Untracking," for more ideas on managing the classroom and monitoring progress when students are reading different texts.)

In lieu of reading a book, one of the groups can be assigned the task of compiling an oral history, interviewing survivors of the Holocaust. Rabbis in local synagogues or grandparents of Jewish students make good sources of information. During in-class working sessions, students could first generate a list of questions to ask their interviewees. Their homework would be to find survivors in their community, meet with them, ask questions, and take notes on their answers. In class they could then share their information and talk about ways to write up their interviews into an interesting report to present to the class. They could each prepare a separate report, summarizing common experiences of all of their interviewees. One of the members of this group might contact a Dutch or German embassy or travel bureau to find out about the Anne Frank annex in Holland or Anne Frank house in Frankfurt. Another might interview someone who has visited the United States Holocaust Memorial Museum in Washington, D.C.

When the groups have discussed their books, prepared quizzes, and taken the tests, they can prepare a group summary of their texts and present that to the class in some way that ensures participation by each group member. Nancy's role is to encourage aesthetic as well as efferent responses. In other words, the small groups tell the class how they feel about their book as well as what the book is about. After each small group's report, Nancy expands the discussion and links it back to the history lessons of the first week.

After a whole-class discussion of the Holocaust, the groups that have read *Anne Frank* in Nancy's class present their reports. They will have written as a group a single essay on the most important thing they have learned from this book. (Because the rest of the class has read it, these groups will not need to summarize the text.) Their reports too can be a springboard for another class discussion and review for the final essay exam on the unit's work. This might be a good time to show the video version of the *Diary*.[5]

Evaluation

Grades for this total *Anne Frank* unit of work can be based on the quality of the students' Readers' Theater presentations, their grade on the quizzes on the book, the quality of their group essay or report (each person in the small group should receive the same grade), and a final essay exam on the whole unit, in which the students are asked to tie together what they remember from reading *Anne Frank* and what they learned from the reports by other class members. One useful question in this exam is to contrast what they used to know or believe about the Holocaust with what they now know or believe.

Conclusion

We need to recognize that there is a trade-off in Nancy's choice of the collaborative learning model for this unit of work. She loses her control of the class discussion and she has less opportunity to address deficiencies in the students' understanding of *Anne Frank*. She probably gains the support of those students who would have resented having to study a book they have already read. She also may gain a greater assumption of responsibility by the students for their own learning. Students who have a chance to respond aesthetically and who have some choice in how they are to engage with and present an important part of a text to the rest of the class usually connect more deeply with the material. The activities Nancy initiates in this second scenario respect the students' prior knowledge, build on it, and expand their learning into a broader arena.

---

[5] *The Diary of Anne Frank*, Video 0-7939 (New York: CBS/Fox Video; Key Video, Playhouse Video, 1990; Copyright 1987)

CHAPTER 10

BUT IS IT SHAKESPEARE?

SITUATION

"Why don't we just see the stupid movie and forget about this dumb play? It's so boring."

Ed has just finished the first act of *Romeo and Juliet* with his freshman class. They struggled a bit at first but stuck with the text for a week. Now they have begun to complain. It's getting so boring! He can handle that, he thinks, because he remembers complaining about the same play himself when he was a freshman just ten years ago.

But now, entering the second week of the unit, he notices that at the beginning of the period, instead of leafing through the book in preparation for the daily quizzes, kids are huddled around copies of *Cliff's Notes*. Some kids arrive with just the *Notes*, not even bothering to carry the play around anymore.

Ed's first tack is to tell them he knows how they feel. When he was in school, if there was a shortcut he'd take it. "Even though I ended up an English teacher, I confess I used the black and yellow pamphlet myself. But let me tell you what you're missing. You're missing the beauty of Shakespeare's language, his turns of phrase, his incredibly rich vocabulary, the word play, the details, the symbolism, the rich irony! You are depriving yourself of some wonderful reading and the pleasure of finding yourself becoming absorbed in a book."

The students are silent at first; then Doug, often their spokesperson, says, "Well, that's OK, Mr. Wright. Guess we can survive without that."

Then Ed gets tough and tells them he is going to write quizzes that ask questions about material not covered in the *Cliff's Notes*.

The kids are angry. The next day the discussion goes nowhere, and the quiz grades drop because the students aren't prepared. Finally Alice, a disciple of Doug's, seems to speak for them all: "Why don't we just see the stupid movie and forget about this dumb play? It's so boring."

At lunch, Ed talks over his problem with Jennifer, a colleague, in her cubicle. She reaches to her shelf and hands him a copy of a shortened *Romeo and Juliet*, written in modern English.[1] "Or," shoving another small volume into his hand, "try this parallel text edition."[2] Ed sighs. "Hey, if that doesn't grab them, there's this one," and she hands Ed a comic book version.[3] The complete, unabridged text is squeezed into the word balloons of the comic book illustrations. Jennifer is enthusiastic. "I've been using it since it first came out, and the kids really love it. And that is what we want, isn't it? For the kids to love it?"

Ed cringes. "There's more to Shakespeare than plot. What is it, if it isn't language? I didn't go into English to teach comic books!" He looks at the comic book jacket that insists that this style "achieves the energy and immediacy of an actual performance." What message would this give the kids about literature—that it has to have unimaginative illustrations to get through to them?

"It's not that I don't appreciate your help, Jen, but I couldn't give that to them. It's like putting a fine steak in a lidded Styrofoam box."

"Without that box, they might never come to the table. Suit yourself. How about the Zefferelli film? You will use that, won't you? It works great! I even have a transcript of the dialogue for the kids to read. Wanna borrow it? It *never* scares them off."

QUESTIONS TO CONSIDER

1. Would you teach a watered-down or updated version of *Romeo and Juliet?*

2. Is there any way you might use a simplified version as a lead-in to the authentic text?

3. What other alternatives does Ed have than to take Jennifer's advice?

---

[1]Diane Davidson, *Romeo and Juliet*, Volume 3 of *Shakespeare on Stage*, (Fair Oaks, Cal.: Swan Books, 1979).

[2]William Shakespeare, *Romeo and Juliet*, edited by Janie B. Yates-Glandorf, *The Shakespeare Parallel Text Series* (Logan, Iowa: The Perfection Form Company, 1985.)

[3]William Shakespeare, *Romeo and Juliet*, illustrated by Von (New York: Alfred A. Knopf, 1983).

4. Is there any place for *Cliff's Notes*?

5. What can Ed do now to change the students' attitude toward Shakespeare?

PERSPECTIVES

Most school boards see the secondary English teacher as the person who teaches traditional, canonical works. No matter that these teachers feel themselves to be saddled with the task of reaching disaffected and uninterested students. Their job is to get them to learn. Unless Ed can get students intrigued by the challenge of Shakespeare's language, all his informative lectures and quizzes will thud like a stone falling on sand.

Ed's own commitment to having his students appreciate Shakespeare's language is inhibiting his capacity to engage them. Everything he is doing now makes them feel more and more powerless to understand this play. He has by his teaching strategies convinced his students that they cannot read *Romeo and Juliet* on their own, so they have glommed onto the *Cliff's Notes* in desperation.

One of Ed's options is to forget the language of the play long enough to stimulate student interest. Until he does that, Shakespeare's language will forever be foreign to them. He might have students improvise the scenes and then write scripts in a dialect of their choice. Another approach is somehow to empower the students to struggle with the language, setting up a structure in which they feel confident enough to try to puzzle out for themselves a text in antiquated and off-putting language.

If Ed can forget Shakespeare's actual text for a while, he might stir up some interest by taking at least some of Jennifer's advice. He could start with the movie *West Side Story*.[4] He could focus the discussion on the elements in common with *Romeo and Juliet*. Then the students could read the old Greek myth of Pyramus and Thisbe and discuss its similarities to *West Side Story*. He might next present the Zefferelli film, having the students watch twice—first as a purely aesthetic experience in a darkened room, then with a copy of the script in hand so they can begin to see some of Shakespeare's words. Ed might pick out parts of the film to focus on, having the students follow the script closely as they watch. Then he might have students meet in small groups, assign students the parts of the characters in

---

[4]Warner Home Video, Inc., Warner Brothers, Inc., 400 Warner Blvd, No. 19, Burbank, CA 91552.

those scenes, and have them read the script aloud with appropriate actions. Ed could encourage them to reinterpret the lines, if they wish, so their presentation of this scene has a slightly different mood than the film version. All the groups could meet simultaneously, and only if they volunteered, would they present their interpretation for the rest of the class. What the students will gain by this approach is an enthusiasm for the play; but they will lose the experience of reading the entire play, and they will lose the experience of interpreting the play for themselves.

A second option, one that helps students become aware of the "subtexts" of the play, is to have them improvise scenes from *Romeo and Juliet*, changing Shakespeare's words into their own modern English, or sub-dialects of it. This way they will feel more ownership over their interpretation of the play and recognize there are a wide range of ways to interpret any script. They might start the first day of the study of *Romeo and Juliet* by taking turns saying this line of Romeo's from Act I, Scene IV:

"I dreamed a dream tonight."

Ed might ask for five volunteers to perform that same line in five different ways. They go outside the class to plan and practice first. When they return, each person says the line, but each *means* something different by the line. Sample subtexts are:

I was in the arms of a perfect lover.

I was in great danger.

I caught a vision of my own death.

I am very tired.

I found it very funny.

Then Ed could have the class read either *Cliff's Notes* or another synopsis in order to get an idea of the entire plot. He might want to read some key scenes aloud to them or have them listen to a recording as they watch the text, but at this point he'll need to curb his urge to explain the play to them. The class then divides into small groups, each of which will select a scene they will be responsible for. Ed may decide that each group should choose a scene that no other group is going to use.

Each group then fills out together a worksheet answering such questions as:

What is happening here?

What is the subtext of each character's lines?

How does each character feel?

What does each character want to achieve?

How does this scene fit with the plot of the play?

After Ed reads their responses, Ed may need to lecture a bit on the context behind each of the scenes the students have selected, perhaps directing them to one of the versions of the play written in modern English to be sure that they understand what is going on. This is not the time to untangle the language, however. Ed must leave that challenge to the small groups, as he cruises from group to group, coaching unobtrusively, to help them get to the heart of each scene.

After each group arrives at an understanding of the gist of their scene, and (with Ed's help), sees how it fits in the larger play, they improvise the scene, either putting it into another idiom, such as modern slang, African-American street English, valley-girl/surfer dialect, soap opera style, or their own heritage language. They need to keep the mood and subtext of the original as they have identified it on their worksheets. They improvise the scene several times, revising each time, and then write it up as a script. Then the groups take turns performing their scripts for the class.[5] After each group performs, they read the Shakespeare text of the same scene as the class follows along in their own copies.

If Ed chooses, he can have each of these scenes performed in the correct order, and in between he will fill in the other scenes briefly, reading aloud or having students in role read passages central to the development of the plot, as the class follows the text. He only explains lines that impede the class's understanding of what is happening, but he tries not to tell more than they need to know in order to understand the next student improvisation.

A third tack is for Ed to put the students in role, not as characters in the play this time, but rather as famous Shakespearean performers. His goal is to cloak them in what Dorothy Heathcote has termed the "mantle of the expert."[6] When the teacher metaphorically drapes a "mantle of the expert" onto the shoulders of students, it has the effect

---

[5]Elise Ann Earthman, "Enter the Madcap Prince of Wales: Students Directing *Henry IV, Part I*," *English Journal*, 82 (1993) 54–60. Most of the articles in this issue focus on the teaching of Shakespeare. When the call for manuscripts on this topic went out, the editors of the journal received more manuscripts than they had in several years, showing that, at least among the readers of *English Journal*, Shakespeare is robust.

[6]Gavin Bolton and Dorothy Heathcote, *Mantle of the Expert* (Portsmouth, N.H.: Heinemann, 1995); and John Hughes and Philip Taylor, "Researching *Mantle of the Expert*: Australian and U.S. Experiences," paper presented at the International Conference on the Work and Influence of Dorothy Heathcote, Lancaster University, Lancaster, England, July 28, 1993.

of elevating them, at least in their own minds, to a status that demands that they perform like experts. In the process, their confidence is boosted, and they often try out a register and language that is beyond the level of their everyday speech. In Vygotsky's terms, they are moving into their "zone of proximal development,"[7] the level just above what they can achieve by themselves, the level at which they *can* perform with an appropriate context or scaffolding. The "mantle of the expert" becomes this enabling context.

This strategy appears to work best before the students have been given any background to the play, not even a bare bones introduction to the plot. Ed comes in the first day of the unit and tells them they are to become world-renowned Shakespearean actors and interpreters. He asks the class where such talented persons are likely to be found, and he lists on the chalkboard their suggestions. After they, with his help, have listed such centers as Stratford-upon-Avon or the Royal Shakespeare Company in England, the repertory theaters in Stratford, Ontario, or in Salem, Oregon, he divides them into groups of three and has them decide which of these centers they represent.

Then he assumes the role of the Executive Director of the National Endowment for the Arts who has convened a scholarly meeting at the Faculty Club of the Yale Drama School. He starts out:

> I have brought together you Shakespearean scholars from all parts of the globe to help us decipher a new manuscript that has just come to light. It is a fragment, mind you, but since some of it includes parts for such famous Shakespearean characters as Romeo and Juliet, we have a suspicion that it belongs in that play, but we cannot figure out quite what it means. I apologize that this fragment is so short; I know this will be frustrating to you because you do not have enough to go on in most cases, but do the best you can. I know your many years of experience with the bard will guide you in your interpretations.

Then Ed hands each of them a copy of the Prologue to *Romeo and Juliet*, saying, "See what sense you can make of this." They are to work in triads, and he encourages them to use the dictionary or *Cliff's Notes* or *Outlines of Shakespeare's Plays*—anything that might help them interpret the lines. When they think they have figured out the meaning, each group of three presents its reading to the class, explaining the text line by line. Ed, still in role as the con-

---

[7]Lev Vygotsky, Chapter 6, "Interaction Between Learning and Development," *Mind in Society: The Development of Higher Psychological Processes* (Cambridge: Harvard University Press, 1978) 79–91.

vener, does what he can to point up contradictions and urge the various groups to defend their interpretations against those of the others. He tries never to step out of his role as the facilitator of the discussion, and to avoid the roles of arbiter of disputes or the teacher who knows.

After the class has reached some tentative consensus on the meaning of the Prologue, they work as a whole to decide on the best way for a chorus of voices to present the Prologue to an audience. They determine if some phrases or lines should be read by a solo voice, if high and low voices should be separated and assigned certain parts, if some should be read by the whole group of performers, and so on. Ed stays out of this discussion completely.

Then they meet again in triads. Each group appoints a director and rehearses its choral reading until they are satisfied with the rendition. This experience helps all of the students, under the cover of other voices, to become familiar with and even somewhat comfortable with four-hundred-year-old English. Then each triad in turn reads its interpretation. Ed congratulates students on the lines they render particularly aptly, reminding them again of the value of their considerable collective expertise on Shakespearean language.

Then he assigns each group a different short scene from *Romeo and Juliet*. He might pass out copies of the complete play so the students can look through the list of characters. (Possible scenes for this activity are Act I, Scene I until the entrance of Benvolio; Act I, Scene I from Romeo's entrance to end; Act I, Scene III; or other scenes that are not central to the plot. Then Ed needs to give his "experts" as much time as they require, maybe several days, to puzzle over, discuss, look up word meanings, and rehearse the lines in their segments until they can interpret them, providing any needed background information for the class. Finally, they perform them. On the last day before the lectures and performances, Ed might speak, with a pronounced British accent, not as the Executive Director who called the meeting, but this time as another renowned Shakespearean scholar, just arrived from Oxford. His expertise may be tapped if any of the groups still have questions about their segment of the text. This would be his chance to "teach," but he would frame any suggestions in the context of his admiration for their remarkable scholarship and insight.

After these fragmentary scenes are performed by each group, the students, still in role as experts, can read together the more important scenes in the play.

CHAPTER 11

THE WRITING
COMPETENCY TEST

SITUATION

"Hey! Who the hell graded this?" Shyla shouts. . . .
"I hate these tests. They don't make no kinda sense!"
Jeremy turns his paper face down and slaps it with
his hand.
"Does this mean I'm, like, writing incompetent?"
Nathan wonders aloud.

Janice has been teaching for two and a half years. Until she gets
tenure next year, she plans to teach by the book and play according
to the rules, following the prescribed curriculum with almost obses-
sive care. But that is becoming more difficult to do now.

By the end of the first quarter of this year, she found she could
no longer deny the frustration and dissatisfaction she felt with her
students' writing. It was bland and uninspired, produced grudgingly when it was produced at all. And recently, more and more
kids had begun not turning in the required work. She knew something had to change. And she felt confined by the strictures of the
curriculum.

At first, she blamed her own assignments and tried to enliven
them and to tie them more closely to the kids' interests. She moved
from giving assignments like the classic, "What three qualities do
you look for in a friend?" to more engaging topics like "Would you
eat a bucket of live worms for a million dollars?" Their pre-writing
discussions were lively and interesting, but when the papers came

in—the ones that did come in—they were just as dull and limp as they always had been. She tried starting each day with a story from the newspaper. Her students, she discovered, loved to discuss current events. She gave writing assignments based on news stories. This helped a little. A few kids who had never written before, suddenly turned in an essay or two. Jeremy, for example, who had announced on the first day of class that he *hated* writing, wrote an essay on whether high salaries for sports figures are a genuine problem. It really surprised Janice with its passion and clarity. She asked him why he suddenly decided to write and he told her simply, "'Cause I had something to say."

One day, as an experiment, she announced that they could write on any topic that interested them that week.

"Anything?" they asked, an incredulous chorus. *"Really? Anything?"*

"Anything," Janice assured them, soaking in their excitement, "So long as it interests you."

A few kids had trouble coming up with a topic, insisting that nothing interested them. For these students, she produced a list of twenty-five topics. But, for the most part, the kids approached the assignment with unusual enthusiasm. In the days before the paper was due, they would gather at her desk before and after class or stop her in the hall.

"Can I write about the day my father died?" Shyla wanted to know.

"I want to write about legalizing drugs. Is that OK?" Jeremy asked.

Taylor waved a handful of pages in front of her teacher's face and said, "Would you accept a fairy tale if I wrote one?"

"Yes. Yes. Yes!" Janice said, again and again.

She collected the papers on a Friday. A few students turned in nothing, as usual, but unlike on other due dates, these students were in the minority. Several papers were typed for the first time, some were bound in plastic folders, and Shyla had even created a title page that incorporated a picture of herself with her father who had passed away earlier in the year.

Janice took the papers home and for the first time in a long while, read them all in one sitting. She loved the variety, the depth of feeling, and particularly the care that was evident in these papers. On Monday she returned them to her students and told them what a special weekend it had been for her. The classroom came alive with excited voices. Some kids traded papers and read each other's essays.

Then Shyla asked, "Can I read mine out loud?"

Janice had something else planned for that day and was a little worried about how the other kids would react to so personal an essay, but she nodded to her. Shyla read the paper she had written about the morning her father fell dead in the driveway after letting the dog out: how, when she first saw him on the ground, she thought he was joking; how the paramedics tore open his pajama shirt while he still lay on the pavement; how she woke her younger brother and said, "Daddy might have died." The class sat silently when she was finished, which Shyla seemed to take as appreciation. Then Rachel wanted to read, and after her Nathan.

Near the end of the period, Janice asked the class what they would think of turning in one essay every week on any topic they chose. The chorus of their approval came in the form of hollered ideas—"short stories? film scripts? sit-coms? horror stories? letter to the president?"

"Yes," she said. "Yes, yes, yes."

For two months, the papers rolled in with varying degrees of success. Not all were wonderful, not everyone produced, but something was very different in her classroom now. Ideas began to generate more ideas, and the more ideas the more excitement. And the more excitement, the higher the quality of the writing.

Janice kept the juices bubbling by starting each class period with ten minutes of free writing; she made it clear, "You can say anything at all that you want."

"Can we swear?" Jim asked.

"You can swear at *me*," she said, "if that's what's on your mind. I'll never see it. This writing is for you. Write whatever is on your mind." Although some students balked at first, by the second week some were coming into class early just to get started in their free writing. They wanted more than ten minutes, and several wanted to read aloud what they had written. Janice encouraged them to write without worrying about mechanics. "Concentrate on saying what you really want to say. We'll worry about spelling and all that later."

Now comes March and with it the English department's annual reminder of the school-wide writing competency test. Each fall Janice had been told about it, but this year, in the excitement of the writing the students were doing, she had forgotten about it. For the test, students are asked to write a five-paragraph essay on a given topic. They have one forty-five-minute period. The essay must be well-organized with a clear topic sentence, three supporting arguments with elaboration, effective transitions, and a sound conclusion. Student papers are expected to be reasonably free of mechanical errors and to follow a strict manuscript form with a heading, title, one-inch margins, and legible handwriting in black ink on only one side of the paper.

The essays are read by two different teachers who do not know the students' identities. Each reader assigns a score between zero (for very poor writing) to four (for excellent writing). The two readers' scores are added together for a student's final score, which can therefore be between zero and eight points.

At the bottom of the memo is this year's topic, which is *not* to be announced to students in advance: *What three qualities make a teacher effective?*

Janice sighs. If there ever was a ho-hum topic, this has to be it.

Two weeks after the test, the results come back. None of the papers has so much as a one-word comment. Just a digit. Most of the kids in her class receive a four, a "competent" grade, the evaluation sheet tells her.

"Hey! Who the hell graded this?" Shyla shouts.

"I thought I did what they wanted, and I got a stupid 4!" Taylor groans.

"I hate these tests. They don't make no kinda sense! I hate this!" Jeremy turns his paper face down.

"Does this mean I'm, like, writing *in*competent?" Nathan wonders aloud.

They want the names of the anonymous readers. Some want home addresses, too! A lot of kids ask Janice to read the papers and tell them what she thinks.

She looks at them and listens to their complaints and concerns, and it hurts her to see them so hurt. She has a strong, almost aching desire to say, "I haven't been lying to you about your writing."

She knows she cannot tell them to dismiss the test results. How would that affect their attitude toward such tests in the future, not to mention their developing feeling toward institutional tests? But what can she say?

She wants to talk to her department chair, but he is the one who writes the test and organizes its evaluation. As a matter of fact, when she went to him the year before, he had handed her his "format" and told her it "always worked beautifully."

John's Format

Sentence 1: TOPIC SENTENCE
Sentence 2: follow-up (elaboration on the above)
Sentence 3: FIRST SUPPORTING SENTENCE
Sentence 4: follow-up
Sentence 5: follow-up
Sentence 6: SECOND SUPPORTING SENTENCE
Sentence 7: follow-up
Sentence 8: follow-up
Sentence 9: THIRD SUPPORTING SENTENCE

Sentence 10: follow-up
Sentence 11: follow-up
Sentence 12: CONCLUSION

Janice tried to write something interesting herself following this pattern, and the results were so disastrous she was demoralized. She threw out his mechanical approach immediately. How could she lay such a format on her students?

She would like to initiate a conversation with her colleagues, but with only two-and-a-half years under her belt, she may not be taken seriously. She knows many of the other teachers believe in the value of the test. Besides, what if *she* is wrong about the test?

QUESTIONS TO CONSIDER

1. What can Janice tell her angry students?

2. Should she have had them follow "John's Format" for this test?

3. What can she do to reconcile her goals as a writing teacher with her desire to help her students perform well on the writing competency test?

4. What should be her long-term strategy to avoid a repetition of this situation another Spring?

5. Are there other, more valid ways to assess student writing competence?

PERSPECTIVES

Shyla and Taylor and Nathan have a right to their outrage, and the teacher, Janice, knows it. Throughout the year, her instincts have guided her well. The students are writing with an authenticity that comes from the heart. Writing has become significant and personally valued, and Janice knows it. How can she demonstrate this fact to the department chair, and, more immediately, to the students themselves? They expected their scores on the competency test to be higher, and Janice knows they had every right to.

One way for Janice to approach her dilemma is to set out for herself short-term and long-term goals. Her most pressing short-term challenge is to restore confidence in her burgeoning writers without feeding their cynical tendency to believe the whole school system is rigged against their best efforts. As a representative of adult authority, she has to defend the writing competency test as a fact of life, if not her ideal of an assessment device.

After the anger over the grades has died down a bit, she might say something like this: "Real writing is what we do when we want to communicate with other people. We write because we want others to know how we think and how we feel. We write to sort out our minds, to organize our thoughts, even to find out what we really do think about a something. This is what we have been doing all term." (See Appendix F for a diagram showing the various genres from which students might choose.)

"There is another kind of writing. It's not the opposite of real writing, not actually 'unreal writing,' but it is writing we do for another reason. It is writing to demonstrate that we can write. Its purpose is to put ourselves out there for others to evaluate. It is common in schools, but, unlike the real writing you have been doing at school this term, it is uncommon in the world outside of schools. You find it in essays that are required for college admission, in paragraphs written as part of job applications, such as writing tests for secretaries. Sometimes you have to prove to other people that you are a competent writer.

"How do you do this? Start by reading the test very carefully. Then, instead of trying very hard to respond to the topic in a creative and original way, spend your time outlining what you might say about such a topic that would meet the requirements of the prompt and yet could be written within the time constraints.

"For this writing competency test, you were asked to list three qualities that make a teacher effective. Here is one that received a top score of 8." Then Janice passes out a paper like this one, and they go over it together.

> Walking into a classroom on the first day of school is usually cause for nervousness, if not fright. However, if the teacher shows interest in the students' quest for knowledge, is open with students and concentrates entirely on education instead of discipline, the students will relax and enjoy a better learning environment.
>
> First of all, the teacher must show she cares about the students' interest in learning. The teacher should listen respectfully to a student's questions then react thoughtfully. The teacher should encourage questioning by allowing the students to analyze their thoughts and opinions. If a student's question is rebutted by a sarcastic remark, that student won't feel that he is good enough to have an opinion on the subject. Hence, it is important for teachers to have an interest in their students' want of knowledge.
>
> A second necessary quality for a teacher is openness with students. A student feels more comfortable and thus more inclined to participate in class if he feels that he is on a person-to-person basis instead of a teacher-to-student one. Students do not like be treated

like naive three-year-olds. Therefore, it is important for teachers to treat their students as people rather than just as students.

Lastly, a teacher should not waste time on discipline problems, just eliminate them. If two students are in the back of the room talking loudly, they should simply be asked to leave. Spending time reprimanding them will only cause more of a disturbance. Also, other students might think the teacher is a softy and then not actively respect the teachers. So, it is important that a teacher treats discipline problems by eliminating them and not encouraging them.

In conclusion, to receive a better education, it is important for a student to have a quality teacher. This teacher must express an interest in the student's learning, speak only with the students and not waste time on discipline problems. If a teacher portrays herself in this manner, the students will have more interest in learning and therefore, a better understanding of the material.[1]

Janice notes,

As you can see, the first sentence gets the reader's attention, and the second presents a preview of what is to follow. That is exactly what many writing-test scorers are looking for. Then each paragraph develops each of the three qualities that are presented in capsule form in the second sentence. The final paragraph is simply a rewording of the first paragraph.

The student who got a score of 8 did not waste energy on this timed test thinking of fifteen or so other qualities he or she might have added. Instead, I suspect the student thought of three qualities, jotted these in a list, then wrote a summary first sentence, described the three qualities, and concluded the paper. Then he or she had a good portion of the time to reread the paragraph carefully, to be sure there were no careless punctuation errors, omitted or misspelled words, or missing capitals. The shorter the piece, the more time the writer has to reread, proofread, and fix up his paper. The goal is simply to show someone you can write without making simple errors. It is not the time to sort out all you know or think about a subject.

It's like wearing appropriate clothes to a party of strangers. Some people will look at the way you look as you walk in the door and make a judgment as to whether they want to meet you or not. This is not fair because who you are is more than what you are wearing, but when you walk in you make your first impression. This is what a writing competency test is. If you get a 4 you pass minimum muster. What you are really like is what you say in your writing the rest of the year. Try not to worry about the score you

---

[1] Actual student test paper that received an 8 in a suburban secondary school. The score is the sum of two scorers who each gave it a score of 4.

got on this test, and next time you do it, think about how to write
something short and simple and how to allow yourself time to go
back over it to correct any little mistakes. Now to help us get back
into the place where we do our best writing . . .

At this point Janice can go into the best prewriting strategies she
knows, helping the students with guided imagery to stir up their
memories as they return to writing on topics of interest to them. (See
Chapter 1, "Defending a Grade" for prewriting suggestions.)

So much for the short-term goal for this year. The next year,
Janice can introduce the writing competency test as an important
but comparatively perfunctory exercise to demonstrate mastery of
minimal skill in writing. She should not even return the test essays
to the students unless she plans to use them to teach students how
to take tests in the future. Somehow, she needs to make clear that
a timed test of this sort, a single writing sample, is useful in deter-
mining averages of large groups of students, but it is notoriously
unreliable as a measure of the writing of a single individual. She can
tell them that the collection of papers they have done for the term
is a far more important and valid test of their writing ability.

Her long-term goal has to be to convince the rest of the department to change the method of evaluation of student writing. One of
the hottest issues in the field of English pedagogy these days is the
effect of inappropriate testing on instruction. If we want students to
write well, we need to ask them to engage in writing tasks that challenge their best thinking. It is easier to get test scorers to agree on a
score if each student writes on the same topic. Selecting topics, however, is problematic. Any topic is likely to turn off some students as
it engages others. Thus, the most valid way to assess students is on
the basis of a body of work.

If Janice's department members are open to an alternative
assessment that does not involve administering a single writing
prompt for all of the students, she can introduce the way to measure
growth that is the most authentic and least disruptive of all, namely,
portfolio assessment. A portfolio is simply a folder of samples of a
student's best writing efforts. Growth can be measured in terms of
the difference between the papers produced earliest in the year and
those written fairly late in the spring. To assign grades, the teacher
need only rank the folders in terms of overall quality. (See Chapter
1, "Defending a Grade.")

The greatest value of the portfolio, however, is in helping students reflect on their own growth. As they, in consultation with their
teacher, select a paper for inclusion, they look critically at their own
work, and the process of selection breeds criteria for good writing.

Appendix B is an actual memo written by one of the authors of this book to make a case for portfolio assessment to the members of his department. After Janice has tried out portfolios in her classroom, she might write a similar memo to convince her colleagues. At least such a memo might start a departmental discussion of alternatives to the writing competency test and the scoring criteria Janice finds problematic.

If Janice's English department wants to assess students on the basis not of a portfolio, but rather on the basis of a single writing sample, then she should advise them to adopt one of the excellent writing tests developed by the California Department of Education in 1991. (See Appendix A for a sample.) There is no reason why a writing assessment could not also be a test of a student's reading. In the California state assessment, students are assessed through two separate essays: (1) interpreting a character in a short piece of literature, and (2) reflecting on a broader theme emerging from the literary selection. Because students are expected to write their first responses freely and to write down any thoughts, questions, or opinions before they are asked to draft a coherent essay, they are nudged toward reflection and examination of the meaning of a piece of literature. Having students share their ideas about the story in a small group mirrors good classroom practice and helps students verbalize their interpretations, get feedback, and often revise their ideas before they are asked to commit these to paper. The goal is for all of the students to produce the best possible final draft. In actual writing settings, collaborative efforts are honored; why not in the classroom?

CHAPTER 12

INHERIT THE WIND

Situation

"These are God's words," Steve shouts.
Rachel adds, "Who is Charles Darwin compared to
the Almighty?"
"Darwin actually existed, for one thing!" Jim
laughs.

Inherit the Wind has always been one of Alan's favorite plays. When he was in high school, he was a juror in the senior class play, and ever since has been interested both in the play and the actual Scopes trial. Although the play is not required reading for his honors-level juniors, it is on the list of alternative texts approved by his board of education. So in his first year as a teacher, Alan begins the year with *Inherit the Wind*.

He starts with three days of background. The first day, he presents creation stories from all over the world, which the students find interesting and entertaining. On the second day, he hands out photocopies of Genesis and reads aloud. He explains that at the time this story came into being it may have been the closest thing to science people had. The third day, he presents, in simple terms, Darwin's theory of evolution, ending with a newspaper article reporting on fossil microorganisms discovered in Australia that "are likely to prompt a reexamination of rates at which species are presumed to have evolved on the early Earth."[1] On the fourth day, he distributes copies of the play.

---

[1]"Life Gets Earlier Date of Origin," *Chicago Tribune*, May 2, 1993, 28.

Before he has finished handing them out, several students ask him which account or theory he finds the most plausible. At first he tells them that what one believes about such things is a personal matter. But they persist. He says, "Genesis is a beautiful story. But I think it is just that, a story. There is no concrete evidence to back it up. Evolution, on the other hand, has a great deal of scientific data to support it—in fact, more is being unearthed all the time."

Brenda throws her hand in the air, her eyes locked on some point in the middle of the floor. "So you're an atheist."

"My religious beliefs should not be an issue here," Alan says. "I simply intended to present the two points of view which will come into conflict in this play."

"But you said you're an evolutionist," she says, her eyes still fixed downward.

"I didn't. But I find the scientific evidence plausible."

"So the Bible is all wrong," she snaps. Now her eyes meet his. Alan sits, crosses his arms. "Look, Brenda, let's back up. I'm not here to preach to you what I believe. My intention was to give you information that would help you understand the play. If I erred in answering your direct question, I'm sorry. But that should not be taken as a challenge to your beliefs."

Jim, always eager to wrestle an intellectual point to the mat, jumps in. "Brenda. Let me ask you. How do you explain the complete lack of evidence for the Biblical story and the abundance of data supporting the theory of—"

"I know what the Bible tells me. God created the heavens and the earth."

Someone in the back says, "Amen!" Alan wonders if it is genuine concurrence, or sarcasm. Several students groan, some laugh and shake their heads.

Brenda raises both hands close to her shoulders, palms out and shakes them. "I don't want to talk about this. I don't want to talk about this at all."

Jim rises to his haunches on his chair. He's a pouncer. "Brenda, I want to ask you something 'cause I'm really interested. So don't get defensive. You believe exactly what the Bible says and that it can't be disputed in any way? I mean, like when Jonah was swallowed by the whale, or Christ rose from the dead—all that's real? Not just a story to make a point."

"Do you have a copy of the Bible?" Brenda turns to Jim.

"Yea, man, I keep it on a shelf with my other mythology."

Alan interrupts, seeing that Brenda is shaken, coiling and uncoiling her hair around her finger. "Jim, we'll let it be."

Now Steve and Rachel jump to Brenda's defense. "These are God's words," Steve shouts.

Rachel adds, "Who is Charles Darwin compared to the Almighty?"

"Darwin actually existed, for one thing!" Jim laughs.

Alan is relieved when the bells ring, though the class, as they prepare to leave, seem to have formed two camps—one gathered around Jim, the other around Brenda.

The following morning, Alan receives a call from Brenda's mother.

"You have no right, Mr. Davis," she says, in a tone very much like Brenda's, though more confident. "No right whatsoever to be teaching religion in a public school."

"I'm not teaching religion," Alan says.

"Brenda told me that you taught Genesis. I have a duplicated copy of it here in my hand."

"I read it in class, but I didn't try to teach it. I also read nine other creation stories."

"I do not look kindly, Mr. Davis, on your lumping the holy word together with what you call other creation stories."

"I am trying to set up some background material for our study of a play. I really am not trying to push one or the other point of view."

"You are out of line. Just so you know. Everybody already knows Genesis, so I don't know why you should have to read it in class."

"Well, that's not really true," Alan says. "We have students from a variety of backgrounds here. Two of my students are Muslim."

"Are you a Christian man?" she asks.

"Mrs. Underwood . . ."

"Just answer my question."

"Mrs. Underwood, I think this is a very private issue."

"Well so do I, Mr. Davis. And I want you to keep your mouth shut about it in your classroom. Am I understood?"

"I have 120 other students. I'm not going to change my plans. If you wish, Brenda can read an alternate book."

"Do your superiors know you teach such things to our children?"

"We do not have to go over our plans with our . . ."

"You may rest assured they will know before this morning has passed."

Rebecca, Alan's department chair, calls him into her office at the end of the day. She has received four calls today: one from Brenda's mother, demanding that he not teach a play that requires an "informal and cavalier" study of the Bible; one from Steve's father who wants his son excused from having to read *Inherit The Wind* and from any classroom discussions relating to it; one from a woman who does not have a child in the school but had heard about Alan's classroom discussion and wanted to know what "the heck Mr. Davis is trying to do!" The last call came from Julie Crowell, a member of the board, who said she had received phone calls from each of the same three people and felt Mr. Davis's motives ought to be looked into.

"So what are you saying?" Alan asks. "Do you want me not to do the book?"

"I'll tell you what I want, Alan. I want no more phone calls on this matter. I don't care how you accomplish it, I just want you to accomplish it. No more calls."

QUESTIONS TO CONSIDER

1. What do you think of the way Alan has handled the students and the parent, so far?
2. Should Alan continue with this play?
3. If he does continue, should he present alternatives for those who do not want to read it? If so, how does he solve the logistical problems?
4. What if Alan continues, but Rebecca gets more phone calls?
5. If he chooses not to continue, what should he say to the class? What if some members want to go ahead and read the play?

PERSPECTIVES

As a first-year teacher, Alan needs support. He is teaching an approved alternative text, so he is clearly within his rights to continue with this play. However, Rebecca, his department head, is not going to defend his choice if phone calls persist, and there is no way for him to guarantee they won't. His commitment is to educate his students truly—showing them that in our pluralistic and multicultural society, there are profound differences in belief. How better than to introduce them to a court trial in which differences in belief are hotly debated?

What are Alan's options?

He can abandon his plan, taking the message from his department chair as a directive. As a first-year, untenured teacher, this course of action is tempting. To do so, however, would be to abandon his commitment as a teacher—to open student minds and stimulate critical thought. To take this course will, in the long run, damage Alan's sense of integrity. As an educator, he has taken on the challenge of introducing young persons to significant major issues of human experience. To give up that goal is to turn his back on the major reason he went into teaching in the first place.

He can ask those students who prefer to read another play to meet separately during class time and read an alternate play aloud together, either in the hallway, library, or at the back of the room. He might give them an equally challenging text, such as Arthur Miller's *Death of a Salesman* or *All My Sons*. These students will not have the benefit of the classroom interaction with Mr. Davis, but they will have an opportunity to discuss issue-laden material. Alan can have them report on their progress daily and do a polished Readers' Theater presentation, to the entire class, of a cutting of the play they have read.

This option will probably placate the most irate parents, and most of the students will have the benefit of discussing one of the hottest and most controversial issues of our day. Creationism has been in the news repeatedly over the past decade.

Alan is more fortunate than some English teachers because his school board has agreed to include *Inherit the Wind* as one of the plays he can teach. He might have been in a community where the school board has been taken over by certain fundamentalist Christian groups, who are adamant that *they* control what their children read in school. Parents have, after all, a strong commitment to seeing that their children grow up believing as they do, and whenever their power to make this happen is challenged, they can make the professional lives of more moderate teachers extremely difficult. If Alan were in such a school district, he would be wise to get involved in public forums and book discussion groups, working toward the eventual election of a more moderate school board. The school has a responsibility to educate the community, as well as its children, and extremist parents and others need to be invited to participate in a broad-based discussion of issues.[2]

A third course for Alan is to decide courageously to barrel ahead with *Inherit the Wind* for the whole class. He first needs to identify as many allies in the community as he can find. He also needs to share

---

[2]To understand what happens when groups who are bent on censoring student textbooks are excluded from public dialogue, read James Moffett's account of the Kanawha County, West Virginia, textbook burning in the mid-seventies: *Storm in the Mountains* (Carbondale, Ill.: Southern Illinois University Press, 1988).

his plans and problem with other members of his English department and science department colleagues as well. It would be tempting but self-indulgent and unproductive to whine about what the department chair told him. He does not want to put her on the spot, but at the same time he needs to broaden the dialogue and to find other faculty who will support his decision. It might be a good time to alert the president of the local American Civil Liberties Union of the pressure he is under. He can also call the National Council of Teachers of English[3] to find out who is chairing the Standing Committee Against Censorship and ask that person for advice and help. He can also request a copy of an NCTE position statement on censorship and see if they have a defense of *Inherit the Wind* or plays like it. Members of Great Books discussion groups, local library board members, and book store managers and clerks are among others are likely to support his decision should the parental complaints escalate.

After Alan has marshaled some allies and if he feels up to the challenge, he might invite Brenda's and Steve's parents to visit his class and participate in the discussion, along with a parent who is not complaining about the class. The discussion the parents have might be very enlightening to the class. After all, the Tennessee law under which John Scopes was tried and convicted in 1925 was not repealed until 1967, so the parents who disagree with Darwin are not alone in their views.[4]

---

[3]Phone: 800-369-NCTE.

[4]The Louisiana "Creationism Act," which prohibited the teaching of the theory of evolution in a public school unless accompanied by the theory of "creation science," was struck down by the U.S. Supreme Court *Edwards vs Aguillard*, 482 U.S. 578 (1987). In Arkansas, a similar statute was declared unconstitutional. *McLean v. Arkansas Board of Education*, 529 F. Supp. 1255 (E.D. Ark. 1982).

CHAPTER 13

DIVERSITY OF HERITAGE

SITUATION

"If you were in a class of all black students, Ms. Goldman, and everything they read was by black writers—with one tiny exception—and the way they acted, when they talked and when they were quiet and the way they spoke—everything—was black— wouldn't you want a little break now and then, a chance to get out of the room?"

Sue has one problem in her honors class—Henry Sheffield. But it didn't start out that way. Henry is one of three African-American students and the only African-American male in that class. He's bright and articulate; he charms with his quick wit. Sue liked him immediately for his blunt and apt assessments of events and people. He is equally capable of turning his laser-accurate perceptions on the literature they read. There have been times when Henry could throw Sue off-balance with his on-target remarks—like the time Sue was giving a test, and, after a steady stream of students had stepped up to her desk with questions, she had announced, "There is a set of thirty dictionaries in this room. If you have trouble with any of the words on this test, you can look them up." Henry had said, "Translation: Don't bother me."

And it was true. Sue had hoped to grade essays while her students were busy with the test. Could this kid read her mind?

But recently Henry has started arriving late. The first time, Sue wagged a finger at him and Henry rolled his eyes. When it happens again two days later, Sue asks him why he is late.

"I'm not late."

"But you are."

"No."

"Henry, the bell rang."

"So?"

"So you're late."

"Do you see my books on my desk?"

Sue nods.

"Then how are you going to try and tell me I'm late?"

Sue has heard this argument before, expressed with the same attitude, but in the lower tracks. She is surprised to hear it from an honors student. The next day, Henry is on time. The day after that, he's not yet in the class ten minutes after the bell rings. Sue sees him in the hall, leisurely parting company with another boy. She meets Henry at the door and stops him quietly while the class is taking a quiz. "What's going on?" Sue asks.

"Nothing. What's your problem?"

"You're late again."

"The bell hasn't even rung."

"Yes, it has."

"No, it didn't."

"Look around you, Henry. Everyone else is in his seat and has already begun the quiz."

"That's their problem."

Next, Sue begins seeing Henry in the halls when he should be in another class. Sometimes he has a pass, sometimes he does not. At the same time, his academic achievement begins to slip. He stops doing his homework and fails reading quizzes. When the class discusses current events, he is as interested and involved as always. But when talk turns to the text at hand, he either puts his head down, talks to other students, or demands a pass to the washroom.

Conferences with Henry seem to make no difference. It is time to call his parent. Sue reaches Henry's mother at work.

"Do you have a moment to talk?" she asks.

"About my son? Any time, day or night."

Sue explains the situation. Mrs. Sheffield wants to come in some time in the next week. A meeting is set up for three days later.

"Coming late, is he?" Mrs. Sheffield says as she shakes Sue's hand. "Why do you think that is?" She sits down with her purse in her lap.

"I don't know. Henry had been doing great. He was one of my top students in every way. Things, though, started to fall apart about three weeks ago."

"Fall apart." She pulls an envelope from her purse and writes a note to herself on it. "Not doing his work? What else?"

"Getting disruptive in class, too."

"Talking out of turn?" she adds.

"Yes."

"Sassy."

"I suppose you could say that."

She snaps the purse shut. "We will take care of this." She rises and extends her hand. "There will be no more trouble from Henry."

Then the next day Henry is not in class. The following day he is fifteen minutes tardy, but has a pass. He extends it to Sue, but then as Sue is about to take it, he lets it fall to the floor. Sue picks it up.

Shortly after sitting down, Henry spins in his seat and snaps at Charles, who sits behind him. "Get your feet off my chair. What the fuck is wrong with you?"

Henry has an oral presentation to make on a chapter from *The Scarlet Letter*. He is one of three presenters. He tells Sue he has a headache and wants a pass to the nurse. When Sue gives him one, Henry promises to get a Tylenol and be back in ten minutes. But the entire period passes and Henry does not return.

Sue calls home that evening. Mrs. Sheffield is unaware of the absence and disturbed to hear that Henry has cursed in class. She will come in the next day. Henry will be at the meeting, too.

The next afternoon Mrs. Sheffield, Henry, and Sue sit in three student desks set corner to corner like the leaves of a clover. Henry keeps his head lowered, staring at the backs of his hands and flexing his fingers slowly. Sue is about to go over the situation one more time when Mrs. Sheffield speaks.

"How many African-American students do you have in this class, Ms. Goldman?"

"There are three."

"Three." She reaches into her purse and this time takes out a small memo pad. "Three. All right. The rest of the students are— "

"Are . . . what?" Sue asks.

"White, Asian, Latino . . .?"

"White."

She scribbles, then turns a glare on Sue. "What are the expectations you have for your students?"

"I expect them to be prepared, to be attentive, well-behaved."

"Explain that one."

"Well-behaved? Not talking out of turn. Being on time. Speaking courteously."

"You don't like Henry, do you?"

"What?" Sue laughs. "Yes, I do." It was a strange thing to have to defend. "I always have. He's very smart . . ."

"Smart for a black child, is that what you mean?"

"Henry, on the contrary, Henry is one of my top students. Until he started acting up."

"Acting up." She makes a note. "I want to hear more about the time he went to the nurse."

"He had a presentation to make, but told me he had a headache. I gave him a pass to the nurse so he could get a Tylenol, but he never came back. He shouldn't have been more than ten minutes. That seemed suspicious to me. So I asked him honestly if he had been prepared for his presentation."

"Why?"

"Why did I . . .?"

"Why did you not trust him?"

"I trust him."

"Why did you ask him if he was prepared? Unless you had a preconceived idea. Assumed he wasn't prepared."

"I wondered. I didn't assume."

"Would you have wondered the same thing about your white students?"

"Mrs. Sheffield . . ." Sue shifts in his seat, trying to signal a transition. To what, she doesn't know.

"I am asking you an honest question. You like honest questions, I believe."

"That's not an answerable question."

"As I thought." More notes. "One last question, then I'll allow you to return to your busy schedule. What African-American writers will you be reading this year?"

"Well, we read, *To Kill a Mockingbird*, but, of course, that's . . ."

"That's written by a white female."

"I was going to say."

"So my original question . . ."

"I do a short story by Richard Wright. Actually it's one chapter from *Black Boy*."

"Good. What else?"

"Mrs. Sheffield . . ."

"Is there anything else?"

"I have long been waiting to introduce more . . ."

"So, 'no'."

Sue nods.

Mrs. Sheffield sets a hand on the back of her son's neck. "Now Henry, I want you to tell Ms. Goldman what you told me. Go on now."

Henry shakes his head downward. "Mom."

"Henry."

Henry speaks softly. "Said, this stuff you be reading . . ."

"You *are* reading," his mother corrects him.

"Yeah. Whatever. Stuff you are reading has nothing to do with me."

She squeezes Henry's neck, then folds her hands and leans over them toward Sue. "If you were in a class of all black students, Ms. Goldman, and everything they read was by black writers—with one tiny exception—and the way they acted, when they talked and when they were quiet and the way they spoke—everything—was black—wouldn't you want a little break now and then, a chance to get out of the room?" She drops the notepad in her purse. "I'm asking an honest question."

QUESTIONS TO CONSIDER

1. Does Mrs. Sheffield have a valid concern, or is she just defending her son's misbehavior?

2. What should Sue do about her questions? Can she change the curriculum in the middle of the term, and, if so, how should she go about it? Who else in the school might be affected by such a change?

3. Suppose the next novel scheduled is *The Great Gatsby*. Is that any more likely to attract Henry's interest than *The Scarlet Letter?*

4. What should Sue do next to solve her problem with Henry?

PERSPECTIVES

Mrs. Sheffield's questions are not so much about Sue's attitude toward her son as they are about the message implied in the selection of literature in Sue's secondary school. In part, this message is that the "best" literature in our culture has been written almost exclusively by whites. Thus, Mrs. Sheffield's concerns need to become part of the ongoing department discussions of the literature approved in the English program.[1]

---

[1] A good resource for Sue's English department is the Committee on Racism and Bias in the Teaching of English of the National Council of Teachers of English, 1111 Kenyon Road, Urbana, Ill., 61801 (phone: 800/369-NCTE).

There is no such thing as a neutral curriculum. The current debate over cultural literacy merely focuses national attention on the conflict inherent in any selection of reading matter. Anyone who is teaching reading and writing is inevitably making judgments as to what is worth reading and writing about.

It is likely that Henry's attitude and behavior will improve markedly if the next novel the class reads is written by an African-American, and his mother then will probably be a wholehearted supporter of Henry's becoming a more responsible student. Sue's best course of action would be to ask Henry and his mother to recommend a list of novels they think would be of the greatest interest to him. Sue could promise either to select one from this list or to choose another comparable novel that she feels more appropriate for this age level. For example, a book written by Nobel and Pulitzer prize winning novelist Toni Morrison would probably meet Mrs. Sheffield's implied criterion that the artist's work reflect Henry's heritage, particularly centering on the effect of the legacy of slavery on African-Americans; and, at the same time, such a work would be likely to be considered by the other members of the department as worthy of being substituted for *The Great Gatsby* as another classic of American literature.

Another alternative is to have the three African-American students read a different novel from the rest of the class, but this strategy would be fair neither to that group nor to the rest of the class. Each group needs the opportunity both to affirm their own heritage and to talk across their culture to the other group. Since the African-Americans in Sue's class are in the minority, they, more than the rest of the class, need literature that represents their racial heritage to enhance their status and comfort level with the other students. Even more important, to be fully educated, the white students need to become immersed in the African-American consciousness and literary imagination. If they get the idea that a novel by an African-American is suitable only for students of that race, they will be learning a lesson that will forever cut them off from a unique and incomparably rich source of aesthetic experience.

Sue's situation should not be viewed as a problem. Diversity of background is not a problem but a plus in a literature class. The differences in the ways students respond to a piece of literature provide fertile ground for the growth of genuine cross-cultural understanding.

A heritage is simply a given. Every person has one, a force that has helped shape values, ways of thinking and knowing, oral and written language, and ways to communicate with others. The more diverse the classroom, the greater the opportunity for learning. If all of the students have a similar heritage, there is less to explain to others. If they differ, they need to teach each other what the differences are. Gonzalez Mena summarizes it this way:

> Children in a bicultural or multicultural program grow up to be highly competent people. People who are able to move freely and comfortably with or away from their own people. They feel good about themselves. They fit, and when they find themselves in situations where they don't fit, they have a better chance of adapting without giving up anything of themselves or their culture.[2]

Thus, Sue owes it to all of her students to immerse them in literature that reflects their own heritage *and* in literature that challenges them to identify, at least for the hours they are reading the book, with a culture outside their own. Expanding experience beyond what one can know directly is exactly what reading literature is all about. We learn from vicarious experience just as we do from actual experience.

It is possible, of course, that Henry's mother is misguided in her assumption that Henry's misconduct stems primarily from the literature he finds alien. If his misbehavior continues even after the required reading has been changed, Sue needs to explore other approaches. From what she has learned about Mrs. Sheffield, she would probably be a strong ally in Sue's efforts to help Henry improve. Mrs. Sheffield wants him to do well in school.

Sue's long-term goal needs to be to recruit more persons of color to teach in her English department. If the members of Sue's department were of diverse racial and ethnic backgrounds, it is likely that the books on the reading lists, from which the required readings are selected, would include substantial numbers of works by African-Americans, Asians, Hispanics, Native Americans, and members of other non-white groups.

One of the major current concerns of the National Council of Teachers of English is the decreasing number of college students of color who are entering the profession of English teaching. Sue needs to do all she can to build into the Henrys of her class a respect for the English teaching profession. We need many more such young persons to join the ranks of secondary school and college English teachers.

In the meantime, Sue needs to recommend titles to be added to the list of approved materials from which teachers may choose their

---

[2]Janet Gonzales-Mena, *Multicultural Issues in Child Care* (Mountain View, Cal.: Mayfield Publishers, 1992), 83.

required texts—be they fiction, poetry, plays, or essays. Six good sources for lists of books to expand the range of racial and ethnic heritages are:

Rochman, Hazel, *Against Borders: Promoting Books for a Multicultural World*. Chicago: American Library Association, 1993.

Schullstrom, Faith Z., *Expanding the Canon*. Urbana, Ill.: National Council of Teachers of English, 1990.

Hardt, Ulrich H., *Literature of the Americas*. Urbana, Ill.: National Council of Teachers of English, 1992.

"Many Voices" compiled and annotated by Ellen Greenblatt. University of California, Berkeley: The Bay Area Writing Project, 1991.

Beach, Richard, and James Marshall, "Teaching Literature of Different Cultures," in *Teaching Literature in the Secondary School*. New York: Harcourt Brace Jovanovich, Inc., 1991. pp. 437-83.

Magill, Frank N., editor. *Masterpieces of African-American Literature*. New York: Harper-Collins, 1992.

Department members might find lists of useful books at their local library or from such groups as the Council on Interracial Books for Children,[3] or the Racism and Bias in the Teaching of English Committee of the National Council of Teachers of English.[4] Other sources are journals such as *English Journal, The Journal of Negro Education*, and *Publisher's Weekly*. Two books that would make good background reading for Sue and the members of her department are:

Banks, James A., and Cherry A. M. Banks, eds., *Multicultural Education: Issues and Perspectives*. Boston: Allyn and Bacon, 1989.

Miller, Suzanne M., and Barbara McCaskill, eds. *Multicultural Literature and Literacies: Making Space for Difference*. Albany: State University of New York Press, 1993.

---

[3]29 West 15th Street, New York, NY 10011.

[4]1111 Kenyon Road, Urbana, IL 61801 (phone: 217-328-3870; fax: 217-328-9645).

CHAPTER 14

SCHEDULES AND SERENDIPITY

SITUATION

"This class is kinda like that, Mr. Oberman. No offense, but we just keep moving along like the old mighty Mississip'." She laughs. "Yeah, just like that. Not stopping for nothin'!"

Bruce lives by schedules. He always has, even as a child. He had a desk calendar when he was six years old and derived pleasure from filling in the squares with important events: "my birthday," "school starts," "sledding with Dad." When he did his student teaching with Margaret Thorsen, he felt immediately at home. She plotted out entire quarters at a time, distributing schedules on the first day of class that told what would be read and discussed on which days, when papers were due and when they would be returned. Bruce found comfort in no surprises.

Now in his first year, teaching mid-level sophomores, he is working from a schedule he had worked out within a week of learning that he had been hired. And it was a good schedule. The students would do some writing first, due on day three, a Wednesday. He would return the essays Friday and rewrites were due the next Monday. They would read *The Autobiography of Miss Jane Pittman* first. At twenty pages a night, they would finish by October 4. On October 5, they would take an exam and on October 6 they would begin *Of Mice and Men.* Bruce believed this had to be among the best laid plans.

Bruce brought in some articles about the 1993 flooding of the Mississippi River on the day they were to have read the chapter, "Of Men and Rivers," that includes this paragraph:

The damage from that high water was caused by man, because man wanted to control the rivers, and you cannot control water. The old people, the Indians, used to worship the rivers till the white people came here and conquered them and tried to conquer the rivers, too.[1]

He initiated a discussion about the power of nature and humankind's inability to govern it. He figured they would spend fifteen minutes talking about that, take the daily reading quiz (ten minutes, tops) then have fifteen minutes remaining for discussion about the rest of the chapter. However, his plan was interrupted.

"Mr. Oberman," Lindy says. "I was in Kansas City the year of the flooding. I always go to spend the summer with my dad. But so here I was in '93 down there when all heck broke loose. You should've seen. I spent the whole summer up to my belt in water or going around streets in a row boat or filling sand bags trying to patch the levee. It was incredible."

"What's a levee?" Nicky wants to know.

Lindy explains a levee and talks about the way people worked together, about the Red Cross and the news people, about rescuing a cat from a rooftop. Ten minutes, twelve minutes, she kept talking. "No matter what we did, that water had a mind of its own," she said, "You get so you—even though you hate it and what it's doing to all these people, you get so you respect it. You got to."

Jonathan says, "Jane Pittman talks about that on page 149." And he reads, "'Well, they stacked sacks and stacked sacks, and every time the river got ready to break through it went right on and broke through that little levee like it was made of match sticks.'"

Seventeen minutes, Bruce is thinking. He takes up the stack of quizzes and thanks Lindy. As he distributes the sheets, Francis asks Lindy, "Did you ever get the feeling the river was, like—maybe a person and had a—mission, like it was doing this on purpose?"

Lindy takes the quiz sheet from Bruce and says, "Yeah! That's what I'm telling you: like it had a mind of its own. The power of nature. Unbelievable."

"All right," Bruce says, "You all have copies of the quiz. We're running out of time, I'm afraid, but, Lindy, thank you again so much for that first-hand account."

Lindy shrugs, "Oh, that's OK."

"Perhaps we'll hear more about it at another time. But now, I'm getting worried that the class won't have time to finish the quizzes before the bell."

---

[1] Jane Pittman, *The Autobiography of Miss Jane Pittman*, (New York: Bantam, 1972), 147.

Andrew asks, "Can't this wait, Mr. Oberman? I want to hear more about what happened."

Bruce looks at the clock. "Well. Thing is, if we wait, that will mean we'll have to take two quizzes tomorrow."

Andrew says, "So?" and the rest of the class agrees that it would not be a problem.

Bruce tries to explain that that would take twice as long and leave very little time to discuss two reading segments. He imagines each square of his quarter schedule being knocked into the next, like a multi-car pile-up. "We have so much to cover," he says and begins to worry now about the time *this* discussion is taking.

"Can't we just chill for once?" Bonita asks. "I mean, dang, I feel like we're on some kind of conveyor belt."

Lindy says, "That's what it was like! This one time we were working on the levee and we pretty much knew it was going to break, but we kept piling up on it anyway because we were trying to save this electrical plant. And we kept watching the river rise and rise." Then she turns to Bruce. "This class is kinda like that, Mr. Oberman. No offense, but we just keep moving along like the old mighty Mississip'." She laughs. "Yeah, just like that. Not stopping for nothin'!"

QUESTIONS TO CONSIDER

1. What are Bruce's options? Is he right to barrel ahead with the quiz?
2. What would happen if he skipped the quiz that day? Would it provide an incentive for the class to prolong a discussion on another day just to keep from having a quiz?
3. Is the idea of having two quizzes the next day a good one?
4. What is the value of Bruce's schedule?
5. What are its disadvantages?

PERSPECTIVES

Bruce's commitment to staying on schedule is in conflict with the real learning that he can see is going on in his classroom. He knows the consequences of getting behind; only he really knows how much of the curriculum lies ahead of the students this term. He doesn't want to have to rush through literature later in the term just because he lets this discussion take more than the time he has allotted.

His wisest choice at this point is to skip the quiz altogether and let the fruitful discussion continue. Linda's first-hand experience with the world Jane Pittman describes is not only pertinent but of great interest to and informative for the rest of the class. If Bruce fears that this will give the class the message that he is an easy target for getting him off his agenda of the daily reading quiz, all he need do is to give the quiz at the first of the class period from now on. That way the discussion can incorporate the questions on the quiz as well as the other parts of the chapter Bruce planned to discuss.

Piling up two quizzes the next day seems unwise. Not only will the discussion of the next chapter be too truncated, but the students do not need to be tested daily as long as they are keeping up their reading assignments. Bruce might congratulate them on the quality of their discussion and the large number of students who participated. He can tell them that he now has a good sense of their understanding of the book so they do not need a quiz.

Since the main purpose of the daily quizzes would seem to be to keep the students energized for their daily reading, pop quizzes might serve the same function. As long as the students don't know which day to expect a quiz, they have the same pressure to keep up as they would with daily quizzes. If Bruce likes, he can always have a quiz ready in case the discussion bogs down, but if it's clear from the discussion that almost all of the students are engaged with the text, he can give quizzes only from time to time. Students will know that if the quizzes are less frequent, it is more important that they do well, since there are fewer scores to average, and one low grade will pull down the rest more than if the quizzes were daily.

CHAPTER 15

FROM GRAMMAR
TO WRITING?

SITUATION

How to proceed? Can she stick to her original intention of deducting one point for every mechanical error, failing a paper with seven or more?

Linda started out her year with the prescribed textbook, Warriner's *English Composition and Grammar*.[1] She felt she should have her one-level sophomores learn the "building blocks" of writing before they moved on to essays. Besides, this was the prescribed curriculum.

From the start, Darlene was her prize pupil. She always caught on to the exercises quickly, finishing them in time to help other students who were struggling. Darlene could identify all the parts of speech and diagram the most complex sentences Linda could give her, and could even grasp the section on punctuating quotations, which many students found particularly difficult.

In late November, Linda assigns the first essay. The assignment is to write about "an unpleasant encounter you have had with one other person." The assignment requires at least one segment of dialogue. Linda tells her students that after two months of grammar study, she feels justified in deducting one point for each mechanical error. More than seven mechanical errors will result in an F. She collects the essays and tells the class how excited she is to see what they

---

[1] John E. Warriner (Orlando, Fla.: Harcourt Brace Jovanovich, Inc., 1988).

can do. "I know how anxious you will be to get them back, so I promise to return them to you tomorrow."

Linda goes home that night with her first stack of essays to grade. She curls up in her favorite chair and sets the papers on her lap, a pile as thick as a pillow. She kicks off her shoes and sets a cup of hot coffee at her side. She decides to thumb down and find Darlene's essay to start with and then ease into the rest.

bad time

Every body they warned me bout old man Fred bout how he always be messin with other people's busyness and stuff. How he could bit off your ear and stuff and shoot you quick as sneeze. But I'am a bullheaded gal. I go up his stair and I go", hey you Mr Fred and he come out is door an he go "who you child? Be messin at my door?" I go "my name Darlene, Mr Fred. My moma she send me to ax you for that money"y" Fred he go, laughing like he going to choke on hims spit, "Gal, you go on hom now hear? Don't be messin with old man fred, gal."

So he turn away like I doan be even existing. Made me feel bad. Was a bad time.

Linda sets the essay down and gulps her coffee. She fingers the stack. Some of the essays look better, many of them worse. She counts: 1 read, 117 to go. She sets the stack on the coffee table in front of her and stares at them. Her chest tightens to think of reading all of them. How to proceed? Can she stick to her original intention of deducting one point for every mechanical error, failing a paper with seven or more? Good Lord! At that rate, she will have to fail almost every paper—seven times over.

Linda shuts off the reading light and closes her eyes, something she always does when she needs to think hard. Is it possible she has just wasted the first crucial months of the year? What is the point of studying grammar if it doesn't result in better writing? How could she have failed so utterly? Where has she miscalculated? Is she a terrible teacher? Can she have harmed these kids in some way, inadvertently stunted their grammatical growth?

She decides to keep reading the papers until she is finished, circling every error, but she'll not assign a letter grade. She will return the essays tomorrow, set a stack of dictionaries and Warriner's on the front table, and while she conducts writing conferences, the kids will correct their errors and then resubmit the papers. Good. A plan. She makes another pot of coffee and divides the thick stack of papers into smaller stacks of ten. After every ten she will allow herself a break of five minutes. She spends the next five and a half hours reading those papers and circling their errors, because she has promised to return them the next day, and, besides, she has no other lesson plan.

The next morning it takes a good fifteen minutes to explain to the first class what she has in mind and what the rules and guidelines will be; then another ten minutes are spent distributing the papers and quieting the students' anger and soothing their hurt feelings. Thank goodness, she didn't also put grades on these papers. Once they are finally quiet and at work, Linda calls Darlene up first to the chair beside her desk. Darlene's lips are tight, and she fixes her eyes on something beyond Linda, outside the window.

"Well, Darlene, do you know what I liked the very most about your essay? I liked the fact that your unique sense of humor came through bright and clear. At home alone last night, as I read this, I almost felt like you were right there speaking to me."

Darlene's foot, set across her knee, flutters like a piston. "Darlene," Linda leans closer, "are you upset about something?"

The girl's eyes go wet, and she waves her hand over the paper. "Look at that thing," she says, her voice flying off into a tiny falsetto. "It's all bloodied, like you whipped it with a bullwhip. Why'd you go and do that if you like it so much?"

"Whipped with a bullwhip. That's an effective simile for describing the way it looks, Darlene."

"Whatever." She swats at her tears.

"Let's see if we can clean up some of these wounds right now. Turn to page nineteen of your Warriner's. What do you remember about titles?"

Darlene looks at her book. "Capitalize the first and last word and any other important words," she reads.

"Yes, very good. Now tell me, why didn't you do that here in your paper?"

Darlene shrugs.

"Well, I'm sure I don't know either, Darlene. Now look here." She points at the words "every body." What do you think is wrong here, Darlene? Darlene takes up a pencil and scratches off the "y."

"Ever body, Darlene? Come now."

"I don't even know, Ms. Johnson. I don't even care."

"Tell you what," Linda says. "I'm going to read this to you and you tell me how it sounds." She reads the essay, glancing now and then at Darlene. Darlene works hard to gain control of a spreading grin. Linda finishes reading and smiles. "What's so funny, Darlene?"

"It sounds funny when you says it."

"It does, doesn't it? Why do you think that is?"

Darlene shrugs. "It isn't your way a talking. You always talk all proper."

"Well, wouldn't you like to learn to talk and write proper, too?"

Darlene shrugs again. "I guess. Don't really matter."

"Well, let's move on, shall we?" Linda glances over the rest of the paper, wondering how to proceed. She looks up at the class. Several students are out of their seats and gathered in the corner, fighting over a radio. Many of the others have packed their bags and are either sleeping, talking, or staring at the clock. Two minutes remain in the period. Linda closes her eyes and wishes she could shut off the light. Will she really be able to have a conference with every student? And even if she can manage to come up with enough to keep the rest of the class busy, how much value will the conferences really have? She feels she is getting nowhere with Darlene.

The bell rings and the room empties quickly. Linda picks up a rubber-banded pile of thirty-one papers and prepares to face the next class.

QUESTIONS TO CONSIDER

1. What went wrong here? Why isn't Darlene able to transfer her knowledge of grammar to her writing?
2. What else could Linda have done with Darlene's paper besides circling the errors?
3. When she held a conference with Darlene, what could the rest of the class have done during that time?
4. What is the best way to help a student like Darlene get a vision of the limitations of her paper?

PERSPECTIVES

What is demoralizing to Linda is the fact that two and a half months of teaching grammar and five and a half hours of hard work the night before seem to have little effect on her students. If Darlene couldn't make the transfer to her own writing, how about all those other students who weren't as good at grammar? What had gone wrong?

It might be some comfort to Linda to realize that summaries of almost ninety years of research show that grammar study has little or no effect on the improvement of writing.[2] Linda assumed that the prescribed usage of the middle and upper classes that is systematically presented in Warriner's would not only be learned but also transferred to the writing her students did. If that wasn't going to

---

[2]George Hillocks, Jr., *Research on Written Composition* (U.S. Department of Education: National Conference on Research in Education, 1986); R. Braddock, Richard Lloyd-Jones, and L. Schoer, *Research on Written Composition* (Champaign, Ill.: NCTE, 1963).

happen, then why waste her and her students' time? What was the point of teaching grammar anyway?

School- and District-wide Proficiency Examinations

Linda can talk with her department chair and fellow teachers about the fact that the emphasis on grammar instruction in a writing program is misguided, but she may feel locked in by the mandated language proficiency examinations. Even though the teaching of grammar is not effective in improving writing, many school districts place heavy emphasis in their district-wide examinations on conventions: spelling, noun plurals and apostrophes in possessives and contractions, capitalization, punctuation, grammar, syntax, and usage.

Some schools and districts list the items to be mastered in each course or at each grade level. Such lists are vestiges of the now widely discredited behavioral objectives or mastery-learning emphasis of the 1970s. The fact that such an emphasis is discredited doesn't help Linda except psychologically, however. She is under pressure to see that her students do well on the punctuation and grammar tests that are not going to go away—at least not until she and others develop more persuasive power over the evaluation establishment, not only in her school district, but in the larger society as well. Even if Linda is convinced that a study of grammar has little effect on writing quality, how can she get her students to do well on these tests? Can they learn punctuation and grammar as they learn to write, or will she need to teach punctuation and grammar directly?

Her problem is not only the text she is using, but the assumption behind the selection of that text, namely, that punctuation and grammar are learned the most efficiently when they are approached directly. Warriner's is characteristic of the majority of English textbooks. They focus on drill and practice activities that do not transfer easily to the real uses of language in the processes of writing, speaking, and reading.

Alternate Ways to Teach Usage and Punctuation

Linda does need to teach punctuation and usage for the Darlenes in her class. Research shows this is best done in the context of student writing.[3] Linda can conduct mini-lessons on problems common to a large proportion of students.

---

[3]Hillocks and Smith, in *Handbook of Research on Teaching the English Language Arts*, 591–603.

Let's look again at Darlene's paper. The important thing for Linda to realize is that there is no way for Darlene to attack all the problems in this paper at once. What is the most obvious problem it presents? Suppose Linda decides it is what Darlene calls "proper" talk. She needs to help Darlene see that this piece reflects non-standard Vernacular Black English (VBE), which in formal school writing belongs inside quotation marks, but not elsewhere. She needs also to help Darlene recognize that a writer may deliberately write in VBE, but this choice is not appropriate when taking a writing test in secondary school!

Linda then points out that good writers often choose to write in a non-standard dialect. A good contemporary book to show at this point to demonstrate the power of Vernacular Black English is *The Color Purple* by Alice Walker[4] For example, Linda might read the following excerpt: "Dear God, My mama dead. She die screaming and cussing. She scream at me. She cuss at me."[5] Then she asks the class, "Is Alice Walker writing as an educated, sophisticated speaker might write, or is she creating a character who speaks a particular dialect." Then Linda reads a sample sentence from the latter part of Walker's book: "Adam was trying to appear unconcerned, but I noticed he was absentmindedly biting the skin around his nails." She reads the two excerpts again, and asks the class which sounds the more formal. "Why would an important contemporary author deliberately write in an informal way at the beginning of a book and in a formal way at the end? What do you suppose she's trying to show?"

Linda hopes the class will recognize that the dialect a writer chooses in a piece of writing can show something about the speaker or literary *persona*. A writer can choose an appropriate dialect only if he or she has the capacity to write in more than one dialect. Linda may decide to point out to the class that one of the realities of school is that it usually rewards the capacity to write in a standard dialect, not the ability to capture non-standard speech patterns, no matter how well this ability may be demonstrated. This is true even though capturing the flavor and style of oral English is one of the most difficult challenges writers face.

If Darlene agrees—and she is more likely to if Linda first congratulates her on her ability to capture oral dialogue—then have her read her first sentence to the class.

> "Every body they warned me bout old man Fred bout how he always be messin with other people's busyness and stuff."

---

[4]New York: Washington Square Press, 1983.

[5]Walker, *The Color Purple*, 12.

Linda asks the class if that sentence sounds informal or formal. Then she asks Darlene to write her first sentence on the chalkboard and then to reword it in formal standard English on the board, as the class members do the same on their papers. Then students read their versions, and Darlene decides if she prefers any of them to her own rewrite.

Linda then asks what is gained and what is lost by the alternative versions the class has presented. She makes two lists on the board as the class answers her question. If the class does not note that the informal lively oral flavor of the piece is lost by the more standard versions, Linda makes this point. At the same time, she lets the class know that her job is to help each of the students know how to put any account into standard English when the situation calls for it. Again she needs to congratulate Darlene publicly for the rhetorical power of her original first sentence—one that conjures up the image of a brash storyteller at the same time it introduces "old man Fred."

If Darlene still feels happy about her piece, Linda can ask her to write on the chalkboard a sentence with dialogue:

> I go, "hey you Mr. Fred and he come out his door an he go "who you child? Be messin at my door?"

She then asks the class to point out the correct conventional use of quotation marks, and the one place where quotation marks need to be added. This is the time for Linda to remind the class of the need to capitalize the first word in each quotation. The class can reword this sentence in standard English. Linda needs to show that the words inside the quotation marks do not get changed. Again they discuss what is gained and lost in the alternate versions. Then she shows the class how changing the non-dialogue parts into standard English makes the writer sound sophisticated, formal, and educated even though the person quoted is speaking informally. This is the time to talk about the formal, "I say" rather than "I go" and the conventional use of the comma after "say" and the period after "Mr."

This might be a good time to firm up their learning with a quiz. Each student writes three different sentences that include dialogue in which the participants are speaking informally but the writer is writing in standard English, punctuating the sentences conventionally. These three sentences can be turned in for a grade on conventional usage and punctuation. This time Linda could comfortably grade each paper, reducing their grade by one letter for each error in conventional usage and punctuation.

If Linda decides this task is too difficult for most of the class, she can give them a few minutes at the end of the period to work in pairs to read and edit each other's papers before they turn them in for a grade. Then she takes home only three sentences from each student, quickly counts errors, assigns grades on usage and conventions only, and returns the papers the next day. This way she avoids making the Darlenes of the class feel "whipped with a bullwhip," since it is not their ideas and narratives that are being graded, merely their mastery of usage and punctuation.

Another way Linda can focus discussion on issues of usage and punctuation is to go through a set of papers, writing brief comments about the parts that work well, and one suggestion for improvement on a revision or in a subsequent paper. In addition to writing these notes quickly, Linda copies onto a large chart five sentences from a batch of student papers for each class, without identifying the author of any of the sentences. These five sentences will have errors that are characteristic of a large percentage of the students. Then during class she discusses with the students how to fix these sentences, but she doesn't make any corrections on the chart. In the last fifteen minutes of the class period the students copy the sentences to correct and turn in. Each error on these sentences will lower their grade one whole grade.

Either way, the next time Linda sits at home editing a set of student papers, she is not making or implying any judgments about the content of their work; she is merely checking their usage and punctuation. (See Chapter 8, "Mandated Language Proficiency Test," and Chapter 11, "The Writing Competency Test," for more ways to help students learn usage and punctuation without circling every error on a student's paper.)

CHAPTER 16

UNTRACKING

SITUATION

He's taught all "tracks," and he cannot imagine one of the "low-level students" reading, say, **Wuthering Heights,** *which his AP [Advanced Placement] English students read.*

Walt Hoekstra usually goes into school the week before it officially begins to "do" his room. And to place his book orders. This August, he stays home. As far as he knows, there are no book orders he can place. The letter the newly hired English department chair sent him last June was bundled with his summer mail at the Post Office when he got back from two months in Spain. Her letter threw his plans awry; it said in part:

> . . . As we look toward the twenty-first century and beyond, we must take into account the diverse nature of our student population—ethnic, social, physical. We can no longer afford to use the English classroom to stratify further and separate adolescents. Literacy in all its guises—verbal and visual as well as print—must be available to all our clients. In order to encourage and facilitate literacy acquisition for all our students, and in keeping with the most recent research in cognitive psychology, the English department will no longer have levels, or tracks. All classes, including required ones, will be heterogeneously comprised. Remember, what's good for the gifted is likely good for everybody.

Walt has no idea what he will do next Monday—or any other day for that matter. He's taught all tracks, and he cannot imagine one of the low-level students reading, say, Emily Brontë's *Wuthering Heights,* which his AP (Advanced Placement) English students read. "Even they struggle with Emily's English," he tells his wife. She nods knowingly, having trudged those Brontean moors more than once herself!

At the pre-term English Department meeting, Walt and his colleagues meet Dr. Deborah Whitehead for the first time. She's pleasant, calm, and very firm about the decision to untrack course offerings. "She means 'de-rail' everything," murmurs the tweedy teacher on Walt's right, "and she'll go on to a bigger job and leave us with the wreck."

There's more than mumbling going on. Dr. Whitehead listens with care, makes notes now and then, and finally says,

> I understand that it seems too hard and too sudden. But I trust your experience and judgment this quarter, and I want you to experiment and do whatever seems sensible. I will field the telephone calls about 'What's Bart going to do without "AP" on his transcript,' and 'You expect too much of Jenny because this isn't a weighted[1] class, you know.' Refer those queries to me.
>
> My only suggestions are these. Perhaps it would help to stop thinking of 'mixed populations' and 'heterogeneous groups' and just think of them as a class or as clients. While you're planning and worrying these first days, ask your students to write. Their own texts can be the first literature you examine. And poems are always good because they're short.

After Dr. Whitehead closes the meeting, Walt and his friend Ellen go out to lunch, as they normally do on this pre-term day, but instead of catching up on the summer, they complain through half a hamburger. Finally, they try to solve problems. Walt keeps returning to his reading list. "Maybe I could show *Wuthering Heights* instead of reading it, and we can read something simpler, like a play. Low levels always like plays. . . ."

Finally, Ellen grows impatient. She teaches primarily middle-level students, and she's accustomed to a diverse population. "Walt, stop it with the books, will you? Let's make the list of the major issues these changes bring up. Then if we decide we're really going to protest, we'll look organized. Besides, it will focus our minds. Let's cast them as questions, okay?"

Walt nods.

---

[1]A weighted class is one in which a teacher expects more of a student because, when the grade point average is calculated, the grade the student earns counts as one grade higher than in a regular class.

QUESTIONS TO CONSIDER

What questions do you suppose Walt and Ellen will pose? Before you read the questions below, stop and make your own list of the questions and issues this situation raises for you. They may come to you in at least two categories: (1) questions that directly relate to a classroom, such as Walt's concern about what books he will use; and (2) those that have to do with broader concerns, such as the future of students previously scheduled for Advanced Placement courses.

Here are other questions that may be similar to those on your list:

1. How can the top students be challenged in an untracked class? Dr. Whitehead said, "What's good for the gifted is likely good for everybody." Is the corollary also true, that what's good for the basic students is likely to be good for everybody, including the gifted?

2. How can an English teacher meet the needs of students who have different motivations, interests, and experiences with reading and literature if the students are not grouped in the traditional tracks or levels?

3. To what extent can individualization take place in an untracked class, and how can a teacher keep up with it?

4. How will students in untracked classes be prepared for standardized tests, both mandated and voluntary, such as the SAT and ACT exams?

5. Is there any way to design a course that maintains high standards and also implements what English teachers know about how people read—that is, that each reader constructs a personal text or interpretation?

6. Is there any way to integrate writing and literature in an untracked class? What would be the advantages or the problems?

PERSPECTIVES

Faced with the necessity to overhaul and rethink the literature courses he teaches, Walt might decide to take Dr. Whitehead's advice about beginning with his students' writings and with poetry. This would leave part of his mind free to read and think and plan the rest of his fall semester.[2]

---

[2]For an account of how one teacher coped with untracking, see Joan Kernan Cone, "Untracking Advanced Placement English: Creating Opportunity is Not Enough," Occasional Paper No. 30 (Berkeley, CA: National Center for the Study of Writing, 5513 Tolman Hall, University of California, Berkeley, CA 94720).

What is Not Working Now

First, Walt might remember that his tracked classes were not perfect. There were problems and things he did not like about his courses as he had taught them before. His list might look like this:

1. Not everybody did all the reading!
2. Reading quizzes turned students off and were a bore to grade.
3. A student who really loved one book might hate the next.
4. The "best" students were not always the ones who read with the most relish and intuition.
5. I never really knew some students; they wouldn't talk, and their writing was sterile, even if competent.
6. I got bored, even with "Emily."
7. I always felt anxious and responsible for everything—that students would accept or like the books I chose, that they would read with enough care, that I could ask questions to help them talk, that my quizzes were fair—for *everything!*

This will help Walt know what he would like to change. He wants his students to read more and to be more invested. He longs for flexibility for himself and his students. He wants to release the top students to read challenging material and at the same time give confidence and recognition to less-able readers. He wants time to talk with his students individually about their responses to texts. He would like them to do some writing in connection with their reading. He still hopes people will read and enjoy "Emily."

Another way of thinking about "what Walt wants" is this: he'd like his literature course to more closely approximate the ways people read when their reading isn't assigned or required.

Student Choice

There is a way for Walt to get what he wants, to a large extent anyway. That is to follow the advice of his old college English methods professor: Let the students choose their own books. Many respected theorists in English Education have long advocated student choice in

---

[3]E.G.: Bruce C. Appleby, "The Effects of Individualized Reading on Certain Aspects of Literature Study with High School Seniors," (Ph.D. diss., The University of Iowa, 1967); Nancie Atwell, "Making Time," in Thomas Newkirk, ed., *To Compose* (Portsmouth, N.H.: Heinemann, 1986), 129–146; James Moffett and Betty Jane Wagner, *Student-Centered Language Arts, K–12* (Portsmouth, N.H.: Boynton/Cook, 1992).

reading.[3] James Moffett proposed this practice in 1968; *Interaction*,[4] the language arts curriculum he developed with a team of educators, was built on the assumption that students would be meeting in small groups to read and discuss books of their own choice. Thus, the idea of letting readers read different texts and of holding individual conferences with students isn't new at all. However, it has not been widely practiced in secondary schools.

In the elementary schools, on the other hand, student choice of reading matter is increasingly practiced. Walt might do well to talk with elementary teachers who are implementing a whole language approach. Using Nancie Atwell, Kenneth Goodman, and Regie Routman[5] as their mentors, they are putting student choice of reading matter at the center of their instruction.

Organizing a Course

When Walt finally sits down to make sense and to organize what he's read and heard about, he can go back to his and Ellen's questions and his list of things he did not like about his courses in the past and wants to change. He can decide to set up a course where everyone reads and everyone chooses what he or she reads. Walt will be able to talk with his students one-on-one, and the classics and the popular literature will exist side by side.

Walt might write the following course description:

> *Independent Literature:* Thousands of titles at your service.
> Spend the term reading books of your choice. A Conference Chair is always open with one actively listening teacher who nods and says "mmmhhhmmm" frequently; two hours of private conference time per student each semester.

This is not the description of some dream course but of a course adjusted to meet the needs of a range of student interests and reading levels. It is commonly found as an elective in secondary schools around the country (those that still have elective programs). Alternatively, it may be used as a three-week to quarter-long mini-course or module inside a non-elective "traditional offering."

---

[4]James Moffett, sr. ed., *Interaction: A Student-Centered Language Arts and Reading Program,* (Boston: Houghton Mifflin Co., 1973).

[5]Nancie Atwell, *In the Middle* (Portsmouth, N.H.: Boynton/Cook, 1987); Kenneth S. Goodman, *What's Whole in Whole Language?* (Portsmouth, N.H.: Heinemann, 1986); Regie Routman, *Invitations: Changing as Teachers and Learners, K–12* (Portsmouth, N.H.: Heinemann, 1991).

What is required, as Throeau says, is to *simplify, simplify, simplify.* Each student in Walt's class designs his or her own literature program. All the students need are access to books, a room with chairs, and a teacher who reads and likes to listen to people who read and talk about what they have read.

Now, Walt has a number of decisions to make.

How will he decide which books to give his students to choose from? There are many ways to do this. He could pull out a list of books that appeal to adolescents. *The English Journal*, published by the National Council of Teachers of English, features many articles each year about books for adolescents. He can consult the school and community librarians as well as other published lists.[6] Or he may prepare a list of suggested titles from books already approved for the courses in his department. He can add his own and his former students' reading choices. The aim is to have available for student choice books likely to appeal to young readers, including books Walt would like to introduce. After students begin to read and to contribute their own choices, the list will grow.

Walt will need to scrounge for as many books as possible from existing stocks and go to secondhand book stores and book fairs and sales. He can suggest his students buy, borrow, or bring from home books they want to read. This will expand his list.

Walt's goal should be a wide variety of reading matter, and, of course, he can privately urge "Emily" on some readers, just as he recommends his favorite Stephen King novel. He won't be able to predict his curriculum; this will keep him fresh and reading himself. Naturally, students will select many books he has not read or at least not read recently.

He might encourage students to choose more than one book (1) by the same author, (2) from the same historical period, (3) with a similar theme, or (4) with similar characters. This might make it easier for the students to write the semester paper outlined below.

Walt can also decide how much reading to require. He might require a minimum of six books per semester, about the same number as in a more traditional literature course. To some extent, this will depend on enrollment and reading choices because Walt will conference with each reader privately about each book read. When? you may ask.

---

[6]Good lists of adolescent literature titles can be found in Joan F. Kaywell, *Adolescent Literature* (Norwood, Mass.: Christopher-Gordon Publishers, 1993); and Robert E. Probst, *Response and Analysis: Teaching Literature in Junior and Senior High School* (Portsmouth, N.H.: Heinemann, 1987), 143–169.

During class. Recall that one of Walt's goals is to integrate composition with literature. He will discover that when students do some of their reading and journal responses in class, time to conference will appear. A room full of readers at work is quiet, and he can meet with individuals then. Walt's students can schedule a conference with him a few days before they think a book will be finished. He can probably meet with two or three readers per day for a minimum of fifteen minutes per reader; he can expect some conferences to be longer.

Walt may find that the conferencing skills that work with writers also work with readers. Appleby and Connor titled their article about a course like this one, "Well, What Did You Think Of It?"[7] This is still a good conference-opening question. Walt's main job will be to listen and respond, as any good conversationalist does. As Donald Graves reminds us, when the student talks in a conference, the teacher learns.[8] This one-on-one literature class allows the readers to talk about books without worrying about how their peers might react to what they say. They can ask questions and concentrate on the aspects that seem most important or relevant to them without the posturing for peers that sometimes characterizes contributions to whole-class discussion. With only the teacher as audience, students tend to be more candid and authentic. The reader, not Walt, will set the agenda, and usually the conference will be successful to the degree that the student does most of the talking. (See Appendix C for a transcript of part of a teacher-student conference.)

The reader will be expected to prepare for the conference in two ways. Walt should ask each reader to write up some information on an index card or a set of cards: the student's name, book title, author, a pithy summary, and three quotations from the text the reader thinks important. Writing on a card gives the students experience in being concise, yet particular, in selecting significant excerpts.

Students turn in the card when they schedule a conference. This card previews or reviews the book for Walt. If Walt has never read the book, he will need to get a copy to read or scan before the conference with the student. Even if he reads only the first two chapters, a chapter or two in the middle, the last chapter, and the card the student has written, he'll know enough to conduct the conference.

The second way the readers will prepare for the conference is to keep a notebook. This will not ensure, but will help ensure, that

---

[7]Bruce C. Appleby, and John W. Connor, "Well, What Did You Think of It?" *English Journal* 54 (1965), 606–612.

[8]Donald Graves, *Writing*, 119–128.

they've read and thought about the book. (See Appendix D for an assignment Walt might write explaining the notebook; and Appendix E for sample index cards, sample pages of a student's notebook, and a sample final reflective essay.)

Another assignment Walt might add is a semester paper. If he teaches juniors and seniors who have done a good deal of writing, they may be ready to write a paper without much help from him. He could ask them to select an aspect of two or three of the books they've read and conferenced about during the two quarters, develop a focus, and write a fairly formal essay. Walt could model this assignment to prepare the students. He would select a couple of books he has read in the past six months and then talk his way through a comparison of the two focused on a particular element.

Evaluation

This approach raises the always thorny issue: grading. One way for Walt to go is to rate each book, taking into consideration its complexity (a lot of weight); its place in "the canon" (some); and its length (some). He may realize that his judgment of a book's place in the canon is somewhat idiosyncratic, but those books that are on an approved reading list usually represent at least some consensus among his colleagues that they are of high quality. For example, the ratings might go from one to ten, from easiest to most difficult. *Crime and Punishment* is a "ten," *Of Mice and Men*, a "six," *The Outsiders*, a "two," and so on.

After each conference, Walt could grade, or rate, the conference from one to five, with one as "not acceptable" and five "terrific." Then, by multiplying the book's rating by the conference rating, he will have numerical records. The point values of each book will be listed and available to students right away; they can, in consultation with Walt, decide what grade they want to try for, and that will help to direct their choices of books and the number of conferences they schedule.[9] Walt might try 100 points per quarter as his A level so that a student who reads five, four-rated books with terrific conferences could get an A-minus, for example. He multiplies five books by four for the rating of the book by the average rating of the conferences. Fifty points and three conferences might be the minimum to pass.

Thus, students of all achievement levels in this untracked class would set a sort of contract, mostly with themselves. Students would not be limited by a teacher's or test's determination that they are

---

[9]Marilyn J. Hollman and Walter J. Kirsch, "Independent Literature" (Communication Arts Department, Naperville Central High School, Naperville, Ill., 1972).

incapable of reading complex or difficult literature, and yet they can choose books that are easier or of greater interest to them without feeling they have failed in some way.

Walt should try out his point system with other members of his department, especially if any of them are considering conducting a similar course. They will then need either to reach consensus on the point values or to abandon the weighting of books altogether.

Problems Walt Solved

Now Walt can look forward to the day when each of his twenty-eight juniors reads a different book. He's ready to begin his new course.

Which of his problems has he solved? Look back at Walt's goals under the heading "What is Not Working Now" earlier in this chapter. Which would be realized by letting students choose their own books? Are there other problems that Walt might solve with the approach outlined here?

In addition to solving his own problems, Walt's school, by eliminating tracks, will be taking a step toward solving a problem that is increasingly being recognized by our profession, namely, the damage done to students who are identified early for a lower track and who thereby never have the advantage of working in classrooms with more able classmates, and in many cases more experienced teachers as well.[10] Even worse, these low-track students all too often are given a limited, even stultifying academic program; what they learn—perhaps for life—is that they are not good students and that they don't deserve the best the school has to offer.

---

[10]Jeannie Oakes, "Can Tracking Research Inform Practice? Technical, Normative, and Political Considerations," *Educational Researcher* 4 (1992) 12–21; and *Keeping Track: How Schools Structure Inequality* (New Haven, Conn.: Yale University Press, 1985); Jomills Henry Braddock II and James M. McPartland, "Alternatives to Tracking," *Educational Leadership* 48 (April 1990), 76–80; Robert E. Slavin, "Synthesis of Research on Grouping in Elementary and Secondary Schools," *Educational Leadership* 46 (September 1988), 67–77.

PART III

FOCUS ON THE STUDENTS

CHAPTER 17

GENIUS IN THE CLASSROOM

SITUATION

"OK. Big damn deal. So you're smart, so what? Why do you have to keep putting it up in our faces for?"

Becky has a senior honors class in which most of the students perform at the expected level. She is teaching the curriculum and presenting the material in a way that is appropriate for this ability group. However, one student, Meredith, not only seems to finish her work ahead of everyone else, but performs at a very high level. She quickly finishes books others are struggling with. In class discussions, she makes frequent references to other authors, such as Dante, Chekhov, and Faulkner, as well as current authors and artists. Recently, Meredith's parents called Becky to say that Meredith would like to do more challenging work but is too shy to ask.

Now, Becky runs into real trouble. Meredith has been asking questions and playing with concepts that are far out of reach of the other students. When Becky tries to answer her at her level, the other students become agitated, discouraged, or bored. Meredith is demanding more and more class time for ideas that only Becky and she can discuss. And even then, Becky is becoming increasingly insecure about her own ability to offer anything of value to this student. There are times when she even finds herself over-preparing her lessons, fearing Meredith's questions and her own inability to answer them will prove embarrassing in front of the rest of the class. As the parents requested, Becky has given her extra work, and has spent time with her outside of class. But it doesn't seem to be enough.

One day in class, during their study of *Hamlet*, which Meredith finished reading in two days, it all comes to a head. Meredith raises her hand and asks about post-Freudian interpretations of Hamlet's relationship to Gertrude. She isn't showing off, that is clear to Becky, she is just curious. But Becky feels on the spot. She can't draw upon her own information on the subject, slight as it is, quickly enough. And besides, it seems inappropriate in this study of the play, which she considers her students' first reading of it. She assumes they will study it in more depth after secondary school.

One student turns quickly and snaps at Meredith, "OK. Big damn deal. So you're smart, so what? Why do you have to keep putting it up in our faces for?"

After that, Meredith's contributions are few. She withdraws, interacting with only one other girl in class, who seems not to be intimidated by Meredith's intelligence.

Becky sees Meredith as a student who could benefit from a program for the gifted who are beyond the level of even the honors class. However, Becky's school has no such program, nor does it have an Advanced Placement class she might transfer into. Meredith must remain in Becky's class.

QUESTIONS TO CONSIDER

1. How might Becky help Meredith without putting undue strains on her own time?

2. How can Becky channel Meredith's curiosity and her eagerness to learn in the classroom? outside the classroom?

3. How might her exceptional abilities be used to benefit the rest of the class?

4 How can Becky help Meredith become a part of the class, rather than an outcast?

PERSPECTIVES

Meredith sounds like the type of student college English professors would kill for, but in this class with these peers, her needs are not being met, and the rest of the class does not benefit from her interests and insight.

Becky's first response to this problem should probably be to talk with the department chair. Have any precedents been set for students like Meredith? How have such students been handled? Is this the first time Meredith has shown herself to be so far ahead of a class? Is she only ahead of the other students in her English classes? What have her other teachers done—in the English department and in other departments?

Next, Becky needs to talk with Meredith's parents. They need to understand that Becky will be doing all she can to challenge Meredith, including giving her extra work to do outside of class. They also must recognize that Becky will not be able to do enough; the parents simply have to know this and, Becky hopes, accept it. One option for the parents might be to see if Meredith can enroll in a junior college, university, or college literature class in the area—this in addition to staying in Becky's class. Another option might be a correspondence course, perhaps in connection with a televised university offering.

If Becky can find no more challenging class for Meredith to take than the honors class she is teaching, she has to modify her teaching and still keep Meredith in the class. She would do well to talk candidly with Meredith about the problem, explaining Becky's problem in reconciling the needs of the class with Meredith's individual needs. She should make it clear she does not want Meredith to retreat from class participation, but she will sometimes fail to respond to her queries if she feels the rest of the class is not ready for a dialogue at Meredith's level. She might ask Meredith how she would feel about the teacher's talking with the whole class about the problem.

Becky faces three very different problems:

- Meredith's problem of finding the class discussions boring and beneath her level

- The other students' problem of feeling left out and inadequate when they are unable to participate in Meredith and Becky's discussions

- Becky's problem of having to spend more time preparing for Meredith's questions and meeting with her outside of class time

The first two problems can be addressed with one instructional strategy—dialogue journals. The third is something Becky simply will have to live with for the term. A student like Meredith challenges her teacher, and so she will have to spend more time than she spends for the other students both in preparing her instruction for Meredith and in meeting with her.

Dialogue journals are one of the most effective ways to individualize instruction. They are written conversations between a student and the teacher. Every day or two, students write a response to the assigned reading in a dialogue journal. The teacher's responses to these are private, informal, and direct. For all of the students except Meredith, they will usually be quite brief, just enough to keep the student continuing to respond to and reflect on his or her reading.

Through the journal medium, Becky can focus just on Meredith's questions; and because the dialogue is private, the rest of the class does not need to feel underappreciated or left out. If Becky feels Meredith's questions merit longer and more thoughtful responses, she can write them without making it obvious to the rest of the students (as it would be in a class discussion) that she is devoting more instructional attention to Meredith than to them. In the dialogue journal, Becky can recommend extended reading, including more advanced critiques of the literature the class is reading. Whenever Meredith is ahead of the class in the assigned reading, Becky can suggest something else to illumine the text.

To be able to keep the dialogue in the journal up to Meredith's level, Becky will have to study more and think more deeply about the literature she is teaching. Since it is extremely unlikely Becky could find an actual graduate literature class where the same selections she is teaching are studied, Becky will need to become her own teacher. Meredith's apt questions deserve an informed response, and for this term, Becky is the best source Meredith has for furthering her literary education.

One way for Becky to catch up with Meredith fast is to go to the literature section of the nearest university library (Dewey Decimal Classification call number in the 800's in most libraries) and examine quickly every book she can find that analyzes the literary work she is teaching.[1] If Becky can check out books from this library, she should take as many of these home with her as possible, look over those that might help Meredith answer her own questions, return them to the library, and recommend that Meredith go to the library and read them along with the play. (Becky may have to make special arrangements for Meredith to use university library materials.) Becky's writing assignments for Meredith can nudge her to use these new resources. They, and not just Becky, will be her teachers, and her papers can reflect all the material she is reading.

---

[1] In the Dewey Decimal System this section is numbered 813.5. She can find the resources on analysis very quickly by looking at the second call number (the Cutter number) for each book. Before the initial for the title there will be a "Z." Thus, the second call number for a critical text on *The Great Gatsby* would start with an "F" for "Fitzgerald," then a number, then a "Z," and then a "G" for the first important initial of the novel.

CHAPTER 18

SPORTS HERO

SITUATION

*"Just 'cause you screwed up and wasted your life,
Mr. Nance, don't take it out on me."*

Greg is twenty-four years old and in his second year as an English
teacher. He is also the freshman boys' softball coach. When he was
in secondary school he excelled at most sports. He was on both the
football and swimming teams. The local paper seemed to run a new
story on Greg Nance every other week. As a senior he was crowned
homecoming king and led his football team to the state championship. He was offered full scholarships to three different colleges.
He played football for his first two years, then grew increasingly
interested in both literature and teaching. His African-American
studies professor convinced him he had more to offer in the classroom than on the playing field and stood a far better chance of getting a job there.

Now he has a student, Deron, who reminds him of himself when
he was in secondary school. Deron plays on both the baseball and
football teams and has achieved the status of high-school sports
hero. His counselor pulled a few strings to pair him up with Greg.

In class Deron had always done passing work, nothing either
exceptionally high nor low. He got a C in his first quarter. He and
Greg got along well. Greg made a point of attending Deron's games,
sometimes offering tips and strategies which Deron took well.

Halfway into the second quarter, Deron's grades were in sharp
decline. The football team was headed for a state championship for
the first time in almost a decade, and the playoffs were occupying all

of Deron's time and energy. At first Greg talked to him, telling him he knew how he felt, but that he had to balance his time. Deron would nod and say, "Yeah, I know. You're right." But the work did not get done. He was placed on "study table," a tutorial requisite for athletes unable to maintain a C average. Greg brought in Deron's father and the three of them discussed strategies for getting through the season. Greg even offered to strike some compromises with him. For example, he reduced the number of papers Deron had to do. Still nothing changed.

Now he is in danger of failing the second quarter. According to school policy, even a D in English would keep him off the team. He had a research paper to write but never did it, and he failed the reading quizzes on *Their Eyes Were Watching God*.[1] In addition, he owes a character sketch and a personal narrative. Greg has sent through the paperwork notifying his counselor of his possible failure.

Greg makes a deal with Deron. If he would just get the research paper finished by a specified date, he would be able to swing a C for him despite the *Their Eyes Were Watching God* grades and the missing papers. Deron is pleased and promises to do his best, saying that he already had the material gathered together and all he has to do is assemble the paper. Greg offers his time and help after school if Deron needs it.

But on the day the paper is due, Deron is absent.

The next day, Deron comes to class but will not look at Greg. "Where is the paper?" Greg asks at the end of the period.

"Man, I just couldn't make it."

"What do you mean? How much is done?"

"Well," he laughs sheepishly. "None. I'm having trouble finding an idea."

Greg slams the door and crosses to Deron. "Trouble finding an idea? You told me you were doing sports medicine. You said you had—and I quote—'lots of stuff.' You led me to believe that you had this well under way."

"It—I decided I didn't like the topic. So what? Get off my back, man." He stands up and starts toward the door.

"Wait a minute, Deron. Don't you even *try* to walk away from me."

Deron turns in the doorway, "You're just pissed 'cause you never made it. You're pissed 'cause you know I'm gonna make it. I don't need this shit and you know it. Just 'cause you screwed up and wasted your life, Mr. Nance, don't take it out on me."

---

[1]Zora Neale Hurston (Urbana, Ill.: University of Illinois Press, 1991).

The next day Deron's father calls and says, in so many words, that Greg has no right to fail his son. "Football is all this kid has got. He's a star, man. You know how it is. Why are you gonna do him that way? I don't understand you at all."

"I tried everything I could," Greg says, "He just didn't get the work done."

"Give him a break. It's not that hard."

The day after that, Dale Hoggin, Deron's coach and a friend of Greg's, asks to join Greg on his morning jog. Before they have rounded the first lap, Dale begins, "Listen, I don't know how to say this without being blunt. So. Here goes. Deron's got to stay on the team. I know there's something you can do."

"I've done everything I could," Greg says.

"Not everything. I need Deron. And Deron needs football. Let's face it, Greg, this kid's never going to be a scholar. And even if he doesn't become the next Walter Payton, whatever he does isn't going to take a whole lot of book learning. And anyway, without football, he's going to give up on school quick as fast as you used to run."

QUESTIONS TO CONSIDER

1. What should Greg do at this point?
2. Is there merit in the father's and the coach's arguments?
3. What are the hazards, if any, of Greg's caving in to the father and coach?
4. Was Greg right to make a deal with Deron earlier in the term?
5. Does Greg have any other alternatives than to pass Deron or to give him a D or F?

PERSPECTIVES

It would be very easy for Greg to buckle on this one. Why go against both the father and his colleague? The coach is right: Deron might well drop out of school without football. But if Greg gives up and passes Deron, what kind of message is he giving the other students? His leniency is not something Deron is likely to keep secret. No, he will probably brag all over school about it. To allow him to pass without doing the work will send a loud and clear message that Mr. Nance is a soft touch. He can be expected to back down under pressure. Students who are not athletes may feel they are unfairly treated because they don't get any "breaks." And next year, Greg may have all the athletes clambering to get into his classes because they have heard Mr. Nance is easy.

Even though he is a second-year teacher, he has to stand his ground. It is time to set up an appointment with both his department chair and his principal, ideally with both at the same time. Greg needs to type out an account of just what Deron has done all term and his current standing in the course. He gives a copy of this account to both the department chair and principal at the time he asks for an appointment. He also mails a copy home to Deron's father with a brief note that this is the current situation regarding Deron's English class performance, which is being reported to the department chair and principal.

It would not be wise to put in writing his memory of the conversation with either the father or the coach, since that memo might get back to one of them, and they might dispute the actual gist of the conversation. When Greg meets with the chair and the principal, however, he should report the two conversations as accurately as possible. Then he should ask for their backing when he takes appropriate action regarding Deron. If his two superiors agree to back him up, have one of them write to the student and to his father apprising them of the situation. At this point, an extension of the deadline and an outline of a schedule for making up the work after the term is over might be decided upon, but Greg should not agree to changing the requirements again for Deron even if it turns out that he fails the course.

What Greg will be risking, of course, is the alienation of his friend the coach and Deron's dropping out of school. Greg has far more to lose, however, by buckling under to the pressure to pass him. The student may never recognize the favor Greg has done for him by insisting there is more to high school than sports, but Greg will be able to sleep nights knowing he has been fair. If passing an English class means anything, it means turning in the papers that are due, even if you are the superstar of the football team.

CHAPTER 19

STEALING PAPERS FROM COMPUTERS

SITUATION

One student had apparently sold a pirated manuscript to a freshman. That's when the deception began to unravel. The freshman had squealed.

Emily is impressed and not just a little surprised that Lucas turned in a research paper on the Gulf War. Lucas is interested in sports—sports and nothing but sports. He had planned to do his paper on Magic Johnson, though the last time she had talked to him, he still didn't have a "controlling purpose." When he handed her the final paper, he looked so proud; perhaps he even surprised himself. She wasn't sure how to read his grin and the accompanying blush. Perhaps he was finally revealing a side of himself that Emily knew nothing about. She couldn't help wondering what part she had played in his sudden display of academic prowess. Had she said or done something right? given a look or a word of encouragement at the right time? Privately, she preened along with him.

"I knew you could do it, Lucas. Congratulations."

He went red again. So did she.

A week later a memo is released by Frank McMillan, the supervisor of the computer lab, notifying English teachers that students had found a way to tap into the system's main files where back-ups of documents are stored. They were calling up the work of others, deleting the author's name and inserting their own. One student had apparently sold a pirated manuscript to a freshman.

That's when the deception began to unravel. The freshman had squealed.

When the topic comes up at Emily's lunch table, several teachers talk about having received papers from students who had produced surprisingly, unexpectedly good work. This, they agree, provides an explanation.

"Lucas!" Emily thinks, though it is not a thought she cares to share. She goes back to his paper and reads it again and again, straining to hear even the slightest echo of the writer's voice she had come to know as his. There isn't a trace.

Will she, can she, confront Lucas? What if he *had* written the paper himself? What would her line of questioning say about her expectations of him? If she doesn't, wouldn't she always wonder? And what lesson would he learn if he got away with this?

When she talks to Frank about it, he says, "Well, there is one possible solution, if you want to be sure before you talk to him. You could go through all the documents that are stored and see if any of them is the one Lucas turned in."

"How many documents do you think are stored there?" she asks, picturing herself sitting down in the lab during her free period and opening every document with a title that might even remotely relate to the Gulf War.

"I'd say . . ." Frank rolls his eyes toward the ceiling in computation, then trains them on Emily, ". . . close to three thousand, maybe more."

QUESTIONS TO CONSIDER

1. Should Emily attempt to find the source of Lucas's paper before she confronts him?

2. Should she bother to confront him, and, if so how?

3. How can she prevent other students from turning in work that is not their own?

4. If she does nothing, what message is she giving Lucas and the other students?

5. What is Emily's moral responsibility and to whom?

PERSPECTIVES

Emily is in a tough spot. The only "evidence" she has to go on is the fact that Lucas's voice is not apparent in the paper, but how can she prove that? To let Lucas know about Frank McMillan's memo might just make Lucas feel he's been as clever as lots of other students. Besides, that paper stealing is going on does not necessarily implicate Lucas.

One option is to set up an appointment with Lucas and ask him some questions about his paper. If he could not tell Emily anything about the paper's thesis or how he went about finding his source material, she can then aver gently that she suspects that he didn't really write this paper. She could say that since she has these suspicions, she wants him to write a supervised short essay right there on the spot outlining the main ideas of the paper. If he prefers, he can admit right then that he did not write this paper. This may be enough. If he chooses to write the short summary, then this paper can be compared with the research paper on the Gulf War. If Lucas, by some chance, remembers well the paper he probably stole, then Emily will have to give him credit, and ask no more questions. If, however, she can show Lucas a great discrepancy between what he turned in as a research paper and what he wrote as its summary, she can insist that he redo the paper, and this time he has to write on the topic he originally planned to use, namely, Magic Johnson.

A second option is to try to control the access students have to the files stored in the back-up disks at the school. Since any coding system to control such an archive is simply an irresistible challenge to the young computer hacker, this strategy is likely to fail in the long run.

A far more sensible approach would be for Emily to have a set of very well written term papers easily available, either in hard copy or on a computer disk, for students to look at as examples of papers they might write. She might give a student a paper written by another student and ask for an update of the material. So if Lucas chose to write on the Gulf War, he could use another student's term paper as one of his references, but his job would be to find more recent analyses of that conflict and its aftermath to answer his own questions about it. In this way, a secondary student would be in the same position as a doctoral dissertation writer who uses the most recent studies of a topic as a starting point.

Part of the goal of facilitating students' entree into the researcher's territory is to show them as many sources of information as possible. Young inquirers need to become competent users not only of books in libraries but also of data bases they can access through computers. In addition, they need to find out how to reach other persons who are pursuing inquiries similar to their own.

Emily might do well to give her students the option of identifying other students in their own school or in other schools who are

pursuing similar research topics and working together on a coopera-
tive research project. Already students are participating in rich coop-
erative research efforts and dialogues with students in other parts of
the world. This process is greatly speeded up through electronic
mail.[1] (See Chapter 30, "Equity in Computer Access" for more on
ways to use data bases and electronic mail for research.)

Another option is to allow students to work together on the
same research project. This will be easiest if the students can work
together on computers that are connected by electronic mail. Even if
the students are in the same room, collaborative writing is much easier to do with computers because more than one student can look at
the screen at the same time.

Researchers are increasingly aware of the social nature of writing, and of the value not only of reading drafts of work in progress
to other students and receiving their feedback, but also of writing
collaboratively. Herrmann's two-year ethnographic study showed
that students who worked collaboratively with one or more sympathetic classmates made noticeable improvement as writers.[2]

When students are together constructing a text on the computer
screen, it is often easier for them to see the text as fluid and thus to
engage in revision, not as something the teacher imposes, but rather
as a dimension of the act of writing. Studies show current school
practice in teaching writing remains far too teacher- and product-
centered, leaving little time for students to draft or revise their
work.[3] Emily will, of course, need to rethink her method of evaluation if some of the students are doing collaborative research and others are writing individually.

One of the effects of introducing computers into English classrooms has been a subtle altering of the relationship between students and teachers, and among the students as well. Collaboration is
easier because the act of writing is less private. Teachers often find
themselves giving up some of their authority in the classroom as students become more adept than they at some tasks—(loading paper
into the printers, for example). Teachers have found themselves
becoming more open to student ideas, more aware of student exper-

---

[1]FrEdMail is a free electronic mail service that is heavily subscribed to by students
throughout the world. To join, phone 619/757-3180.

[2]A. Herrmann, "Using the Computer as a Writing Tool: Ethnography of a High School
Writing Class," *Dissertation Abstracts International* 47, 02A. (University Microfilms No.
86-02-051), 1985.

[3]Susan Florio-Ruane and Saundra Dunn, "Teaching Writing: Some Perennial
Questions and Some Possible Answers" in V. Richardson-Koehler, ed., *Educator's
Handbook: A Research Perspective*, (White Plains, N.Y.: Longman, 1987), 50–83.

tise, and more willing to let students teach each other.[4] Their teaching becomes more holistic, improvisational, and interactive rather than segmented, sequenced, or linear.

To avoid having to confront another Lucas, the next time Emily assigns research papers she could spend at least a full class period discussing ways to find topics for research. She should define research as an attempt to answer pressing questions; small groups of students could then meet together to brainstorm to list pressing questions they would like to pursue. These can be projected from an overhead projector or listed on charts and shared with the whole class. After each list has been shown and read aloud by a representative from the group, the students could be asked to select one question each to pursue for their research topics. If there are topics students might have trouble researching, either because of the nature of the question or the limitations of the school library and data bases students can access, this is the time to talk about that. What is important is that each student choose a research question he or she is genuinely interested in. Interest is what breeds energy for research and writing, and without it, the written products are almost guaranteed to be dull.[5]

After the students have selected their topics, they write down everything they already know about them and also a list of questions they have; then they turn in their topics and lists to the teacher.[6] Before the next class period, Emily can go over the topics and guide those students who need to narrow or redefine their topics. If she has time, she might indicate sources of information they could use as starting points in their research.

Emily's biggest mistake with Lucas was not to check on his progress more often. The next time she has the students spend several weeks on a research paper, she should often, if not every day, ask the students to write quickly a few sentences chronicling their progress in writing their papers. She should make it clear she does not expect them to change their topic and thus lose the momentum they have gained, and in her brief responses to these writings, she can guide them with questions to refine their topics or with suggestions for new sources of information.

---

[4]Hawisher and Selfe, eds., *Evolving Perspectives on Computers and Composition Studies: Questions for the 1990s*, (Urbana, Ill.: National Council of Teachers of English), 114.

[5]For more ideas on how to conduct lively classroom research, see Kenneth Macrorie, *I-Search* (Portsmouth, N.H.: Boynton/Cook, 1988).

[6]See Eileen Carr and Donna Ogle's notes on the K-W-L Strategy for the rationale for this approach. Eileen Carr and Donna Ogle, "K-W-L Plus: A Strategy for Comprehension and Summarization," *Journal of Reading*, 30, no. 7 (1987) 626–631.

On the day the final research papers are to be handed in, she should make it a practice to stack the papers on her desk and then have the students spend that period writing an essay summarizing the research paper in their own words, without referring back to the paper or using any of the quotations from the sources they used. This paper should retain the original outline of the research paper; in a sense, it will be an abstract of the longer work.

This exercise, which students will hand in at the end of the period, will provide Emily with a check on whether the paper actually has been written by the student, since students are not likely to comprehend and remember a copied paper as well as one they have written themselves. More importantly, the exercise will be a good way for the research paper writers to assimilate and boil down their main points. As Langer and Applebee note, writing about a subject a student has studied is a powerful way to "review and consolidate what is known or has been learned."[7]

---

[7]Judith A. Langer and Arthur N. Applebee, *How Writing Shapes Thinking: A Study of Teaching and Learning*, (Urbana, Ill.: National Council of Teachers of English, 1987), 136.

CHAPTER 20

TEACHER-STUDENT CONFERENCE

SITUATION

He knows her ego is fragile. She is discouraged with her progress in school. Her mother . . . fears Jenny will be placed in a "special ed" class.

Jonathan's department chair has recently reviewed the writing files of several of his students and commented to him that he should be marking every error. Jonathan has decided instead to follow the advice of his college methods teacher and work on problems in conferences. He has given this assignment to his class:

Agree or disagree: All Americans are free.

He made it clear to the students they were to consider their papers as first drafts. Jonathan has scheduled ten-minute conferences with each of his freshmen one-level students. He has read all the papers but has written no comments. His goal for his conferences is to help each student develop a vision of what it means to revise a paper.

Jenny is the first of his conferees to arrive, looking at the floor as she walks in and shuffles her book bag beside the folding chair in Jonathan's crammed cubicle. He knows her ego is fragile. She is discouraged with her progress in school. Her mother has repeatedly refused educational testing and has "locked" her daughter's junior high school files.[1] She fears Jenny will be placed in a "special ed" class.

---

[1] As permitted by the federal family privacy law, which every state interprets in its own way.

Jonathan smiles at Jenny as he puts her paper where both of them can see it. He gently invites her to read it aloud to him.

> Well I am hear to tell you about freedom Well I Do not think that all america are free in this country because some of these kids are not free they are about 20 years old and there mom think that they are stil little kids. and that's not freedom or beening free. this is what all about. well for someone to be able to do what he or she wan't to do or go or say or do what they please at any time they are please. well I thought that Martin luther king jr. was a very good man because he always talk about beening free and about freedom and the best thing that I like is when he said in his speach and he said free at last thank god amighty I am free at last. so one in this world I will love for every person in the world to say thank god amighty that I am

FREE AT LAST THANK GOD AMIGHTY AM FREE AT LAST

THE END

QUESTIONS TO CONSIDER

1. How would you respond to this paper—in a ten-minute conference?

2. How would you help Jenny see the essay's limitations—or would you?

3. Try to find a main point the student is making. How might you help her build an essay from that main point?

4. Should you focus on all of the mechanical errors, some, or none?

5. How would you explain to Jenny what she needs to do to this draft to revise it so it merits a good grade on the final draft?

PERSPECTIVES

Jonathan's first challenge is to keep the ownership of the paper firmly in Jenny's hands, no matter how discouraged he might be about her writing ability. Unless she feels that at least some of what she has written has value, she is likely to stop trying. As she reads the paper aloud, he listens intently for the parts of the piece that Jenny reads with energy or conviction. Then he could congratulate her on the power of her voice. This paper sounds like it is something she really believes, and that is what makes for good writing.

Then he should ask her which part of the paper is the most interesting to her—the discussion of young persons who are treated like little kids when they are about twenty years old, or Dr. Martin Luther King's speeches about freedom. No matter what her answer, Jonathan can gently lead Jenny to understand that King's speech had a different aim than freeing teenagers from their parents, and thus the two parts of this paragraph don't actually fit together. Instead of launching into a treatise on coherence, he could tell Jenny that in this draft she has a start on two papers, not one. She might save the half she doesn't want to work on now for a later paper.

Jonathan could then focus his remarks on whichever half of the paper she is the most interested in. If it is the teenagers and their mothers, then he can ask her to list some of the ways mothers actually limit the freedom of their nearly-grown children. At this point, Jonathan needs to tolerate long pauses. Whenever he jumps in to give his own examples, he is taking away her ownership. He is acting as if he knows better than Jenny what she wants to say. His goal is to have her walk out of his cubicle a little more confident about her piece and focused on at least one new way she now wants to develop it. Unless the conference can build up her confidence and sense of control, she will not be able to revise this paper in any fruitful way.

If Jonathan still has any minutes left before his next student conference, he can help Jenny focus on punctuation. Just the suggestion that the paper would be easier for him to read if it had periods where the reader needs to pause may be all Jenny can take in at this point. If there is still time, Jenny can read aloud again the half of the paper she is going to revise, as he points out to her where her pauses call for periods. To discuss commas as well or the inappropriateness of the word "Well" in this piece is too much for this conference. It would be much better to have another ten-minute conference the next week on the second draft of this piece.

Jenny has written this draft with energy; whatever Jonathan does should never weaken her conviction, or the revised version Jenny will produce will be worse than this one. If Jonathan finds that any student's work seems to be losing verve at the rewriting stage, he would do better to let that draft die and urge the student to write about something else. Pointing out the flaws in this paper will no longer generate the kind of confidence the student needs if she or he is going to learn to write by writing. Certainly pointing out *all* of her errors is probably the least effective approach for Jonathan to take. Essentially, Jonathan's advice from his department chair should be disregarded, at least for this student. (For suggestions for teaching punctuation, see Chapter 8, "The Mandated Language Proficiency Test.")

CHAPTER 21

THE SOMERSAULTER

SITUATION

"Don't you believe me?" he shouted.
"That's not it, Darryl. I just want the work."
"You'll get it. Chill down. You'll get your work.
Damn!"

Sarah Simpson, Darryl's English teacher, has been wondering about him since the first day of school when he did a somersault into the room and said his name was Dick. The next day he arrived ten minutes late and argued that the bell had not yet rung. In the first month of class, he managed to arrive on time only twice. Some days he argued, as he had the first day, that the bell would ring any second; other days, he would come with elaborate reasons why he was held up. A common thread ran through all his reasons: the situation was beyond his control; what was he supposed to do?

Darryl continued to be a puzzle to Sarah. It became increasingly obvious each day that he needed concentrated and special help.

Sarah had been assigning English homework every night, but Darryl rarely came prepared. When asked for homework, he frequently insisted he turned it in and that Sarah probably lost it. Other times, he said the work was in his locker and that he would bring it after school, but he never showed up. Once when Sarah demanded that he go to his locker and get it, he became enraged.

"Don't you believe me?" he shouts.
"That's not it, Darryl. I just want the work."
"You'll get it. Chill down. You'll get your work. Damn!"
"Get it for me now, please, Darryl."

He stands up and sets his fists on hips. "You don't believe me, so forget about it. Yesterday that white boy said his stuff was in his locker and you believed him. Don't believe me cause I'm black, bitch. Ain't that right?"

"John did bring his work after school," Sarah says evenly.

"That's what I keep saying. You deaf? I'm gonna bring the damn shit after school. Wha's wrong with you?"

"Please sit down, Darryl."

"You want me to get it? I'll get it. Show you what."

Darryl leaves the room that day and doesn't return. The next day he explains he had been stopped by a security guard who didn't believe he was on an errand. . . . Once again, the causes of this infraction are beyond his control.

At the end of the seventh week Darryl hands in an essay on Harriet Tubman, and it is riddled with problems. Sarah has tried to contact Darryl's home on four separate occasions. Contact is difficult, however, because there is no phone. She must call a neighbor, who sometimes does and sometimes does not relay the message. A woman named Mrs. Carlson called once in response. As far as Sarah could tell, she is a relative of Darryl's, but the relationship was never made clear. She promised Darryl's attitude would improve. Three more calls went unanswered.

Sarah does some digging and slowly pieces together Darryl's history. It is not easy to do because his parent or guardian sealed his files[1] when he entered secondary school. She talks with Darryl's counselor, who shares very little; with a dean, who only knows Darryl's disciplinary problems; and with Larry the social worker, who let out more information than he was supposed to—but Larry understands how difficult it can be to handle a student like Darryl when you are working in the dark.

Sarah tells him she feels like a doctor with a patient who keeps screaming in pain but who has no visible injuries and gives no clues as to the source of the problem. "Where is the pain? Just tell me where it hurts!"

Larry says, "Nothing I'm telling you should walk out that door with you, understand?"

Sarah nods, wondering if she really wants to hear it.

"Darryl was born to an eighteen-year-old heroin addict. He was himself born addicted. He lived for three years with his mother and grandmother. When he was three and a half, his mother was murdered. By the time he was five, he was getting out of control, both in

---

[1] As permitted by the federal *Family Educational Rights and Privacy Act, U.S. Code,* vol. 20, sec. 1232g (1986).

school and at home, and his grandmother, in failing health, had to hand him over to her other daughter (Darryl's aunt) and her live-in boyfriend. That placement lasted less than a year, ending when Darryl's kindergarten teacher reported neglect to the state child and family services department. He was showing up unfed and dressed in filthy clothes. How much more do you want to hear?"

Sarah just shakes her head, wondering what she must sound like to Darryl Miller, insisting on niceties like promptness and daily homework. This is a kid who has known nothing but instability. But how to handle him? Does she make allowances? Expect less? Give him extra help? The help he needs is out of her league.

Larry taps her arm. "More?"

She nods.

"Between the ages of eight and twelve, Darryl lived in five different foster homes. Then, just before starting secondary school, his grandmother wanted him back when, after a Christmas visit, he complained to her that his fifth foster parents 'don't understand nothin'.' During all this shifting around, he missed a lot of school. There are, as you probably have gathered, enormous gaps in his learning. We've recommended a battery of tests, but his grandmother refuses to allow it."

Sarah says, "I talked to a Mrs. Carlson who said she is a relative. Who is that?"

"She's a neighbor who has taken Darryl in at times—times when he would become too much for the grandmother. Carlson has two other foster kids. She is also very outspoken about the matter of African-American kids being placed in special ed. She works for a community organization called Family First. In some ways she has the right idea and her work is important, but her methods are—well, she favors intimidation."

Sarah winces. "So what do we do? He's extremely difficult to deal with in the classroom, and I feel terrible because all I seem to do is create trouble for him. I'll be honest with you; he's not learning anything from me. Nothing except, perhaps, how to hate school."

Larry asks, "Is there any extra time you can offer him?"

"I offer it all the time. My office hours are always on the board. I keep saying I'm free after school. But I never see him. I try to help him in the classroom, but that's difficult because he appears to have trouble with oral instructions. They just don't sink in. Once I have given the instructions to the class, I have to go over to Darryl and literally speak directly into his face. I have to go over it and over it for him. Even the simplest tasks. Then there's trying to keep him on task once he understands. He's a handful."

"Does that help?" Larry asks. "Giving him very direct instructions?"

"It helps some, but it creates problems, too. While I'm giving instructions to the class, Darryl is screwing around; and when I'm talking to Darryl, the class is screwing around. I mean, I think this kid is quite salvageable. But in this setting, it's . . . I hate to use the word, but I think it's . . . hopeless."

"Right now we're stuck without the testing [for learning disability]. We can't move up, down, or sideways. The only thing I can recommend is that you put through a testing referral to see if it will help push things along a bit."

"*Will* it help?"

"Maybe a teeny tiny bit."

Two days after Sarah makes the referral, she learns that Darryl's grandmother wants to have a conference with Sarah, Darryl's counselor, the principal, and Larry. An appointment is arranged, but the grandmother fails to show up. The meeting is rescheduled. This time, the grandmother arrives with Mrs. Carlson. She has with her a list of students whom Sarah has, in the past, recommended for testing. It is, she says, probably only a partial list, "as it is culled from conversations I have had with other parents."

Sarah shifts in her seat and glances at Larry. Mrs. Carlson folds her arms across her chest and says, "My first question to you, Ms. Simpson, is this: Why are there only black children's names on this list? Do you ever recommend white children? I await your response."

QUESTIONS TO CONSIDER

1. Is Mrs. Carlson fair in implying that Sarah is a racist?
2. Are there, in fact, more African-American students in special education classes in most schools?
3. If so, why?
4. Should Sarah try to change the grandmother's and the neighbor's view of the role of special education?
5. Is this a school or a societal problem?
6. What should Sarah's next step be?

PERSPECTIVES

The grandmother and Mrs. Carlson are right about one thing, at least at Sarah's school: there are far more African-American students than white students in special education programs. But Sarah knows that the special ed programs in her school are good, and the students in them often do well. However, what she may not recognize is the strong movement toward mainstreaming special ed students into regular classes and providing in-class support, rather than pulling out learning disabled students into separate classes. Darryl's advocates, whether they know it or not, have some prestigious allies among educational professionals in their effort to keep Darryl out of a special ed class.[2]

One of the reasons for the large proportion of African-American students in special ed in Sarah's community is the big discrepancy between the average incomes of the families of the white students and those of the African Americans. Since the one measure that correlates with school achievement more strongly than any other is socioeconomic level, it is no surprise that, on the whole, the students from families with more money (who in Sarah's community tend to be white,) do better in school than those from economically impoverished homes—with notable exceptions, of course. This has nothing directly to do with race except that a higher proportion of African-Americans in the U.S. live below the poverty line. There are some very important historical reasons for this, but that does not solve Sarah's problem with Darryl.

Darryl's grandmother and Mrs. Carlson probably remember there was a time in the sixties when special education programs became dumping grounds, not just for African-American kids, but for kids whose behavioral problems the school couldn't or refused to figure out how to handle. Mrs. Carlson might have gone through the system at that time and know first hand what it was about. Sarah's challenge is to convince her that things have changed.

Clearly these two women do not trust the school setting, and their goal is to confront what they perceive to be a system designed to put and keep Darryl down.[3] He obviously reflects this attitude. However, in their zeal to achieve their own political or personal ends, they might lose sight of the real issue, which is what to do with Darryl. Since the special education class is such a red flag for them,

---

[2]E.g., William Stainback, Susan Stainback, and Gary Bunch, "A Rationale for the Merger of Regular and Special Education," in Susan Stainback, William Stainback, and Marsha Forest, eds., *Educating All Students in the Mainstream of Regular Education* (Baltimore: Paul H. Brookes, 1989), 15–26; Margaret C. Wang, Maynard C. Reynolds, and Herbert J. Walberg, "Rethinking Special Education," *Educational Leadership*, 44, 1 (1986), 26–31; Madeleine C. Will, "Educating Children with Learning Problems: A Shared Responsibility," *Exceptional Children*, 52, (1986), 411–415.

[3]Their perception that the educational setting may be stacked against students of color is echoed in Lisa D. Delpit's article, "The Silenced Dialogue: Power and Pedagogy in Educating Other People's Children," *Harvard Educational Review* 58 (1988), 280–298.

and since current advocates for students with learning disabilities recommend for them the least restrictive environment possible, it would be better to keep Darryl in Sarah's class.

If possible, Sarah should arrange for him to participate in some kind of high-status activity that could feed back into the classroom work. He could do this either during his free periods or during some of the English class periods. For example, while Sarah's class is reading a biography of Harriet Tubman, Darryl might join a class that is learning to create slide shows using a software program like *Kid Pix*.[4] Darryl's assignment could be to pull together a map showing the route of the underground railroad, appropriately decorated with clip art, which students have such fun incorporating into their computer documents. If the computer lab has a scanner, he might enhance his show with pictures of Harriet Tubman from library books.

Any student who somersaults his way into the first day of class is crying out for an audience, and Sarah needs to back away from his obvious problems with written language and give him a way to succeed in her class. He has had precious little recognition in his short life, and the more ways she can find for him to shine in front of his peers, the better. If she has students read their compositions in triads to each other, she can have each triad select one of the pieces to rehearse and present as a Readers' Theater performance. (See Perspectives in Chapter 9, "The Book They Have Read Before.") This will give Darryl an opportunity to volunteer for a major reading part in a piece written by a peer. Students like Darryl often rise to the challenge of performing before the class, in part because their literacy skills are not up to those of the rest of the students and they look for another way to be in the limelight.

Riding hard on Darryl to get him to bring in his homework is not working. Although she may risk making the rest of the class jealous because Darryl "gets by without doing his homework," Sarah may find it helpful to stop expecting Darryl to do anything at home. Instead, she can concentrate on his doing as much of his assigned work in class as possible, even if it means sitting there writing while the rest of the class carries on a discussion. She needs to expect hard work from him when he is in her presence, but she probably will have to give up, at least for the present, the hope that she could persuade hm to work outside of class.

---

[4]Craig Pitman (Broderbund Software, 1991).

CHAPTER 22

THE CONCRETE THINKER

SITUATION

"Like, if you hated my tie, but you said, 'Oh, real nice tie, Mr. Dillman,' that would be sarcasm."
"Not really," Jessica says. " I'd be being nice. I'd be being polite. People do that all the time."

The administration at Burris High School has announced some unusually strict policies this year that include a closed campus for all grade levels, penalties for students who don't carry their identification cards, and a ban on T-shirts that bear lewd or drug-related messages or pictures.

Adam Dillman's students open up the controversy one morning in class. Expectedly, the students—all freshmen—are indignant. One girl, Jessica, is so furious about what she perceives as gross infringements of her "rights as a human being and a U.S. citizen," that she is crying openly. Although the class knows her as one who is prone to quick tears, the tone of the discussion suddenly turns serious just as the bell rings.

The next day, *Burris Banner*, the school newspaper, runs the following editorial:

> I applaud the strict measures taken by the school board to insure that the students are safe, and consider them a step in the right direction. However, we must have more.
>
> First, the rule on T-shirts is a good one, but it's not enough. Ban all clothing that offends anybody, I suggest. The administration must form a special security corps who will enforce the new rule by requiring that students wear acid-washed black monastery-style robes.

For identification, ID cards can be lost. To avoid this, I advocate having everybody's I.D. bar code tattooed on their foreheads, in the appropriate color for their grade level.

Finally, regarding a closed campus: it is still not enough. Most students get hurt at home. The incidents involving fights and firearms last year took place after school, outside of the building. To avoid the risk of having students being harmed, we should never leave the building, ever.[1]

Adam gets enough copies of the paper for his entire class and distributes them. Not only will it lighten the mood of the class, he thinks, but he can lead into a lesson on satire from it.

Most of the students laugh and applaud as he reads. But Jessica is upset. "I don't understand why you showed this to us. I don't understand why people were laughing."

At this, a few of the students laugh, thinking she is being sarcastic. Adam explains that the views were not really the columnist's. "He has a purpose in mind. What do you think he wants to accomplish?"

Jessica says, "Wait a minute. If they're not *his* views, whose are they then?"

"He's mocking the views of people who think very differently than he does. He's using satire to poke fun at our school board."

"Then why is he saying it? He says, '*I* applaud . . .' and '*We* should . . .'"

"But he is pretending to take their point of view," Anne-Marie, Jessica's close friend, says, trying to help out.

"Why? That's stupid."

"Because," Adam tells her, "it aims to show the folly of that point of view. He's exaggerating to make a point. What do you think his point is? Frank?"

"That these rules are really totally stupid," Frank says. "And they are."

"Yeah," Adam says, "and rather than just come out and say, 'These rules are stupid,' he uses humor, exaggerates them. That's satire."

Jessica is getting frustrated now. "Then he should *say* that because lots of people are going to think he's serious."

"He's being *sarcastic*," Ann-Marie says.

Adam adds, "Sarcasm is saying one thing and meaning another. We all use it."

"That's really stupid," Jessica says. "How's anybody going to know what you really think?"

---

[1]Mike Medintz, *The Evanstonian*, September 17, 1993, 3.

Adam lifts the end of his tie and lays it in his palm. "Like, if you hated my tie, but you said, 'Oh, real nice tie, Mr. Dillman,' that would be sarcasm."

"Not really," Jessica says." I'd be being nice. I'd be being polite. People do that all the time."

"It's different," Adam counters.

"How?"

"It's different. Trust me. It's *sarcasm*," Ann-Marie says, growing exasperated now with her friend. "Trust me."

"Well, *sorry*," Jessica says, now teary-eyed again. "I just don't get it, OK? So sorry. Forget it."

Adam says, "Jessica, I'd like for you to understand . . ."

"I said forget it, so I mean forget it. I don't care about it. OK, it's satire or sarcasm or whatever, OK? I learned that, OK? Can't we talk about something else?"

QUESTIONS TO CONSIDER

1. If Jessica's classmates can't get through to her, how is Adam going to make any headway?

2. What activities might help enlighten Jessica on sarcasm?

3. How is Adam to move beyond sarcasm to satire with students like Jessica?

PERSPECTIVES

Jessica is probably unaware not only of sarcasm but also of other ways our language does not always match our meaning. She probably doesn't realize that even in straightforward verbal interchange, the words we say have an intention that is different from what the literal words say. As speech act theorists have pointed out, we often speak indirectly.[2] Thus, a person tasting her baked potato might say, "This needs salt," but mean, "Please pass me the salt." She does not mean only to convey information, as the literal interpretation of her words might lead one to think. Instead, she is making a request. For another example, a person might say "It's chilly in here" looking at someone sitting by the window. What he or she means by this remark is, "Will you please close that window?"

---

[2]Paul Grice, *Studies in the Ways of Words* (Cambridge, MA: Harvard University Press, 1989).

In other words, even in ordinary conversation, not to mention sarcasm, persons frequently say one thing but mean another. Perhaps some illustrations of this phenomenon might be a way to help Jessica recognize that she too sometimes speaks indirectly, intending something different than what she actually says.

The next step is to understand that persons sometimes say just the opposite of what they mean. Jessica needs lots of examples. Adam might ask her to suppose her best friend agreed to come by and pick her up to go out for the evening, but the friend did not show up. Jessica might phone her and ask angrily, "Do you mean to tell me you had no intention of coming by for me tonight?" but not mean this as a real question. Instead, she would mean, "I can't believe that you deliberately decided not to come by for me, and I'm angry about it." Or he or she might say, "A fine friend you are!" and mean just the opposite.

Jessica may well be one of those students who expects teachers, especially, and also texts she reads to tell her the truth. She needs more experience with playful, unserious language. Adam might ask the class to bring in copies of *Mad Magazine* or comic strips that are making fun of human foibles. The more exaggerated and zany, the better. He can have the class divide into small groups and make lists of the targets of the material they have brought in. Then they can discuss as a class the comparative effectiveness of the satire.

This may not be enough for Jessica, of course. To appreciate satire, students must have moved from egocentrism to decentering and must have reached what Piaget has identified as the highest level of thought: the stage of formal operations.[3] They need to be able to entertain a hypothetical to decide how to describe, for example, a dismal rainy day as blazing and brilliant, but do it in a sarcastic way. Perhaps all Adam can do is to give examples, hoping these will be like dropping water on a stone, but he may have to wait until Jessica reaches a higher level of thinking before his examples will be understood.

Concrete thinkers pose a problem for the teacher because their lack of understanding of a central concept often bogs down a whole-class discussion as in this case with Jessica. The solution is not to place such students in a different class, however. They are much more likely to develop higher-level thinking if they work in heterogeneous classrooms because the way their classmates operate influences them. However, Adam may need to hold some out-of-class conferences with Jessica to help her understand satire in a way that does not make her more defensive as in this situation.

---

[3]Barry J. Wadsworth, *Piaget's Theory of Cognitive and Affective Development* (New York: Longman, 1984), 136–171.

Adam should organize as many small-group collaborative problem-solving activities as possible to give Jessica repeated opportunities to watch and hear her peers at work. For example, the first time the class reads Jonathan Swift's classic *A Modest Proposal*, Jessica will probably be more shocked than most students, but her response will give the others in a small-group discussion an opportunity to explain why her reaction is, in part, what Swift was aiming for. Immediate recognition of the irony reduces the shock value of the essay, and Jessica's honest reaction may help the other students understand why Swift was so effective.

Adam might then have the students take a contemporary issue, like homelessness, and come up with collaborative essays written by small groups that present preposterous solutions to the problem in order to persuade the larger society to consider more reasonable alternatives. Although such an assignment would be beyond Jessica's ability, through collaboration with peers she just might be nudged toward the higher level thinking Adam hopes for all his students.

CHAPTER 23

SECOND-LANGUAGE
LEARNERS

SITUATION

Two girls in the back smile and giggle; one says, "We are from Polish. Polski books."

Robin has been looking forward to her first day as a freshman English teacher at a large urban public school, but little did she expect the welcome in store for her: In a class of twenty-eight students, four do not speak English at all! She quickly discovers this when she asks each student to tell his or her name and something interesting he or she has read recently. Two girls in the back smile and giggle; one says, "We are from Polish. *Polski* books." A completely tacit boy at the end of one row does not look up at all and declines to say a single word; he looks Asian or Southeast Asian. The fourth, a stocky Hispanic boy, makes some eye contact but still looks uncomfortable when he answers, "I from Mexico. No espeaka *Ingles*."

Robin learns their names from the roster, but can't begin to pronounce them. She feels awkward asking them to pronounce their names in front of the rest of the class: Javier, with its unfamiliar "kh" sound; Xiao Ha, which looks easy but is unrecognizable to its owner when she calls it out; and the challenging "Malgorzata" and "Jadwiga," both mysterious mouthfuls.

After the fifty-minute class, Robin rushes down to the office on her ten-minute break before the next class, to ask if there has been a mistake. She is told the students have been put there because "after all, this is an English class, and they need to learn English," as one

175

assistant neatly puts it. The school has no ESL (English as a second language) program in place, although there have been rumblings that the state is about to require one. (Weeks later, there is still no ESL teacher to be found in the school, and Robin learns that all the other English teachers dread that they might be designated the ESL "draftee.")

At lunch time, Robin discovers that there is little documentation on her four immigrant students. The office does know that the Polish girls are cousins who arrived in town the previous summer. Xiao Ha has an older brother, also new at the school; they may be either Chinese or Hmong from Laos. Javier has spent six months at a secondary school somewhere else in the city where there is a large Spanish-speaking community.

After school, Robin rushes to the ERIC (Educational Resources Information Center) database in the library and calls up "ESL" and then "Secondary Education" on the computer. There are a lot of references—too many, in fact, to absorb, so she makes a printout and vows to work her way through it at her earliest free moment.

Meanwhile, the next day is coming. The first day it was possible to coast, with the first-day handout, introductions, and the like. The second day, Robin plans to get down to the business of English. First, she will put the students in pairs for a warm-up activity, asking them to meet together to share basic information about themselves. After that, she will assign them their first short essay on their most significant experience of the summer, to be written in class. This will be followed by a reading selection from Ray Bradbury's *Dandelion Wine*, a nice youth-centered passage to start reading activities on a positive note. Whom to pair the "foreigners" with? Each other? Would they even understand the warm-up activity and the writing topic? Robin worries about it, but is too busy gearing up for her four other classes to spend much time thinking about the problem.

The next day the classroom is full of activity, but Robin notes a few strategic seating changes. A moat seems to have formed around Xiao Ha—there are empty seats on all sides of him. His silence and reticence seem to create a black hole which is too formidable for these brand new freshman to enter. Malgorzata and Jadwiga, on the other hand, seem quite merry and chat happily in their spot in the back of the room. Robin notes the frequent "ch" and "z" and "sh" sounds they are making—even their whispering is different from English. Javier is absent.

"Let's get into pairs," Robin directs resolutely, assigning them partners from the roster, splitting the cousins into two pairs with boys—one African-American and one Italian-American. Xiao Ha is paired with a white girl, Alexa, who seems to be one of the brightest and most responsive class members. As Robin circulates, she is impressed by the valiant efforts the native speakers of English are making with the immigrant students, and the equally dynamic efforts of the foreigners to communicate.

She notices that Alexa has taken out a pencil and is trying to explain something to Xiao Ha by drawing. Xiao Ha whips out a pencil box, takes out a sharply-honed pencil, and responds with his own drawing, using quick strokes. Robin smiles to herself and thinks, almost smugly, "A perfect choice of partners. Maybe this will work after all."

Flushed with success, Robin moves on to the composition topic. As the class settles down to work, all three limited-English speakers quickly deflate and stare at their blank papers intensely. Jadwiga manages to keep busy, and Malgorzata is trying to copy Jadwiga's paper word for word, while Xiao Ha just keeps sharpening his pencil and looking at the paper.

When Robin reads and responds to the compositions that night, she sees that Jadwiga has some considerable ability to express herself in English, despite phonetic spellings of many words. Malgorzata, on the other hand, in copying her cousin's sentences, found one too daunting even to copy, so reverted to Polish. She did produce one sentence of her own in "English," however: "I'am from polish." Xiao Ha wrote his name and nothing more. Robin responds to the compositions non-evaluatively with simple messages to each of the immigrant students, such as:

> I will try to help you learn English. Please come to class every day and keep trying. Do you have a dictionary that translates from your language into English? If so, please bring it every day.
> Sincerely,
> Your teacher, Ms. Williams

When she hands the papers back the next day, she sees the three students puzzling over her comments. Javier, meanwhile, has reappeared, and Robin tries to move him to a nearby work area to write the first essay, but can't seem to explain to him what she wants him to do. She directs, "I would like you to sit down here and write an essay about the most significant experience of your summer. The rest of the class did it yesterday."

Javier replies amiably, "Sorry, Teacher, I no understand." She gropes for a response, exasperated, then breaks down and laughs. Javier laughs too, and although the communication has by no means been successful, there is a certain camaraderie in their shared sense of helplessness.

She manages to take Javier down the hall with her while the students are doing small group work and asks the Mexican-

American janitor to translate for her. "Could you please tell him to write a composition about his summer vacation?" The translation is made, and Javier grins. "*No problema*," he says confidently.

That night she reads over Javier's paper, which is full of "Spanglish" and shows very little sense of conventional English syntax. She realizes that Javier, Xiao Ha, and Malgorzata are more or less at the same level—zero—while Jadwiga is considerably above them.

Jadwiga is quickly bonding with the American students, and this seems to be a powerful motivator. Maybe she can get some help out of the class, Robin surmises. Sure enough, the next week Jadwiga hands in a well-proofed paper. She is either making stunning progress or her American boyfriend, a junior, has written the paper for her. Obviously her extracurricular English practice is helping her, probably more than anything she is doing in Robin's class. Robin decides not to raise the issue of plagiarism for the moment and to rely on in-class quizzes to monitor Jadwiga's progress.

The three others, though, are almost worse off attending than not coming at all, Robin reasons. So she talks with her department chair, who advises her to set up an appointment with the assistant superintendent for academic affairs, Stan Sordillo. This she does, and, at their appointment the following afternoon, she shares the four writing samples, their (mostly blank) first quiz papers, and the grade book with their empty columns. "They desperately need an ESL teacher or tutor," she says, "because three of the four are sinking quickly into defeat. And the best one is a far cry from being at a level of reading literature and writing essays. Besides," she adds to drive things home, "the other students are beginning to resent all the time I need to spend on them. Today one of them started whistling and catcalling while we were all waiting for Xiao Ha to answer."

Sordillo is noted for his prowess in the humanities, and is also very much a humanist himself. "OK . . . we'll put a notice in the central placement office for a part-time ESL teacher," he says, "but at most it will only be part-time, and it will be at least three weeks before the whole process is complete—maybe more. There's a very good chance there won't be the budget for this. Meanwhile, we expect you to keep all the students in your class. Do the best you can."

QUESTIONS TO CONSIDER

1. How can Robin prevent setting a precedent by agreeing to the assistant superintendent's stop-gap measure of assigning all the foreign students to Robin's class?

2. What's the best use of class time for meeting both the foreign students' needs and the needs of the majority of the class?

3. Are English teaching and ESL teaching completely separate and distinct, or is there a significant overlap? If there is an overlap, where are the areas, and how can Robin take advantage of it?

4. What can Robin do about grading? It would be wrong to imply these students are meeting the class requirements, but wrong also to punish them for not speaking English and being placed in a class where instruction is in a language they don't know.

PERSPECTIVES

Robin has been plunged into a tough predicament in her first teaching assignment. Never in all her education and English courses was this situation even mentioned. However, the challenge she faces is increasingly common for teachers at all levels.

Robin has already figured out two of the cardinal rules for approaching any problem: (1) use the library to find out what you need to learn; and (2) consult with the administration about finding a formula to solve a problem you can't solve alone. Now she can begin to pick her way through the printout and arm herself with some basic information about effective ways to address the needs of students whose heritage language is not English. She also might call another secondary school with an ESL program and talk with the ESL teacher.

Further, by raising the problem with the department chair and the assistant superintendent right away, she has lessened the chance the administration will see the status quo as a viable solution for the long run. She must continue to agitate politely on behalf of these students until they have a more appropriately trained advocate and instructional leader on the faculty or staff. This is not for altruistic reasons alone—it is also to spare everyone the awkwardness of a class with such a wide range of proficiency.

Stop-Gap Approaches

Robin needs to think fast. By instituting the partner tutoring she has hit upon an effective instructional strategy, one that has proven advantageous in a wide variety of curricular areas, including English as a Second Language. Working the first day with Alexa, a conscientious, friendly peer, helped Xiao Ha feel more at home, thereby lowering his inhibitions and opening up his receptivity to learning. Peer tutoring also lends a social aspect to communication, which provides an opportunity for the learning to serve not just a practical or instrumental purpose but also a global or integrative one. Therefore the learning is more likely to be well motivated and successful.[1]

She might be tempted to have the three lowest-level students use first-grade basal readers. This approach may well embarrass the teenage students; they may feel demeaned by the childish texts that are not developmentally appropriate for teenagers. It is also unlikely to help because, although the students are learning a new sound-symbol system (especially Xiao Ha, who comes from a language background that uses characters, not sound-connected letters), they are probably not learning to read for the first time.

The happy prospect is that Robin can expect her three foreign students to pick up reading more quickly than a first-grade native speaker might. The parallels between children acquiring a first language and older children or adults learning a second one is an imperfect one at best, and can lead to many false analogies.[2] Still, when the students are being quizzed in succession on their reading, Robin will need to skip over Xiao Ha to avoid some of the long, tense waits.

Robin cannot depend on students to pick up writing as quickly as they do oral language or reading, however. Writing is usually the last of the four language skills (listening, speaking, reading, and writing) to reach a high level, and it is critical to these students that they learn it well. All their other course work will depend upon it.

To help her LEP (limited English proficient) students, Robin might institute dialogue journals for the whole class. (See Perspectives, Chapter 17, "Genius in the Classroom.") Dialogue journals are one of the most effective ways to individualize instruction. They work just as well for students at the lower end of the class range as they do at the upper end. They do take a great deal of teacher time, but that is time spent outside of the precious class time, which is always far too limited.

In a dialogue journal, the non-English-speaking students can carry on a conversation with their teacher in the form of a series of letters. Even if Robin herself has to get a translator to read their journal entries, she can always reply in English, focusing on the content and not the errors, and thus provide the students with high-interest reading matter for them to translate and respond to. All she need do

---

[1]H. Douglas Brown, *Principles of Language Learning and Teaching*, 2nd ed. (Englewood Cliffs, N.J.: Prentice-Hall, 1987), 115.

[2]Brown, *Principles of Language Learning and Teaching*, 40.

is congratulate them on their hesitant efforts to communicate in English and point out a few areas to work on, such as troublesome English idiomatic expressions.

If Robin runs out of time to respond to dialogue journals, she can pair up the students and have them respond either orally or in writing to each other's journals. The difficulties the LEP student's partner has in reading his or her journal poses an ideal opportunity for cross teaching. The one thing all native English speakers can do is help others know how English is spoken and written idiomatically. Peers are more likely than the teacher to be up on the latest teenage jargon, which is usually what the immigrant student wants to know most of all.

The dialogue journal gives the LEP students a chance to practice their writing in a non-judgmental setting. That does not mean, however, that the teacher or peers never give feedback on the students' problems in English. Although it is usually better to avoid correcting the journals with a heavy hand, the teacher's response can often point out places where the students need to work on their expression.

Will the LEP students have to do more homework than their classmates? No doubt about it, they will (and so, alas, will Robin, until an ESL teacher takes over). They, through no fault of their own, have a deficit, which must be overcome as soon as possible. If the students don't learn quickly and don't learn structures correctly (sometimes contradictory goals), they are likely to "fossilize" mistakes and misconceptions, making it much more difficult ever to learn the correct forms later.[3]

However, these four may have time on their side. Some ESL theorists have postulated that the critical age for learning new languages to a fluent level is the beginning of adolescence. Others place it earlier,[4] but the motivation for teenagers to assimilate tends to be strong, so the odds are in their favor that, with expert assistance combined with patience and understanding on the part of the faculty, staff, and student body, they will learn to speak English well.

---

[3]Fossilization has been defined as: "a cessation of interlanguage learning often far from target language norms," Larry Selinker and John Thomas Lamendella, "Two Perspectives on Fossilization in Interlanguage Learning," *Interlanguage Studies Bulletin*, 3.2 (1978), 144–91.

[4]Recent research is placing cerebral laterelization, the time during which language functions are established in the brain, at about age five: Stephen D. Krashen, "The Critical Period for Language Acquisition and its Possible Bases," in Doris Aaronson and Robert W. Ruber, eds., *Developmental Psycholinguistics and Communication Disorders*, 263(New York: New York Academy of Sciences, 1975), 211–224.

Long-Term Solutions

Robin should not give up on her pressure to get an ESL or a bilingual program at the school. She has neither the time nor the know-how to be both a good English teacher and an ESL specialist. If the English department chair checks in periodically on Robin's class and is pleased with her stop-gap measures toward the successful integration of the immigrant students, she should beware: stop-gap approaches have a way of getting institutionalized. The department chair might even decide to bestow on Robin the honor of being the designated "ESL liaison" for the English department. She will then be the victim of her own success, and all that before she even knows what she should be doing!

She should always keep her mind on her goal: to continue to build up support in the department for pressuring the administration to institute an adequate program for immigrant students at the school. This will mean hiring a specialist in this area. She should look into state guidelines on this matter. It is quite possible her school is out of compliance with a state mandate.

To forward the LEP students' needs to the administration most effectively, Robin might want to write to International TESOL (Teaching English to Speakers of Other Languages), the dynamic professional organization serving ESL and EFL (English as a Foreign Language) teachers worldwide. They have position papers on many ESL teaching issues, including one on secondary education resources. They also publish numerous books, conference proceedings, and two major journals, one specifically on classroom techniques.[5]

Once an ESL teacher or tutor is in place, that person will undoubtedly go over the immigrant students' papers with them in detail for idiomatic and structural correctness, but Robin will continue to be the one who actually shows these students how to write papers that are appropriate for an English class.

Robin should try as quickly as possible to find her LEP students appropriate ESL reading textbooks, which are carefully graded for difficulty and contain supplementary reading comprehension exercises. These and many other excellent materials can be found by browsing through the major ESL publisher and distribution catalogs available free through the mail.[6]

---

[5]International TESOL, Inc. is located at: TESOL, Inc., 1600 Cameron St., Suite 300, Alexandria, VA 22314; (phone: 703-836-0774; fax: 703-836-7864).

[6]Three of the biggest catalogs are: Delta Systems Co., Inc. (phone: 800-323-8270), a distributor of books, classroom aids, teacher training materials, etc.; Alta ESL (phone: 800-ALTA-ESL); and Prentice Hall/Regents Publishers (phone: 800-663-0033). There are at least two dozen other excellent publishers, and most of their titles are included in Delta and Alta catalogs.

Robin also needs good integrated textbooks that present grammar systematically in ways that will not overwhelm or bore students. Robin would be well-advised to get her hands on some beginning integrated skills series and have the students work their way through them for homework. If the catalogs seem too meaty, she could ask an ESL teacher at another school for help. Failing that, she could also get the address of the president of the state TESOL organization through the International TESOL office, and call that person. The president will undoubtedly know of nearby resources.

Grading

Robin will need to get consensus from the rest of the teaching staff on this issue, but the best course will probably be to grade these LEP students on their progress rather than on their achievement. Robin can keep a file of their papers and look over how much they've improved by the end of the year. If an ESL teacher is hired, Robin can also consult with that person to see how their English is progressing in those classes or tutorials as well. Of course, all the other teachers in the school will be in the same predicament, so together they need to decide a strategy for evaluating LEP students.

Increasing Diversity of Students

We ignore the trend toward diversity of heritages at our peril. Our classrooms are changing at a dizzying pace. As Sarah Hudelson has pointed out, "In 1982 fewer than two million school-age children were dominant in a language other than English."[7] At that time 6.2 percent of the population was foreign-born; in the 1990 census, this shot up to 7.9 percent, or 19.7 million people. "Projections show that in the year 2000, over 3 million students will be non-English dominant, and two decades after that, American schools will house 5 million such students."[8] The shift is away from European immigrants to Asian and Hispanic populations. By 2000, the majority of school-age children will be of non-European ancestry.[9]

Our challenge is to keep alive the dream on which our nation is built. We are a people who are not bound by a single ethnic and religious heritage but by an ideal—a common commitment to freedom

---

[7]"Bilingual/ESL Learners Talking in the English Classroom," *Perspectives on Talk and Learning* (Urbana, Ill.: National Council of Teachers of English, 1990), 267.

[8]Hudelson, "Bilingual/ESL Learners Talking," 267.

[9]Hudelson, "Bilingual/ESL Learners Talking," 267.

and democracy. The test for this nation is whether in the face of severe economic stress we can still ascribe to Emma Lazarus's words inscribed on the Statue of Liberty:

> Give me your tired, your poor,
> Your huddled masses yearning to be free,
> The wretched refuse of your teeming shore.
> Send these, the homeless, tempest-tost to me.
> I lift my lamp beside the golden door!

No matter how we feel about the United States' immigration policy in this time of rapidly increasing poverty in this country, we must inevitably adjust to an increasingly diverse student population. If present trends continue, this situation will become more prevalent, and we need to learn how to use the diversity in fruitful ways. If we cannot do this, the specter of the alternative looms large— increasing ethnic and cultural isolation. We only have to look to eastern Europe or Africa to see the effects of ethnic violence. One of our highest priorities as teachers has to be to educate our children to live in harmony with persons whose heritages differ from theirs.

If Robin continues to learn and experiment with ESL teaching techniques, she may herself suddenly hear the call of the ESL field echoing in her ears. If she follows the call, she won't be the first secondary-school English teacher who got into ESL accidentally, and then fell in love with the field. After all, ESL teachers can have the whole world at their fingertips, right in their local school.

PART IV

FOCUS ON THE SCHOOL

CHAPTER 24

DRAWING THE LINE

SITUATION

Why does he come home exhausted more often than excited now? Why is he so often on edge and frustrated? Why is he so much less patient with the kids?

Max had been teaching at a large suburban secondary school in an affluent community for six years. He loved his job, had loved it from the first day. He was paid relatively well, the benefits were good, the staff were generously supportive, and the students were basically well cared for, stimulating kids reared by a community that had always prided itself on the emphasis it placed on education. Education mattered here, and that fact showed in the students' performance.

And yet, as Max approaches the end of the first semester of his seventh year, something is different. Or is it? A question had been nagging him for the last two or three years. Now, though, that question has grown into a suspicion. Were the kids changing—getting more defiant, less involved, unmotivated, meaner, more easily given to anger, less capable—*far* less capable—than before? The question had always before been easy to dismiss. What generation has not shaken its head over what the newer generation is becoming? And yet. . . .

The question arrives with a new weight on the day he sits down to write his first-semester exams and finds himself wondering what he actually has taught them in the first semester. They have only finished one novel, written a few essays, and completed a smattering of mini-lessons on usage and writing conventions. What have they been doing each day? Where has the time gone? Why did he have to revise his schedule so often that he finally scrapped it altogether and began daily putting the next day's assignment on the board? Why does he come home exhausted more often than excited now? Why is he so often on edge and frustrated? Why is he so much less patient with the kids?

The following morning, in the first ten minutes of the first period, he has his answer. Antoine and Billy have gotten into their usual argument over something that may or may not have been said about one of their mothers. Angie and Samantha have to be restrained from throwing books at each other, and Donald will need to be written up (his inappropriate behavior reported in writing to the school counselor) for sending Gloria into tears with his observation about the size of her butt.

It takes Max a good ten minutes to get everyone seated and calmed down. Then there are the tardies to deal with and Donald's write-up. Next, he collects the homework and receives papers from less than a third of the students. Finally, it all comes to a head in a discussion of the scene in *To Kill A Mockingbird* where Bob Ewell spits in Atticus's face. The class unanimously supports Godfrey's idea that Atticus should kill Bob Ewell; *kill* him, literally kill him. This discussion shakes Max to his core. The kids, he realizes, are serious. They think Atticus was a "chump" for not fighting back, for just standing there and taking it. Max tries to get them to explore other options Atticus had for handling the situation. They can see no others. They laugh at every suggestion he makes. This business of retaliation has come up before. Violence, in so many of their minds, seems to be the only honorable way to end any dispute. He can't crack it. He finds himself wanting to shout. He wants to pick up a book and throw it at them. He wants them all to leave, to just get out of his sight. In that moment, he no longer recognizes himself and knows it is time to draw the line.

So where is this class headed? He can't get them to read, to write, to explore and evaluate values, to take responsibility for themselves—not even to do their homework. He spends an unusual amount of time on the phone with parents, many of whom seem to throw up their hands themselves. He talks to counselors who say they need to concentrate on the more "critical cases." He tries himself to help the students, but tactics that have worked in the past seem to have no lasting impact. He is getting nowhere.

Has it always been this way? Is his memory flawed? Is he doing something wrong, differently? What is he missing? Is it just he? But more and more it seems that every newspaper and magazine he reads has an editorial that moans over the state of our kids. And now there is the study, released by the bipartisan National Commission on Children, concluding that the future of millions of our children is imperiled. "We catch glimpses of this future in the violence that stalks children in school yards and neighborhoods, the homeless who crowd city streets, and prisons filled to capacity. We see it in the growing number of children without fathers, students without skills, teenagers without hope," the Commission reports.[1] Well, yes, there is a national educational crisis, but their school has somehow seemed immune because it is a good, strong school with a community that backs it. And yet . . .

Looking back over the first semester, Max realizes how much more time he spends these days on intervention than on teaching. He feels as though he spends at least as much time filling out forms and contacting parents and counselors as he does preparing assignments and grading papers. One colleague has scolded him for that, saying he must not forget that he is there to teach, not to solve the students' personal problems. And yet, their personal problems seem to exert more and more control over their academic performance.

He scans his grade book and reflects.

MONICA: Academically strong; rarely missed an assignment, worked hard at everything she did, took pride in her work. However, she frequently lost control of her behavior. She talked incessantly and became furious if Max tried to stop her.

DONNA: Spent a lot of time in the hall when she should have been in class. In the first semester she had eighteen tardies to Max's class.

JOAN: Absent close to seventy-five percent of class days in the first semester. She has a medical problem which no one can quite put a finger on. There appear to be psychological problems as well. Being absent made her fall behind, falling behind made her nervous, being nervous worsened her medical condition, which made her absent again, which made her fall further behind.

TOM: English skills among the lowest of all Max's students. His attention span is very short, and, partly because of that, he can make class sessions extremely difficult. He bursts into laughter, talks incessantly, and generally creates problems for the teacher and the class.

RON: After a meeting with his parole officer, father, and counselor, Ron was given this ultimatum: attend class or go to the boys' correctional home. His attendance and his attitude immediately improved. His work in class was among the best Max received. Then suddenly he disappeared again. He had fired a weapon and was in trouble with the law.

---

[1]*Beyond Rhetoric: A New American Agenda for Children and Families* (Washington, D.C.: The National Commission on Children, 1991), 7. Available from the Superintendent of Documents, U.S. Government Printing Office.

YOLANDA: Lethargic and reluctant to contribute to discussions. She is way behind in her work. She is in distinct danger of failing the class. When Max called home, her father told him that Yolanda's grandmother had suffered a heart attack a month earlier and recently passed away. Because she was very close to her grandmother, the illness and death has had a profound effect on her.

Max talks to other teachers, most of whom have been teaching two and three times as long as he has. Many of them have the same feeling he does. Something is happening with these kids, something new and frankly quite frightening. But, as one colleague tells him, you cannot allow yourself to slip into despair. Somehow you have to find the hope so you don't get pulled under by this.

But how does one do that? The students' needs are pressing and often all-consuming. He hates to see so much pain, and he tries to help, but he feels that in many cases the needs of these kids are beyond his expertise, certainly beyond anything he has encountered in his training.

He needs to draw a line, to find a way to say, "This is where my responsibility ends." But how will he do that?

QUESTIONS TO CONSIDER

1. What can Max do with these students? What are his options? Should he insist, for example, that Yolanda make up the work she never finished during her grandmother's illness? If so, what sort of deadlines should he establish?

2. What does "drawing the line" mean under these circumstances? Does it mean he simply chalks these kids off as beyond hope?

3. What adjustments should he make in his instructional strategies?

PERSPECTIVES

Max's school is not unique. Students are facing an increasing number of pressures from outside the classroom, and a higher proportion of young persons are living under duress.[2] The problem has many

---

[2]See, for example, Mike Rose, *Lives on the Boundary: The Struggles and Achievements of America's Underprepared* (New York: Free Press, 1989); and Alex Kotlowitz, *There Are No Children Here: The Story of Two Boys Growing Up in the Other America* (New York: Doubleday, 1991).

causes, the most significant of which is that the adults who are responsible for the kids' care are themselves unable to cope because of their own financial problems, poor health, addiction to alcohol or drugs, or limited opportunities to learn how to become effective parents. It is no wonder their children have difficulty with school.

Max is wise to see that his problem is to know where to draw the line. It is not only that he lacks the expertise to meet the varied needs of these students; he also lacks the time. If he is like most secondary teachers, he meets with approximately one hundred students a day, and their grievously unmet needs are not something he alone can address.

He has already implemented one option: to ease up on the students somewhat. When only a third of them are doing their homework, he will have difficulty finding time to determine which of the parents are going to be able to give support at home to help students complete their assignments. He may need simply to accede to the reality that homework is not something he can count on. Thus, he needs to see that students use their class time as productively as possible, since for most of them that is the only time they are supported in studying English. Perhaps he should not feel guilty about the paucity of the reading and writing the students have done. They have accomplished something, against overwhelming odds, and most of them have continued coming to class. Max needs to recognize that this itself is a plus.

If he allows some students to get out of certain assignments because of home pressures, he opens himself up for charges of unfairness—legitimately one of a teacher's greatest fears. He needs to provide generous amounts of class time for all his students to do assigned work. If school policy allows it, it would be better to arrange for the Marias in his class to take an incomplete at the end of the term, with the proviso that the missing work must be made up during the vacation period and turned in on the first day of the new term or else that work gets averaged in as a zero.

Because such a high proportion of the students have enormous pressures outside of school, Max should do all he can to expand opportunities for students to work in supervised study halls. However, there may not be enough of these scheduled during the school day for these students. Another way to help such young persons is to provide a place after school where they may study, ideally with tutors available. They desperately need a calm place to study.

One way for Max to proceed would be to work together with his colleagues to expand the number of social workers and counselors who can meet regularly with these troubled teens and their families. At the same time, he has to draw the line between what he can and cannot do to help students in the classroom sort out their lives through personal journals and discussions of literature. To stay in the profession, he needs not only to draw that line, but also to continue to respond positively and hopefully to his students without blaming them for what is beyond their control or himself for what he cannot change.

Max is not alone in sensing that something has profoundly changed for the worse in the communities that should be nurturing America's young persons. A recent National Research Council report has concluded that the "problems facing America's youth are so severe that the situation amounts to a 'human and national tragedy.'"[3] To face and to deal capably with something as overwhelming as a national tragedy, teachers need supportive professional communities themselves.

The Center for Research on the Context of Secondary School Teaching at Stanford University has looked closely at teachers of today's troubled teenagers. It identified three broad patterns of teacher response to today's challenging students: (1) continue traditional practice, (2) lower their expectations, or (3) change their practice.[4] Those who continue traditional practice tend to blame the students and to become cynical, frustrated, and burned out. A high proportion of their students fail or drop out, and the teachers are very likely to leave the profession. Those who choose to lower standards and water down the curriculum find themselves bored and disengaged. (See Chapter 5, "The Disaffected Teacher.") The third group of teachers do not stop believing that their students are capable of learning at high levels and that all of them should be actively engaged with challenging content. According to Ms. Milbrey W. McLaughlin, Director of the Center, the critical difference between this last group of teachers and the other two groups was the fact that they belonged to an active professional community that supported them in transforming their instructional strategies.

Max should join local professional groups such as his state Association for Teachers of English, the Teachers Applying Whole Language (TAWL), a local writing project affiliated with the National Writing Project or his local teachers' union. He might enroll in graduate classes. He must learn, from other teachers who also face the challenge of today's troubled students, effective ways to adapt to his students' needs while maintaining high standards and expectations.

---

[3]"Adolescents at Risk of Becoming 'Lost Generation' Report Says," *Chicago Tribune,* 24 June 1993, p. 15.

[4]Robert Rothman, "Study Urges 'Learning Communities' to Address the Isolation of Teachers," *Education Week,* 12, No. 25 (March 17, 1993), 1, 25.

CHAPTER 25

THE ABUSED STUDENT

SITUATION

"Carlos," Penny asks, "What happened to your eye?"
"Coach hit me in the eye."
"Accidentally?"
"I don't think so."

The quiet rustling of papers in her fifth-period freshman class reminds Penny Miller of wind dancing through dry autumn leaves. These are welcome sounds, telling her that everything is normal in the classroom on this snowy January day. The squeaking sound of chalk against the board, as she writes the assignment directions, mimics the sounds made by their resident family of mice.

Penny turns from the board and her eyes do a quick inventory of the empty seats. Yes, she has enough handouts. It is then that she sees Carlos's eye. It is almost swollen shut. His eyeball, the visible part, is red, and the surrounding outside area is various shades of black, blue, green, and yellow.

Carlos, a slightly built fifteen-year-old, is a typical Gheri-curl wearing, inner-city, black high school student. He has a sharp intellect. He moves slowly, but when he volunteers in class, what comes out of his mouth is usually deliberate and profound. Penny loves to call on him because he is sure to supply the spark needed to ignite a lively discussion. Although she has known Carlos for only for a few months, he has grown on her because of his unique personality and his mature, street wise mother wit. His fellow students appear to like him a great deal.

"Carlos," Penny asks, "what happened to your eye?"
"Coach hit me in the eye."

"Accidentally?"

"I don't think so."

"Hmmmmm . . . " Penny murmurs, trying to remain calm as her apprehension level begins to rise. "He hit you deliberately?" she asks.

"Something like that."

"Why?" Penny asks.

"Cause it's the same old mess, Miss Miller."

In a weary tone, Penny says, "See me after class, Carlos," as she returns his medical excuse to him. Carlos has not been in school since the previous Thursday and has been under the care of a physician.

When the bell rings and the students have all hurried on to their next classes, Penny motions Carlos to her and says, very softly, "Tell me about it, Carlos."

"I was playing b-ball, with Timothy, in the small gym, last Thursday, during seventh-period lunch. We always play ball during seventh period. There aren't any classes in that gym during seventh. At first, I don't think Coach saw me, or he didn't really know it was me. He must have thought I was one of Tim's jock friends. Tim is my best friend. He's a junior, but we're friends, anyway. He's a linebacker on the varsity team."

"How did you and Tim get to be such good friends?"

"We take the same train in the morning. We both get on at Thorndale. One day, a whole bunch of guys tried to take my gold chains. We had all just gotten off of the train. Tim saw what was happening to me and made them give back the chains. Tim is a big guy. Nobody messes with him."

Penny asks, "How did he do that? You said there were a lot of them."

Carlos looks at her with disbelief, and says, "Miss Miller, Tim just picked one guy up and threw him at the others. They all ran, after that, including the guy that he threw."

"I see."

Carlos continues with his story:

"Anyway, when Coach came out of his office, he was headed for the outside door, until he recognized me. He turned, immediately, and came over to where we were still playing. When the ball was coming down from the hoop. The Coach caught it. He said. 'Get your ass outa here, Timothy.'

"Tim asked. 'Why do I have to leave? We're not doing anything.'

" 'I said, get outa here, *now*.' " Only this time, Coach sorta yelled it.

"Tim picked up his shirt and books as he headed toward the door and said to me, 'Man, I'll see you later. How long you think you gonna be?'

"Before I could answer, Coach beat me to it. 'He's going to jail, don't wait for him, or you'll be waiting a long time . . .' When Tim left the gym, Coach threw the ball down and headed toward me."

Carlos says this with a heavy sigh.

"He grabbed my left arm and pulled it up behind my back, real hard. I told him he was hurting me. He said, 'Good. That's exactly what I had in mind.'

"I said, 'Man, I ain't done nothing. Why you trippin'?' By this time, he was dragging me with my arm still bent up behind my back, through the back door of the gym, across the hall toward the Discipline Office. The bell hadn't rung, so the hall was totally clear of other students and teachers. It was like he was in a hurry to get to the Discipline Office before the bell rang, 'cause he was moving real fast—as fast as he could and still drag me. All the while, I was trying to get away from him, you know, like wiggling as much as I could, but his grasp was too strong. Every time I moved, it hurt my arm."

Carlos pauses and starts to rub his arm, remembering the pain.

"When we got to the Discipline Office, Ms. Grady, Mr. Gordon, and Ms. Vogenthaler, all of them white, were, as usual, in the office.

"Miss Miller, why are almost all of the teachers in this school white? Most of the students are black. We only have about a hundred and fifty white kids in this school."

Penny replies, "This school has always had a majority of white faculty. I don't think Chicago is adhering to the Faculty Desegregation Decree,[1] Carlos; the decree was supposed to integrate faculties according to a specified student-to-teacher racial ratio."

Carlos looks down at his hand and raises his eyebrows in a look of doubt as he says, "Well, all I wanna' know is this: Are all of Chicago's public high schools staffed like this one?"

Penny thinks for a moment, before responding, "This is my first teaching assignment; but, according to my friends, many of whom have taught for several years, ours is not the only school out of compliance with the decree."

Carlos goes back to his story:

"Faschin Wallace, the Student Aide, was also in there, in the Discipline Office. She's black. When the other white folks saw us, they told Faschin to leave and to go on to her next class, even though the bell had not rung to end seventh period. When she left, they started hollering at me. By this time Coach had let my arm go, and I was standing next to him, at the counter, rubbing my aching

---

[1]Effective in 1979.

arm. I tried to tell them that I was only playing basketball and hadn't done nothing wrong. They just kept on hollering stuff at me, so I turned away from them, toward the chairs, and started to sit down."

Penny listens, in horror, until the anger takes over. It comes rushing up from the pit of her stomach, until it rises like bile to her throat and her lips. "Did you say anything to him or the others while all of this was happening?" she asks.

"When I was walking over to the chairs to sit down, I tol' 'em to kiss my ass, 'cause I hadn't done nothing wrong." Carlos said sheepishly.

"That wasn't polite, you know." Carlos nods. "What happened, then?" Penny asks.

"Coach ran over to me and grabbed me by the arm, turning me around and at the same time, he punched me in my right eye, with his fist. He hit me so hard that he knocked me backward into the chairs. I fell and my eye must have been split 'cause blood was flying all over everywhere, before I fell. Coach was cursing and breathing hard as he jumped on me and started punching me. The others pulled him off of me. I got up and had one hand over my eye. It felt like my eye was coming out. I was holding my other hand out in front of me to keep anybody else from coming at me. Then Coach yelled, 'Look, he's trying to hit me. You are all witnesses. I hit him in self-defense.' He was coming toward me again, and the others pulled him away. He acted like he was going wild or something. I thought he was going to kill me."

"What did you do, then?"

"I knew I had to get out of there, or they were going to hurt me some more. I tried to get to the door and open it, but they wouldn't let me. Mr. Gordon sorta' stuck his arm out and over my head, and held the office door closed, so that I couldn't get out. Coach said, 'Call the police.' He tried to hit me again. He was talking to Ms. Vogenthaler. She called 911 and told them that a teacher had just been assaulted by a student. She told them that they needed the police to come to the school. When Ms. Vogenthaler finished the call, she told Ms. Brady to stand outside the door to make sure that no one else entered the Discipline Office."

"What were you doing, while all of this was happening?" Penny asks.

"I was trying to see if my vision would come back to my eye and I was sorta' crying. We waited about ten minutes before the cops got there. During that time, I was leaning against the far corner wall of the office. I was trying to stay away from all of them and be in a place where nobody could get behind me. When the police arrived, Coach told them that I had tried to hit him. Everybody else just nodded their heads while he was telling that lie. I tried to tell 'em that it wasn't like that. They just handcuffed me and put me in one of those little private offices. They hand-cuffed me to the desk, also."

"Did the police say anything to you?"

"Naw. They just told me to shut up, when I tried to interrupt those lying teachers."

"You mean they didn't say *anything* else to you?" It is really hard for Penny to believe that they didn't ask the child if he needed help for his obvious injuries.

"No way. They just marched me to the back door, in handcuffs and put me in the police car. When we got to the police station, the man at the desk asked me how old I was. I told him that I was fifteen. They took me into a little room, and the Youth Officer came in to talk to me. He asked me, 'What did you do?' I told him that I hadn't done anything. He said, 'You did something wrong. That's why you are here.' I kept saying that I hadn't done nothing. He asked, 'How old are you?' I told him I was fifteen. He looked at me for about two or three minutes and said, 'Get outa here and go home.'

"I said, 'I don't have my coat, and, Man, my eye is killing me. Can't you see that it's all full of blood and stuff?'"

"He yelled, 'I said, get outa here, now!' I guess I must have rolled my eyes at him as I was getting up to go. He got up and came behind me. He started pushing me out of the office; so I left and went home."

"You mean you went home, in this cold January weather, without your coat? Did you call somebody or did you take public transportation?"

"I took the bus home. When I got there, Mama had to open the door for me 'cause my keys were in my coat pocket, at school. I tried to duck my head down so she couldn't see my face, but she saw all the blood on my clothes and started screaming questions at me. She took me to the emergency room at Illinois Masonic Hospital."[2]

QUESTIONS TO CONSIDER

1. If you were Penny, what is the first thing you would have done, after hearing Carlos's story?

2. What do you think should happen to the coach?

---

[2]This vignette was written in the Multicultural Collaborative on Literacy and Secondary Schools (M-Class) teacher research project sponsored by the National Center for the Study of Writing, Berkeley, Cal., 1993.

3. What do you think should happen to each of the other staff members who were present in the Disciplinary Office?

4. Is there any way that Penny can see that Carlos's side of the story gets told?

5. When did the police officers act appropriately, and when didn't they?

6. Should Penny contact Carlos's parents, and, if so, how should she advise them?

7. What are Penny's legal obligations, if any, after hearing Carlos's story?

8. What are the possible legal ramifications for the school?

PERSPECTIVES

Unlike the other cases in this book, in this circumstance Penny's first course of action is prescribed by law. In most states, she would be required to report as soon as possible any situation for which she has reasonable cause to consider it a case of child abuse. All she has is the child's story, but this is reasonable cause, and before the day is out she should call the state child welfare agency and report Carlos's story. In some states there is a hot line for such calls. She will be asked some questions and probably be expected to file a written report within a few days. In most states, an investigator should arrive within twenty-four hours.

Her next responsibility is to call Carlos and his parents and tell all of them what she has done in response to his injury. Either she or they should call the attending physician at the hospital because the investigator may want to interview the doctor as well. She should make it clear to the parents that she will do all she can to see that Carlos's side of the story gets a fair hearing and that she hopes her action will prevent such maltreatment in the future. She can ask Carlos if he told his story to any of his other teachers that day, and she should get from him his schedule of classes so she can talk with his other teachers and let them know of the action she has taken.

Surely another teacher must have seen Carlos's eye, prior to Penny's fifth period class. After she has called the state child welfare agency, she should alert Carlos's other teachers who have seen his injury that day and alert them to the fact that an investigator might be asking them some questions and that all of them are required by law to report a case like Carlos's. They may be grateful that she has done this for them. Like Penny, Carlos's other teachers are bound by the Child Abuse and Neglect Reporting Act[3] to report incidents that suggest reasonable cause that there is abuse to the appropriate governmental agencies. In addition, if Penny or any of Carlos's other teachers had not inquired about and had not reported the incident, they could lose their teaching certificates.

Next, Penny should find out if Carlos told his story to the physician. If so, the attending physician is also bound by the provisions of the Reporting Act.

As a new teacher, Penny may feel hesitant to press this case, but she does have the law on her side, and she needs to remind everyone else of that fact. During the investigation of the incident, Penny can expect the coach and the other staff members who were in the Discipline Office to react defensively, denying Carlos's story and possibly charging her with meddling. The coach and the three other staff members involved will have their own stories to tell. She will probably be considered a troublemaker since she will be perceived as Carlos's advocate in this matter. Because the coach could face criminal charges if Carlos's story is believed, Penny can expect a strong case to be made denying any wrongdoing on the part of the school personnel and insisting the coach acted in self-defense.

At this point, Penny needs to be very conversant with her legal responsibilities and very even-tempered about the whole matter. She can tell anyone who asks that she is not simply accepting Carlos's story without question; she just feels the situation merits investigation.

She would be wise to seek the support not only of any other African-American teachers but also, along with Carlos's parents, legal counsel, since the school authorities will want to do all they can to avoid legal repercussions or publicity of an incident that would jeopardize the reputation of the coach or of the school. Another group she might want to report this incident to is the Human Relations Commission of the city, since she suspects that Carlos's race was significant in affecting the way the coach treated him.

As a fairly new member of this school's faculty, Ms. Miller would be wise not to confront the coach herself. If he is like most secondary school coaches, he carries a great deal of influence, and his story of the incident is much more likely to be believed than is Carlos's story. Every member of the school administration stands to lose a great deal if charges are brought against the coach, so it is in their self-interest to protect him, if at all possible. The playing field is dangerously tipped, with Carlos and his teacher on the top end and

---

[3]Illinois, *Child Abuse and Neglect Reporting Act, Revised Statutes* (1991), 23: Sec 2051.

probably the entire administration solidly together holding down the other end.

The coach seems to have enough influence to get the three staff members in the Disciplinary Office, flagrantly to break the law. Their acquiescence to his claims of self-defense, when they had witnessed his abuse of Carlos, is indicative of the tacit assumption that his authority is not to be questioned, at least not in the Disciplinary Office.

As an African-American teacher, Penny is justified in suspecting this might be a case of racism, because everyone in authority who could have come to Carlos's aid was white. If Carlos's story is to be believed, the only two blacks who could have witnessed the abuse were summarily dismissed from the scene: one, Tim, who was large and strong, was sent away by the coach; and the other, the Student Aide, was dismissed by the staff members in the Discipline Office.

Penny also knows that the arresting officers should have found out how old Carlos was before they took him away. As a fifteen-year-old minor, he should never have been removed from the school without notice to his parents. In addition, whatever the reason for Carlos's obvious injuries, he should have been taken to the emergency room of the closest hospital. The arresting officers, like Penny, were obligated by the Reporting Act to report this incident as soon as possible to the hospital personnel as a possible case of child abuse inflicted by a teacher.

Since none of these steps was taken, Penny could make a case that the arresting officers were grossly negligent. The Youth Officer at the police station was probably as negligent as the other officers since he did not get Carlos's side of the story or call Carlos's parents. He also forced an injured minor to go out of the station without a coat into the cold January afternoon.

The aftermath of Penny's report of this incident may not be pleasant, but unless teachers like her become strong advocates of justice for all students, some may remain powerless and vulnerable to injustices that hark back to race relations of a century and a half ago.

CHAPTER 26

STUDENT COMPLAINTS ABOUT ANOTHER TEACHER

SITUATION

"Mr. Holst, do you think Mr. Price is a bad teacher?"

Of everything he had accomplished in his first semester as an English teacher, Brad Holst was most proud of the rapport he had cultivated with his students. He believed a solid and trusting relationship with his class was the foundation of a successful year. When he made mistakes or didn't know the answers to their questions, he admitted it. When he was angry with them, he told them why. In return, the students were honest with him. Many of them liked to stick around after class to talk, both about their work and their personal lives.

Today, after the bell has rung and Brad has finished taking attendance, he looks up to see a cluster of three girls around Francine's desk.

"Seats, please, ladies, if you don't mind. Seats, please."

"Just a minute," Lila says, tossing a look over her shoulder, then quickly turning her attention back to the center of the group. Brad moves toward them and they grudgingly disperse. Lila touches Brad's shoulder as she passes him and whispers, "She's really upset."

Now he sees Francine for the first time. Her eyes and cheeks are red and wet. She sees Brad and covers her face with her hands.

"I'm so sorry." Brad crouches beside her desk. "What is it?" She only sobs harder.

Lila says, "She just got her semester grade, right at the end of the period, would you believe it? from, that big, fat jerk, Mr. Price."

"The science teacher?" Brad asks.

"Yeah," Chip chimes in. "I got mine, too. This guy's a complete and total idiot."

"How do you tell a teacher he is rude and obnoxious?" Hope asks.

"Very politely?" Chip suggests; a few students laugh.

"He's so totally unfair. He didn't give *anyone* in his class higher than a C." Hope is shouting now. The rest of the class gasps. Some curse this man they don't even know.

Brad rises, "So he's a tough teacher, huh?"

Chip says, "Naw, man, that's not even it. Tough I can deal with. He doesn't even teach anything. He just makes us read stuff, take quizzes, and watch movies. That's totally all we do."

"He doesn't even bother to explain," Hope adds. "If you ask him questions he says, 'Check your book.'"

Chip moves to a desk beside Francine and touches her arm. "You OK?" Francine nods, but keeps her face covered.

Hope is seething now, she's got her momentum up. "If you say you can't find it in the book, he says, 'Go ask another student.' If you say you already did that, he says, 'Then you should reconsider staying in an honors class.'"

The class, most of whom do not have this teacher, are now ready to string him up. They identify with Francine's misery, Hope's anger, and Chip's frustration. They turn now to their own teacher, their confidant.

Doug asks, "Mr. Holst, do you know him?"

Brad has heard bad things before about Mr. Price from other students. There has even been some concerned talk among faculty members about his lack of connection to his classes. He is one year from retirement and seems to be coasting to the finish line. Brad often thinks he might feel the same way himself when he reaches that stage of his life, but he also realizes how unfair such an attitude would be to his current classes. He answers, "I know him, yes. Not well. But we are colleagues of course."

"Have you heard anything about him?" Hope says.

Brad shifts his footing and checks the clock, clears his throat. "Well. I've heard . . ." He thinks of what he has heard about what Charles Price was like before Brad joined the faculty: tough, demanding, conscientious. "I've heard that he is a fair person, and he does know his subject."

The class sits stricken a moment. Can Mr. Holst be lying to them? Is he siding with a teacher—*against* them? Then they verbalize:

"He hates kids!"

"He's unfair!"

"He doesn't care!"

"He's so boring!"

"He's anti-Semitic!"

Chip raises his hand in the midst of all this noise and Brad acknowledges him with a nod. "I heard Mr. Price is retiring in a year. Is that true?" Should Brad answer this? It's harmless information, isn't it? Most people probably know anyway. But he does sense Chip's intention to use the information as a weapon.

"I'm not sure," Brad says. "Maybe so. But that doesn't have to mean that—"

Hope cuts him off, "Do you think it's fair for a teacher to show movies, give quizzes, and not explain stuff?"

"Well, . . ."

"*Do* you?"

"I . . ."

"Let me put it this way," Hope says, seeming to turn her anger on *him* now. "Would *you* do that?"

Brad is not used to this hostility. Why are they mad at *him*? "Mr. Price and I probably have a different teaching style, but that doesn't mean—I don't know. Listen. I think we should get back to the poetry I had planned for us."

"Mr. Holst, do you think Mr. Price is a bad teacher?" Here's the question he didn't want to hear. And it's from Francine, who has dried her eyes and is using them to look right through him. "Huh?"

Brad thinks of the rapport he's shared with these kids, the honesty it's built on, the trust they have come to rely upon. He feels that rapport all being drawn out of the room, leaving a chilly silence.

"Huh, Mr. Holst? *Do* you?"

QUESTIONS TO CONSIDER

1. Should Brad side with the students on this issue?

2. Is there anything else he can do both to reestablish the rapport he has had with this class and to be fair to his colleague?

3. Should he approach Mr. Price, and, if he does so, what strategy would be the most effective?

PERSPECTIVES

Brad has a lot to lose if he sides with his students based only on their complaints and hearsay. As any teacher knows, it is easy to whip up student enthusiasm for vilifying a teacher, whether or not the charges are well-founded. Besides, as a new teacher, he needs to cultivate the respect and trust of his colleagues as much as that of his students. Other teachers might rush to Mr. Price's defense just as readily as Brad would like to rush to Francine's. It is always difficult to sort out the legitimate from the specious in complaints students make about other teachers, parents, and students.

At this point, the best Brad can do is to offer to sympathize with the students, to look into the matter, and to get back to the business of the English class. As he wisely recognized, any negative thing he says about Mr. Price in the context of a whole-class rebellion like this one is likely to be misinterpreted and to come back to haunt him. However, he can again empathize, saying, "What I've heard about him is simply very little. I just don't know him as a classroom teacher as you do. I have to plead ignorance. I can't get into a discussion about something I know almost nothing about, which means I actually can't be much help to you. Sorry."

He could suggest that since he is ignorant about Mr. Price as a teacher, perhaps two of the students in Mr. Price's class could agree to represent the class. After the two students have discussed the problem together, they need to reach consensus on a list of facts about Mr. Price's teaching that they and their classmates agree are causing problems for the whole class. Then the two representatives of the class can make an appointment with the department chair to present to him or her their list of facts.

There is one legitimate area in which Brad might offer to be an advocate of the students, however, and that has to do with Mr. Price's timing. By letting Francine and the other students know about their semester grades at the very end of the previous class period, Mr. Price has created a problem for Brad. To address this problem—which is his, not his students'—Brad could promise the class he will talk with Mr. Price about the way he let the students know about their semester grades. This might placate them somewhat, and Brad would not be promising more than he could deliver.

Brad might open the dialogue with Mr. Price by simply reporting on Francine's reaction to her science grade and the problem it posed in his English class. Next, he needs to listen patiently to Mr. Price's defense of his evaluation of her work, which would likely follow. Then Brad could suggest that Francine seemed to be very surprised and upset by her semester grade, and ask Mr. Price if he could apprise the students of their possible final grades earlier in the semester, so their final grade would not be such a shock. If it is true that many are totally unaware that they are going to get a low grade, Brad could suggest that all of the teachers give more frequent summaries of student averages. Ideally, such a discussion might make a good topic for a department meeting.

Brad should probably talk as well with his department chair about the students' concerns, and perhaps tell the students that he will do so.

CHAPTER 27

AN ATTACK ON THE TEACHER'S COMPETENCE

SITUATION

"Have you ever given any consideration, Ms. . . ., uh, whatever, to the possibility that Charles is not 'performing,' as you put it, in your class because he does not like or enjoy your class? Or you for that matter? Did you ever consider that possibility?"

Terri Roth has been assigned her first freshman honors class the semester before she is eligible for tenure. For her first year and a half she taught two middle-level and three low-level classes. When she was assigned this honors class, she couldn't help feeling that she had, in a way, been promoted. And the class is wonderful. Gone are the boisterous and often belligerent kids from the lower tracks; gone are the days of collecting homework from less than half the class. The honors students are enthusiastic, motivated, eager learners. There is no assignment they won't try, whether it is making vanity license plates for characters from the *Odyssey* or acting out scenes from *The Tempest*. Discussions on literature and current events are lively and well-informed. Homework is consistently well-prepared.

But there is one problem student in this class: Charles, a lanky kid with a ponytail and two earrings puncturing one earlobe. He seems to enjoy class discussions, but appears to have difficulty keeping up with the other students. He also has an adult demeanor that makes him seem older than he really is. But Charles isn't turning in his homework. When Terri questions him about it, he produces elaborate but plausible explanations. "I had it all totally finished, but my dad's printer broke down. So I took it to my mom's office, but they didn't have the same program we had, so it all had to be converted, but then the guy who did it lost part of it, 'cause he didn't know what he was doing. Should I bring a note from my dad?"

"That won't be necessary," Terri would say.

Three weeks into the first quarter, Terri realizes that most of the work that Charles promised would come in "tomorrow or the next day at the latest" never seemed to arrive. His quizzes on the readings and his test scores are also consistently in the D range.

Terri speaks to Bonnie Gonzalos, Charles's counselor. She digs out his file and discovers his placement test scores from junior high school are solidly in the average range. Based on those results and recommendations from eighth-grade teachers, Charles would not normally be recommended to the honors level. So Terri goes to Gene Tully, her department chair, who makes the final decisions on who is placed at what level.

Gene pulls out his own records. He has, in fact, recommended that Charles Nelson be placed in a middle-level class. Attached to his recommendation, however, is a lengthy letter from Charles's parents in which they formally waive the recommendation, which is their legal right. "So what's happening?" Gene asks. "Wait. Can I guess? He's drowning, isn't he?"

"He is," Terri says, "though I didn't realize that was it until just now."

"Not surprising though, is it," Gene responds, with some satisfaction, "considering he really is at the wrong level?"

Terri calls Charles's father and explains her concerns about Charles. On Bonnie's advice she does not mention anything about the test scores or the waiver. Mr. Nelson does not make a sound as Terri speaks. But when Terri finishes, Mr. Nelson asks sharply, "You through?"

"Yes."

"Have you ever given any consideration, Ms. . . ., uh, whatever, to the possibility that Charles is not 'performing,' as you put it, in your class because he does not like or *enjoy* your class? Or *you* for that matter? Did you ever consider that possibility?"

Terri thinks, "The question is hypothetical, isn't it?" but remains silent.

"Well?" Charles's father barks. "Well? Did you ever think of that?"

Terri admits she has not.

"Did you ever think that maybe Charles is not challenged enough in your class? This is a very bright boy we are talking about.

This is a very unusual young man. He tells me what goes on in your class. Drawing projects and little skits. Come on! And he tells me that you have no control over the class. Kids talking all the time, getting out of their seats. "Chaos" is the word Charles used. Is this some sort of new educational philosophy?"

"Rhetorical question?" Terri wonders. "Mr. Nelson . . ."

"How long have you been teaching honors classes, Ms., er?"

"This is, well actually, this is my first year."

"Dear Lord. Can you give me the superintendent's extension?"

In class the next day, Charles does not show the slightest indication that his father has related any of the conversation to him. He participates in a discussion of an upcoming election, as animated as always, as animated as the rest of the class. This is the kid who complained about a chaotic classroom? Terri wonders.

Two weeks later, a major paper is due. Charles does not turn it in. It is on a friend's disk. He'd have it Monday. But Monday comes and goes and the paper never materializes. The following week he fails a major test on *The Tale of Two Cities*. At this rate, he is in danger of failing the quarter. Terri has to call Charles's home again. She sits in the teachers' lounge for five minutes, staring at the phone, bracing herself, then finally dials. She is relieved when Charles's mother answers. Her voice is more gentle than her husband's and she greets her cordially. "Oh, hello, Ms. Roth. Good of you to call." But then she summons her husband to the extension.

Terri's mouth goes dry. She explains, as gingerly as she can, about the paper and the test. Mrs. Nelson listens with verbal nods of affirmation. "I see. Oh, uh-huh." Mr. Nelson's end of the line is quiet until Terri says, "That's where we are right now."

"You finished?"

Terri says she is, then leans back in the chair and closes her eyes, holding her hand over the phone to muffle her sigh.

She is a terrible teacher. A novice! She is probably doing more harm than good. She "has no business with these high-level kids. They need a pro! Idiot classroom games! License plates! Come on! Kids out of control! Not enough challenging work. No wonder Charles rebelled! Hell, who wouldn't?"

Then he hangs up.

After a pause, Mrs. Nelson speaks softly, "We're just concerned, Ms. Roth. Charles is clearly a gifted child. We want him to get the education he needs. We don't want him to go unchallenged. You understand."

Before the week is over, Terri receives a copy of a two-page, typewritten letter that the Nelsons have written to the principal, the president of the Board of Education, and the English department chair. It declares that Terri is an unfit teacher who "seems intimidated by and hence harbors resentment against our son's high level of intelligence." It goes on to relate reports Charles has made about what Terri was supposed to have said and done in the classroom. Most are outright lies. Could Charles possibly have said all this? "Ms. Roth passes days at a time," the letter goes on, "assigning no homework whatsoever and showing full-length movies that seem wholly unrelated to curricular expectations."

Three weeks before the end of the quarter, as Terri reviews her gradebook, it is clear that no matter how she adds it up, Charles will fail her class. School policy demands that if students are likely to fail a term, parents are to be notified in advance.

Terri sits down in the teachers' lounge clutching her can of Diet Coke and stares at the phone. She takes a sip, then she dials. Mr. Nelson answers. . . .

QUESTIONS TO CONSIDER

1. What is the best strategy for Terri to use at this point in response to Mr. Nelson's confrontation?

2. Should she make any more allowances for Charles given the fact that both the department chair and the counselor agree that he is clearly unprepared for the challenge of this class?

3. What would be the advantages and disadvantages of a face-to-face meeting with both Charles and his parents? Should any of Terri's colleagues join this conference?

4. How is she going to counter the false charges that Mr. Nelson has made, and the attacks on her "educational philosophy," or should she try to?

5. What, if anything, should Terri do about the fact that the department chair, superintendent, and president of the board of education have all received a copy of the letter the Nelsons sent to her?

6. Should she try to reply to the Nelsons' letter, putting in writing her own side of the story? Should she actually send the letter to the Nelsons, or only to Gene, her department chair, and Bonnie, the counselor? Or should she just write the letter for her personnel file?

PERSPECTIVES

Whenever a parent attacks the right of a teacher to make a *judgment* about a student's work, the problem becomes a departmental problem. Terri was wise to share her concern with her chair and Charles's counselor. Unless she has some support from her colleagues, she is in a vulnerable position. The charge that she has "kids out of control" could jeopardize her being granted tenure if it were affirmed by other teachers. What are her options at this point?

She might do well to ask Gene or another department member to visit her class, both (1) to assess the over-all tone of the classroom, the educational appropriateness of the activities she initiates, and the effectiveness of her classroom management; and (2) to observe Charles. The invited visitor could write up this evaluation along with detailed notes on assignments that Terri has made on the day before and on this day, noting Charles's response to the previous day's assignment. Copies of this evaluation could go to Terri, her supervisors, including the principal, and her personnel file.

She could, of course, go ahead and pass Charles. This would get the Nelsons "off her back" and make Charles happy. Such a course of action, however, does Charles a permanent disfavor. What he would be learning is that he is not responsible for his own behavior, and that no matter what he does or does not do, his parents will bail him out. To give this message to a teenager is to deny him the consequences of his own misdeeds. Such a lesson is a powerful incentive never to grow up; Terri would be the "enabler," to use the term popular in self-help groups for addicts.

Clearly, Terri is the victim of the Nelsons' unrealistic expectations for their son. Although it might seem reasonable to get all the parties involved in a conference—Charles, his parents, and Terri— such a dialogue might degenerate into confrontation and give Charles the idea that his teacher is not someone to respect because she is not on his side. Mr. Nelson has drawn a line in the sand, with his family on one side and Terri on the other. In such an antagonistic setting, a better strategy might be to meet with the parents face to face, without Charles.

Before the meeting with the parents, however, Terri would do well to have a brief meeting with Charles, doing everything she can to help him realize that she is his ally who wants very much to help him succeed. This is no time to remind him again of his deficiencies and missing assignments. This is a time for active listening, not more directives. Ask him how he thinks he is doing in this class and what he thinks she might do to help. Of course, Charles needs to know

Terri is going to have a conversation with his parents. She could ask him if there is anything he would like for her to tell his parents about his work in this class.

The meeting with the parents will inevitably be difficult for Terri. After a few brief and friendly questions back and forth, Terri needs to get right to the point and to hold the floor, presenting her account of Charles's performance in the class as accurately and non-judgmentally as she can. Only then should she ask the parents if they have any questions. Since Mr. Nelson's previous stance has been to try to put Terri on the spot and to defend their son, Terri will need to listen to their viewpoint. If she can agree on any point she should do so as long as nothing she agrees to undercuts what she has just presented.

She needs to arm herself with samples of Charles's papers, quizzes, and tests. If possible, she should have at her command an example of Charles's confusion during class participation. An audio-tape of a brief interchange in class might be just the article to have to help convince Charles's parents, especially if the taped interchange demonstrates Terri's commitment to helping Charles understand the material under discussion. If other students' more apt responses on the topic were also on the tape, that might help.

A copy of an A paper by another student, with the name deleted, might provide a much needed perspective for the parents. Of course, the grade book with a listing of dates homework was due and when it was missing is essential grist for the discussion.

Terri's tone needs to be reconciliatory and undefensive. Mustering all the courage of her brief two years of teaching experience, she needs somehow to demonstrate both (1) that she has been a caring, conscientious teacher for Charles, and (2) that Charles has not risen to her expectations. If Mr. Nelson charges her again with conducting a chaotic class, she needs to make it very clear she has never before been accused of poor classroom control, even as a student teacher. It is important for Terri to stand her ground, no matter how distasteful conversations with Mr. Nelson have been. It might help at that point cordially to invite both parents to visit her class and see for themselves.

She should avoid the whole subject of how bright or not-bright Charles is. Terri is bound to lose in any argument on that score. Instead, she should state such judgments as: He seems not to understand what is expected of him; he has difficulty getting assignments in on time; he appears to be unprepared for tests. She needs to assure the parents in any way she can that she genuinely likes Charles. She might ask their advice on how she might help Charles.

If Mr. Nelson starts again on the time wasted on drawing projects and doing skits, then Terri should bring out her theoretical underpinnings and talk knowledgeably about the very well-respected theory of Dr. Howard Gardner at Harvard[1], according to which students learn in a variety of modalities. Therefore, it is important to give all of them ample opportunities to graphically visualize the scenes in their texts, and hear the dialogue and other sounds. Important research studies have shown that role playing characters in literature is a profoundly powerful way to help students identify emotionally and intellectually with the characters in the literature they are reading.[2] As they use gestures and postures, they internalize the feelings and interactions of the characters, experiencing the scenes kinesthetically, with their bodies.

Terri could instead write a letter to the Nelsons, but this might simply strike them as defensive, and, no matter what she writes, they are as likely to attack the letter as to attack her. A better strategy might be for Terri to write a detailed chronicle of Charles's behavior, including a detailed account of the assignments that were made, the percentage of the class who completed each, and the response Charles made to each one. This history should be as objective and dispassionate as possible, just laying out the facts as she has experienced them. A copy of a representative homework assignment Charles has turned in might help make her case. This record of what happened could go into her personnel file along with Terri's summary of the face-to-face meeting with the Nelsons.

Clearing herself of the charges made by the Nelsons to the department chair and other administrators will probably be much easier than convincing Charles's parents. She could write a memo describing the meeting with the parents giving a short summary of Charles's behavior throughout the quarter. This memo could be sent to all the persons the Nelsons wrote to with a request that this be put into her personnel folder along with the letter from the Nelsons. Terri should explain her perspective regarding each of their charges. She should show this memo to Bonnie Gonzales, Charles's counselor, and ask her to write a letter for Terri's file as well.

---

[1] *Frames of Mind: The Theory of Multiple Intelligences* (New York: Basic Books, 1983).

[2] Josephine Keeter Demond, "The Use of Role Playing, Improvisation, and Performance in the Teaching of Literature" (Ph.D. diss., Georgia State University, 1977), abstract in Dissertation Abstracts International, 38, (1978): 3906A–3907A; and Beatrice Theresa Green, The Effects of Dramatic Techniques on Selected Learning Outcomes (Ph.D. diss., Clark University, 1974), UMI No. D74-24186 (Ann Arbor, Mich.: University Microfilms, 1974).

The Nelson's charges are not something for Terri to lie awake nights over. Parents have a right to be biased toward their children, and these will not be the last parents she encounters whose perspective is skewed. This type of problem simply goes with the territory of English teaching.

CHAPTER 28

UNDERWATER WELDER

SITUATION

"Lookit. Three weeks from now I'm sixteen anyway, and then I'm outa here forever."

Carl, a student in Simon's middle-level junior class, has been absent fifty percent of all class days. He will fail the first semester, but when Simon told him, Carl's response was, "So?"

"So, you'll have to repeat English," Simon said.

"Lookit. Three weeks from now I'm sixteen anyway, and then I'm outa here forever."

Carl is not an exceptional student in any way, neither unusually accomplished nor unusually weak. He could probably swing Cs if he tried at all, and might be getting Bs if he tried hard. But he hates school and plans to go to a trade school and pursue a career either in auto mechanics or welding. "Underwater welders," he once informed Simon, "make a heck of a lot more than any teacher."

Simon has told Carl he would like him to make use of his remaining school days so his options will be open. But numerous conversations with him have fallen on deaf ears. His parents neither attend parent conferences nor answer his phone calls, though early in the year Simon did talk briefly to Carl's mother one afternoon and explain his position.

"But he wants to be a mechanic," she said. "What am I going to do? A mechanic is a good thing. You ever need a mechanic?"

"Just recently," he allowed.

"Aren't you glad no English teacher talked that fella outa being one?"

QUESTIONS TO CONSIDER

1. Is Carl making a big mistake?
2. Is there anything Simon can do to convince him to change his mind?
3. Should he even try?

PERSPECTIVES

Both Carl and his mother, like a high percentage of Americans, view education narrowly as mere job training. Simon, on the other hand, represents the subgroup of the population who see education as preparation for human experiences that go far beyond the mere making of a living. Carl and his mother have a right to view education otherwise. It will be difficult for Simon to persuade them, and in the case of Carl, it is probably too late.

Persuasive arguments can be made for education as preparation for such life challenges as productive leisure as well as work, enlightened parenting, knowledgeable management of one's own health, or the assumption of a responsible role as a citizen in a democratic society. Leaving these clearly worthy goals aside, however, Simon could present many sound arguments for Carl's staying in school simply in order to become a part of what is an increasingly more highly educated work force. Given Carl's values, this might be the most persuasive line of argument to pursue.

In our post-industrial age, there are no workers, including underwater welders, whose jobs will stay the same over even the next decade, much less over the lifetime of a worker. Like it or not, the Carls of this world will find themselves going back to school over and over to keep up with the latest technological advances.

Changes in the demands of the work force are taking place not just nationally, but globally. Ours is an increasingly global economy. Transnational events and trends increasingly affect the lives of all of us. To advance as a mechanic, or even to keep his job at the same level, Carl will need to learn to work with new technologies that may originate in far corners of the globe. President Clinton's Secretary of Labor Robert Reich, in his book, *The Work of Nations*, claims that the notion of national corporations is out of date. "There is coming to be no such thing as an American corporation or an American industry. The American economy is but a region of the global economy."[1] This means that Carl might well be employed

---

[1]New York: Alfred A. Knopf (1991), 243.

someday by a subsidiary of a multi-national enterprise, and the more he knows about the rest of the world, the better able will he be to serve his firm. Certainly his advancing to a high wage position will depend on his learning new skills.

High-wage enterprises are most likely to locate in places on the globe that have the highest levels of education of the potential work force because it is here the firms would not only find the best employees, but also a superior quality of life.[2] Reich reminds us that the Americans who can cope with the global economy are those who are flexible and have problem-solving skills. We need to educate our population to be jet-setting, big-thinking conceptualizers, or what Reich calls "symbolic analysts." This group is the new elite, linked by jet, modem, fax, satellite, and fiberoptic cable to the great commercial centers of the world. It is not what we own that counts. It is what we do.[3] The choice Carl is making may cut him off from the group of elite workers in our society. If there is any way Simon can help him recognize this, he will be doing him a great service.

---

[2]Reich, *The Work of Nations*, 151.
[3]Reich, *The Work of Nations*, 109.

CHAPTER 29

PRIVACY OF STUDENT WRITING

SITUATION

My boyfriend T. meets me every day before math down by the P.E. where nobody ever goes and he gives me (and me and him both drink) vodka usually, cause he says you can't smell it.

Maria has a class of students who have been reluctant to write. In an effort to loosen them up, she has them keep a journal in class. Each period begins with ten minutes of journal writing. At first they grumbled, doodled, or even refused to do it. The boys thought it was something only girls do. "I don't want to write my feelings," Jacob had sneered. "Anyway I don't have any feelings." He rolled his eyes elaborately.

Marie remained patient. Anyone who wanted to doodle could, and those who wanted to write could, as long as they were putting something on paper. After several weeks, she noticed that more and more kids were beginning to write. A few even volunteered to read aloud. One day, Rachel wrote about an encounter she had just had with a store owner who accused her of shoplifting. Her writing was both funny and poignant. The students clearly admired it. They applauded. That became a turning point. After that, more kids wanted to read their pieces to the class.

Maria collects the journals after the first month. She is surprised by how personal some of the writing is and how painful some of their experiences are. When she hands them back, she compliments the students on their courage and honesty and tells them how flattered she is by their trust. Rachel then wants to know if Maria told anybody about what she read, "like your husband or kids or friends or anything?" The other students seem to have been wondering the same thing because the room becomes very quiet as they await her answer.

Maria promises that what they wrote is absolutely confidential between them and her. She will never show it to anyone. That would be a violation of the trust they have built.

"Promise?" they chorus.

"Promise," she says.

Now Maria collects the journals for a second time. Few students are doodling and almost everyone is able to fill at least a page each day. Near the bottom of the stack she finds one by Veronica, a sullen and withdrawn girl, about whom she knows very little. Veronica is often absent and even more often tardy. Maria has been meaning to talk to her counselor.

Veronica writes:

> At first I didn't like the idea of writing about my feelings and/or my thoughts in this book. I didn't have to much in it the first time you collected because I didnt know what to say. But there is a problem I having that bothers me alot and I didn't know what to do. My boyfriend T. meets me every day before math down by the P.E. where nobody ever goes and he gives me (and me and him both drink) vodka usually, cause he says you can't smell it. Other people are there to. JK and Z. and their girl firends. We ditch lunch cause whats the point? and we drink somemore or sometimes Z. has uppers cause I'm pretty slow in the afternoon from the vodka. Sometimes I'm thinking I maybe shouldn't be doing this.

QUESTIONS TO CONSIDER

1. Is there any way Maria can help Veronica without betraying the trust she has built up with her and the class?

2. Should Maria talk with anyone besides Veronica about her problem?

3. Does Maria have an ethical responsibility to get help for Veronica?

4. What is her legal responsibility in a case like this?

PERSPECTIVES

Clearly, Maria's goal of getting the students to trust her has suc-
ceeded, and even Veronica has risen to the challenge of sharing her
feelings and experiences. Maria has painted herself into a corner
with her promise not to show to anyone else anything they write in
their personal journals, nor to tell anyone else about it. Now she has
found out that Veronica's entry may well be a cry for help, but how
can she be sure?

What are her options?

She can talk with Veronica privately, sharing her concern about
the situation she wrote about and suggesting gently that she has a
problem she may need to share with someone else. She can remind
her that drinking vodka every day can create all sorts of other problems for her and her friends. Maria will need to make it clear she
appreciates Veronica's willingness to share in her journal, and she
doesn't want this conversation to inhibit her writing in the future. It
is just that the situation she described worries the teacher Maria as
well as Veronica.

Because Maria is keenly aware of the school rules, she knows
she should tell a school counselor about this situation, not only for
Veronica's sake but for the welfare of the other teenagers as well.
Suppose, however, that she cannot get Veronica's permission to do
this? After all, she promised that she would keep confidential what
they wrote. Then, to fulfill her obligation as a faculty member, she
will have to break Veronica's trust. Because this trust was so hard
won, Maria might consider telling a principal or counselor in authority to monitor the halls where the teenagers have been meeting, but
not ever to let the students know who tipped them off. That might
solve the problem of drinking at that spot in school, but it would not
necessarily solve Veronica's problem, since the students would only
need to find another trysting place. At minimum, Maria should talk
with Veronica about the seriousness of her problem and her obligation to see that school rules are followed. She should also talk with
Veronica's other teachers suggesting that they be alert to alcohol on
her breath.

Maria might be tempted to give up the idea of a personal journal altogether, but the authors of this book think this would be a bad
idea. The advantages of personal writing far outweigh any risks
teachers might face. The best material for any writer is personal
experience, and the closer students can get to those events that have
shaped their feelings and their thoughts, the more energy they have
for expressing themselves, and the more authentic their voices will
be. However, they should never be required to share their personal

diaries with anyone but the teacher, and the teacher should treat this material as privileged information, not something to be shared with any other teachers or students, unless the contents reveal something truly harmful as in this case.

There are some cases in which Maria would not have an option. Another teacher received the journal below, and in that case he was legally obligated to report the contents to an appropriate administrator or social worker in the school:

> I believe my past has had effect on the way I see the world today. In all my life my dad wip me or slap me very hard. I don't think at first it affect me bad. But he keep slapping and hitting. One day I don't see nothing. But I wake up ok. Now it affects me with everything I see. Whenever I look at something like a light post, when I go to touch it it not really there. All the time I see something I think is there but then it is not there. I sometime jump out of the way of cars that are not there. So all that slapping and wiping has effect on every thing I see in my life time. Now and forever.

Because this journal constitutes reasonable cause for considering the possibility of child abuse, the teacher is obligated by law to report it to the child welfare agency. A teacher who doesn't report it would be subject to suspension or loss of his or her teaching certificate. Any situation in which the students' physical welfare is in jeopardy should be reported promptly. (See Chapter 25, "The Abused Student," for more on this.)

CHAPTER 30

EQUITY IN COMPUTER ACCESS

SITUATION

"You have a research paper due in four weeks. . . . I want it to make one heck of a first impression. Make me want to read this thing!"

Ian grew up around computers. His father worked for a large computer manufacturer and his mother designed software programs for children. He wrote his Master's thesis on the use of computers to improve student writing. When he was hired to teach sophomores at Shaw High School, he was delighted to learn that fully sixty percent of their student body had computers at home.

Now he talks to his classes about the "impression of writing," how everything—spelling, mechanics, organization, word choice—are important elements of writing. A misused or misspelled word or a misplaced comma can break the reader's train of thought, and the impression blurs. "It is also important," he tells them, "that your paper look good." He holds up an old dittoed quiz from his youth. He passes it around the room and lets them get a good look at the faint lavender letters, the "x"-ed out words, the filled in "o"s. Then he holds up a quiz he has produced with a laser printer using seven different fonts and three color graphics. He asks them, "So if you had to take a quiz, which one would you rather take?" The class—no surprise—unanimously favors the computer-produced quiz.

"You have a research paper due in four weeks. Not only do I want it to be well-researched and carefully written, but I want it to make one heck of a first impression. Make me want to read this thing!"

The students' enthusiasm is palpable. "Can we use Kid Pix or PaintBrush?" they want to know. "I have e-mail at home. Can I tap into the on-line data base?"

"Of course," Ian says, delighted that what he had written in his thesis about computers and student interest was true. "In fact, I'll offer extra credit for every graphic you include so long as it is used to make your point clearer. Now go to it!"

Four weeks later, when the papers come in, Ian is so pleased with the results he makes photocopies to show other teachers and sets the originals out on a table for everyone to see. The students gather there at the beginning of each period, for several days, admiring each other's work, asking how a particular effect was created, exchanging ideas for further projects.

The next day, he stops Sarah on her way out of class. She has not turned in a paper. Sarah is a bright and highly motivated student with a deep respect for school and her work. So the fact that she has not turned in this major paper seems very odd to Ian.

"Where is it?" he asks.

She casts a look away from him, then down to the floor. "I'm still not finished. I had a little trouble. I promise it will be in after the weekend."

On Monday, Sarah is absent. Then, during Ian's lunch period, Sarah's mother arrives at his door holding a manila envelope. "My daughter's paper," she says extending it to him. "She has a terrible case of the flu, but she said she promised to get it to you by Monday."

"If she's ill," Ian says, "she could have turned it in on her return. That's one of the benefits of establishing a good reputation for yourself. I have no reason to distrust her."

"You must run a tight ship here, Mr. Mathews. I've never seen my daughter work so hard on a paper. Worked into the night sometimes. She's always been a very conscientious student, but I've never seen her like this. Typing and retyping, gluing maps and graphs, then going to the photocopying shop. I said she could just paste the graphs on, but she insisted on going again to the photocopiers to copy the pages with the graphs. She didn't want it to look pasted, she told me." She smiles and extends a hand to Ian. "I appreciate a teacher with high expectations."

After she leaves, Ian takes Sarah's paper from the envelope. Great care has gone into this typed paper. Every word is perfectly spelled, not a drop of correction fluid on the page. But on the last page, Ian finds a yellow sticky note from Sarah:

"Mr. Mathews. Please do not put my paper on display. Thank you."

QUESTIONS TO CONSIDER

1. What is Sarah's problem? Is she justified in her request?
2. What are Ian's options?
3. Was Ian fair in casting the assignment the way he did?
4. Should he change the way he words the assignment to take account of the Sarahs in his class? If so, how? Will these changes lower the expectations for students whose homes are better equipped technologically? Is modifying the assignment going to reduce the challenge for such students?

PERSPECTIVES

Ian is fortunate to have grown up in an environment where computers were part of his daily experience; in this respect he differs from the average graduate of English education programs. Only a very few of the teacher training programs at the college or university level have computers optimally integrated into the course work. All of them should.[1] The old debate between traditional text-centered teaching and technologically sophisticated interactive learning has been won, and Ian is on the winning side. If his students are to operate effectively in our increasingly information-rich and interconnected society, they will have to become sophisticated computer users. However, Ian as a pioneer needs to consider the implications of assigning papers as if there were no disparity among his students in access to computers.

As in the other situations presented in this section of this book, the source of the problem lies beyond the classroom. Our society is increasingly divided, with the chasm between the haves and have-nots widening daily;[2] one of the ways this is most evident is in the disparity in technologically sophisticated equipment in households. Computer access is just the latest in a long list of advantages of growing up in a home at a comparatively high socioeconomic level. Analysts and researchers have long recognized the correlation between a student's school achievement and a literate parent who provides a home rich in books and other literacy materials.

---

[1]Kathleen Keifer, "Computers and Teacher Education in the 1990's and Beyond," in *Evolving Perspectives on Computers and Compsition Studies,* edited by Gail E. Hawisher and Cynthia L. Selfe (Urbana, Ill.: National Council of Teachers of English, 1991), 117–131.

[2]Reich, *The Work of Nations,* 198–202.

As Nancy Kaplan has persuasively argued,[3] new technologies represent ideological systems, but in this respect they are no different than the entire system of formal education. In any system, certain groups are comparatively privileged or advantaged and others lose out because of the way the system is organized. Whether the new computer technologies will widen the gap between the powerful and the disadvantaged or whether they will serve to increase participation and democratic access to information and power is a hotly debated topic. If those who see the gap widening are right, the entrenched political and economic systems will simply perpetuate themselves by controlling who has access to the new technologies and to the sources of information they can provide.

Another scenario is projected by what Kaplan has termed the "technological determinists."[4] They see a bright future because electronic tools have the capacity to extend opportunities for participation in public discourse to groups who have until now been silenced.[5] For example, thanks to electronic mail connections, students and other heretofore disenfranchised groups can participate in global dialogues without having their voices unheard because of the difficulties of getting themselves published in newspapers, magazines, or books—mediums that tend to exclude the voices of the young or comparatively powerless.

The difficulty Ian faces is an ethical one. Like many of the issues presented in this casebook, this is a professional issue that teachers all over the country increasingly face. As this book is going to press, the National Council of Teachers of English is establishing a Code of Professional Ethics Committee to set standards for dealing with issues like the one Ian faces.

Until then, what are Ian's options?

He could ignore the problem and hope that this experience will lead Sarah and her family to get a personal computer for their home. If he assumes that in her case her family could afford a personal computer and probably would buy her one when she goes off to college, this is not an unreasonable expectation. However, it is never wise to make decisions based on assumptions about the economic circumstances of any student.

---

[3]"Ideology, Technology, and the Future of Writing Instruction," in *Evolving Perspectives on Computers and Composition Studies*, 11–38.

[4]Kaplan, "Ideology, Technology," 34–35.

[5]Some commentators have suggested that the collapse of communist rule in Eastern Europe in 1989 was made possible in part because of the portable camcorders in the hands of the dissidents.

Ian can make clear to all of his students that, for the next assignment, the layout, printer quality, graphics, and other niceties of desktop publishing will not affect the grade. He can still make his point that the overall impression a piece of writing gives is important in a society that has access to increasingly high quality presentations of text, but that he recognizes this is not an appropriate consideration in his classroom because only some of the students have access to powerful word-processing packages, desktop publishing software, and high quality printers. Then, when Ian grades the papers, he will need to be very aware of his own bias toward the quality of the printing and the layout of the paper and try to compensate for this bias, just as teachers who are scoring handwritten essays for content have to try to ignore the legibility of the handwriting. However attractive the paper may look or however difficult the printing may be to read, Ian should concentrate only on evaluating the quality of the writing itself.

There is no way that students will not see each others' papers, even if Ian does not lay them out for display; but in a class with a wide disparity in computer capabilities, it would be well for Ian not to initiate such a comparison. If each student keeps in a file folder in the classroom a collection of her or his own papers, with previous drafts stapled behind the final draft, and if each paper receives comments and feedback from Ian but not a grade, then assigning a grade for a body of work (all the papers completed during the marking period) may minimize the focus on comparing the visual appeal of one student's collection with that of other students' work. (See Chapter 1, "Defending a Grade," for a description of portfolio assessment.)

The ideal option is for Ian to do all he can to provide adequate computer access for those students without computers at home. To do this may take a number of months and a fair amount of school funds, or even a grant from an outside source, but the advantage of this approach is clear: it will improve the learning environment for years to come.

There may be first steps Ian can take right away, such as requesting that computer labs be open more hours of the day or before and after school. Even if he had to offer to supervise the lab before or after school during the four weeks his students were working on the assignment, it would be worth the effort in equalizing opportunity for his students. Most computer teachers want to expand computer use, and they will probably be delighted to find an English teacher who not only values what they are teaching but is willing to help his students become more comfortable with and competent in word processing. A student like Sarah who is new to computers may need quite a bit of hand holding and tutoring for a while, but some of that might be done by other students in the class.

Another goal—a long-term one—for Ian is to see to it that all of the students in his classes learn not only how to write a research paper using desktop publishing software, but also how to access databases and hypertexts and to converse with colleagues in ever expanding networks of information and resources via electronic mail.[6] Our era is termed the "information age" or the "computer age," and secondary school graduates who are not comfortable with computers will be at a disadvantage in both colleges and in the work force. As Hawisher and Selfe remind us, "Power now belongs, to a great extent, to those members of our society who can use technology to access and manipulate the expanding world of information."[7] Typically, the students who use computers most ably are white and male. Just as public schools and public libraries helped equalize access to the tools of literacy for all socioeconomic groups, so they must respond to the challenge of equalizing access to technology.

Ian's first challenge may well be to convince his colleagues in the English Department, who in many schools tend to be the last to embrace new technologies. There is good reason for this, because any technology brings in its wake values that may not be consistent with the goals English teachers and other humanists deem as most worthy. Humanists are concerned with values, ideas, and the search for truth, and most do not want to teach mere mechanical skills. They may think these are skills the students should be able to pick up on their own.

English teachers are not the only ones to be concerned about the effect of technological change. There has always been resistance to new technology, rooted in motives ranging from frivolous miscalculations to awesome misgivings about usurping God's power. Some of our favorite myths and metaphors emerge from the fears of technology's impact on society: Prometheus's hubris in stealing fire from the gods; Frankenstein's monster; genetic engineering gone awry, as in the movie *Jurassic Park*.

Most students, at some point, benefit greatly from formal instruction in computer use. It is likely easy for Ian, who grew up with computer expertise in the air he breathed in his home, to underestimate not only the cognitive difficulties many students face in mastering even a simple word-processing program but also their helplessness in front of the computer screen. This feeling of inade-

---

[6]FrEdMail is a free electronic mail service that is heavily subscribed to by students throughout the world. To join, phone 619/757-3180.

[7]Hawisher and Selfe, *Evolving Perspectives*, 175.

quacy tends to be exacerbated by the perception that most of the hesitant students' peers have no problem mastering arcane computer commands.

Instead of relying on his English department colleagues for support, Ian should find allies among those who teach computer courses; they will be his most likely advocates for setting up requirements in word processing or even desktop publishing for all students. Once such requirements are in place, then Ian can require all of his students to produce pleasingly-designed documents without being unfair to Sarah. Since publishers are increasingly expecting writers to take over some of the functions of typesetters and graphic artists, and businesses are rapidly expecting reports from employees to be graphically sophisticated, Ian's pressure toward pleasing design is not inappropriate, as long as all of his students have equal opportunity to produce such papers.

APPENDIX A
CALIFORNIA READING AND
WRITING ASSESSMENT

The state assessment of reading and writing in California mirrors good practice. Most students who take this test find the tasks challenging and interesting; the test, which takes about a week to complete, can be justified in terms of student learning, even if it did not produce scores the state needs to evaluate its educational programs.

The California test is included here as a sample of the type of authentic assessments that are currently being developed by a number of groups at both the state and national levels. One of these groups is the New Standards Project, co-sponsored by the Learning Research and Development Center at the University of Pittsburgh and the National Center on Education and the Economy in Washington, D.C. As this book goes to press, approximately twenty-five thousand students in grades four, eight, and ten have participated in the field trials of English language arts performance assessment tasks. The tasks and their scoring rubrics eventually will become one part of the New Standards Project's national portfolio assessment system.

We are including here not only the student test pages, but also the scoring guides for assessing reading and rhetorical effectiveness. We hope you will photocopy this exam, try it out with your students, and then advocate the use of this type of test as your local school assessment of reading and writing.

SECTION ONE
READING

"Story of an Hour"

Before You Read
You are going to read "Story of an Hour," a short story written by Kate Chopin at the beginning of the twentieth century. After you read the story, you will be responding to questions and activities that show what you think and feel about it.

Reading Situation
Read the story by Kate Chopin. Make notes of your questions and reactions as you read. You may underline phrases or passages you think are memorable or important.

Story of an Hour   *Notes/Response*

Knowing that Mrs. Mallard was afflicted with a heart trouble, great care was taken to break to her as gently as possible the news of her husband's death.

It was her sister Josephine who told her, in broken sentences; veiled hints that revealed in half concealing. Her husband's friend Richards was there, too, near her. It was he who had been in the newspaper office when intelligence of the railroad disaster was received, with Brently Mallard's name leading the list of "killed." He had only taken the time to assure himself of its truth by a second telegram, and had hastened to forestall any less careful, less tender friend in bearing the sad message.

She did not hear the story as many women have heard the same, with a paralyzed inability to accept its significance. She wept at once, with sudden, wild abandonment, in her sister's arms. When the storm of grief had spent itself she went away to her room alone. She would have no one follow her.

There stood, facing the open window, a comfortable, roomy armchair. Into this she sank, pressed down by a physical exhaustion that haunted her body and seemed to reach into her soul.

She could see in the open square before her house the tops of trees that were all aquiver with the new spring life. The delicious breath of rain was in the air. In the street below a peddler was crying his wares. The notes of a distant song which some one was singing reached her faintly, and countless sparrows were twittering in the eaves.

There were patches of blue sky showing here and there through the clouds that had met and piled above the other in the west facing her window.

She sat with her head thrown back upon the cushion of the chair, quite motionless, except when a sob came up into her throat and shook her, as a child who has cried itself to sleep continues to sob in its dreams.

She was young, with a fair, calm face, whose lines bespoke repression and even a certain strength. But now there was a dull stare in her eyes, whose gaze was fixed away off yonder on one of those patches of blue sky. It was not a glance of reflection, but rather indicated a suspension of intelligent thought.

There was something coming to her and she was waiting for it, fearfully. What was it? She did not know; it was too subtle and elusive to name. But she felt it, creeping out of the sky, reaching toward her through the sounds, the scents, the color that filled the air.

Now her bosom rose and fell tumultuously. She was beginning to recognize this thing that was approaching to possess her, and she was striving to beat it back with her will—as powerless as her two white slender hands would have been.

When she abandoned herself a little whispered word escaped her slightly parted lips. She said it over and over under her breath: "Free, free, free!" The vacant stare and the look of terror that had followed it went from her eyes. They stayed keen and bright. Her pulses beat fast, and the coursing blood warmed and relaxed every inch of her body.

She did not stop to ask if it were not a monstrous joy that held her. A clear and exalted perception enabled her to dismiss the suggestion as trivial.

She knew that she would weep again when she saw the kind, tender hands folded in death; the face that had never looked save with love upon her, fixed and gray and dead. But she saw beyond that bitter moment a long procession of years to come that would belong to her absolutely. And she opened and spread her arms out to them in welcome.

High School Sample, California Department of Education, 1991.

There would be no one to live for her during those coming years; she would live for herself. There would be no powerful will bending hers in that blind persistence with which men and women believe they have a right to impose a private will upon a fellow-creature. A kind intention or a cruel intention made the act seem no less a crime as she looked upon it in that brief moment of illumination.

And yet she had loved him—sometimes. Often she had not. What did it matter! What could love, the unsolved mystery, count for in the face of this possession of self-assertion which she suddenly recognized as the strongest impulse of her being!

"Free! Body and soul free!" she kept whispering.

Josephine was kneeling before the closed door with her lips to the keyhole, imploring for admission. "Louise, open the door! I beg; open the door—you will make yourself ill. What are you doing, Louise? For heaven's sake open the door."

"Go away. I am not making myself ill." No; she was drinking in a very elixir of life through that open window.

Her fancy was running riot along those days ahead of her. Spring days, and summer days, and all sorts of days that would be her own. She breathed a quick prayer that life might be long. It was only yesterday she had thought with a shudder that life might be long.

She arose at length and opened the door to her sister's importunities. There was a feverish triumph in her eyes, and she carried herself unwittingly like a goddess of Victory. She clasped her sister's waist, and together they descended the stairs. Richards stood waiting for them at the bottom.

Someone was opening the front door with a latchkey. It was Brently Mallard who entered, a little travel-stained, composedly carrying his grip-sack and umbrella. He had been far from the scene of the accident, and did not even know there had been one. He stood amazed at Josephine's piercing cry; at Richards' quick motion to screen him from the view of his wife.

But Richards was too late.

When the doctors came they said she had died of heart disease—of joy that kills.

High School Sample, California Department of Education, 1991.

Writing About Your Reading

1. What is your first response to the story? Take a few minutes to write down any thoughts, questions, or opinions you may have.

   _____

   _____

   _____

   _____

   _____

   _____

   _____

2. Below is a double entry journal. In the left column, copy short passages from the story that seems intriguing, interesting, or relates to your life in some way. In the right column, write your responses to the passages you have selected. Your responses might indicate what the passage means, what it reminds you of, what you don't understand, how you feel about it, or any other comments that seem appropriate.

   Remember, copy the passage or quotation on the top of the left column and write your comments *directly* opposite in the right column. Then, copy your next passage and write your response opposite, etc.

Passage from the story	Response to the passage

High School Sample, California Department of Education, 1991.

3. There were several important events in the story. Select the one you feel is most important and explain why you feel this way.

_____

_____

_____

_____

_____

_____

4. Look at the ideas you have generated so far. Now, imagine that you are Mrs. Mallard.

   Below is an "open mind" diagram, a way of making a visual representation of what a character might be thinking or feeling at a particular time. In order to understand Mrs. Mallard more fully, create an "open mind" for her. Inside the drawing, fill in symbols, images, words, phrases, or any combination of these which represent what Mrs. Mallard was thinking and feeling as she was "drinking the very elixir of life through that open window."
   Note: an elixir _is a liquid substance which people used to believe would prolong life. It means "the embodiment of perfection."_

Open Mind for Mrs. Mallard

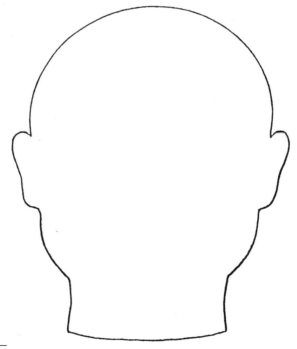

5. Write an explanation of the meaning of the symbols, images, words, or phrases which you included in your open mind and explain why you chose them.

    _____

    _____

    _____

    _____

    _____

    _____

    _____

    _____

    _____

    _____

    _____

6. Discuss the transformation that Mrs. Mallard undergoes as the story moved forward. Explain in the space below.

What the character first thought	What the character finally thought	How do you explain the change?

This is your page to tell us anything else about your understanding of this story—what it means to you, what it makes you think about in your own life, or anything that relates to your reading of it.

_____

_____

_____

_____

_____

_____

_____

_____

_____

_____

_____

_____

_____

_____

_____

_____

_____

_____

_____

_____

_____

_____

_____

_____

STOP!
DO NOT TURN THE PAGE!
This is the end of Section One.

High School Sample, California Department of Education, 1991.

SECTION TWO
WORKING WITH YOUR GROUP

"Story of an Hour"

Guidelines for Working with Your Group
During this part of the test, your group will discuss what you read during Section One. It is important that everyone in the group has a chance to participate. One person should volunteer to act as the discussion leader. The responsibilities of this person are to keep the discussion on the topic, to see that everyone has a chance to talk, and to keep an eye on the clock. The responsibilities of each member are to share in the discussion and take notes or write responses when called for. Select your discussion leader now and write that person's name here:

Discussion leader: ————————————————————————————

What was most memorable about the short story "Story of an Hour"? Quickly jot down you own ideas below.

Now share these ideas with your group and record some new ideas which other people presented.

High School Sample, California Department of Education, 1991.

Now with your group, imagine that Mrs. Mallard has not died at the end of the story. Discuss whether or not this marriage could be saved. In the space below, write down the ideas presented by members of your group on the following:

Reasons the marriage can be saved:

Reasons the marriage cannot be saved:

Based on the group discussion, what is your opinion about this marriage? Why? Briefly write your opinions and reasons here. Take only a few minutes to do this.

_____
_____
_____
_____
_____
_____
_____
_____
_____
_____
_____
_____
_____
_____

High School Sample, California Department of Education, 1991.

Mrs. Mallard felt "free" after hearing about her husband's death. Why did she feel this way, and what were her ideas about the future? Discuss this as a group. Jot down ideas from your group in the following space.

_____

_____

_____

_____

_____

_____

_____

_____

In the space below, draw a visual representation of your interpretation of the last two paragraphs (page 232) of the short story. In your drawing, include characters and depict what is happening when Mr. Mallard returns. Remember, it is not necessary to be a good artist to draw a successful representation of a story.

High School Sample, California Department of Education, 1991.

Share this drawing with your group.

Now consider this broader question:

Does marriage inhibit freedom, or can it be an opportunity for freedom? What is "The joy that kills"?

Take notes while you discuss this question. You may want to use them later.

STOP!
DO NOT TURN THE PAGE!
This is the end of Section Two.

High School Sample, California Department of Education, 1991.

SECTION THREE
WRITING

Interpreting the Character of Mrs. Mallard

Writing Situation

You have read and discussed "Story of an Hour" by Kate Chopin. Think about the changes in the main character, Mrs. Mallard, and the reasons for these changes. You may use your notes from Section Two of this test.

Directions for Writing

Write an essay for your English teacher in which you interpret the growth and change in Mrs. Mallard's character and what it means. As you present your interpretation, support your claims about the meaning with reasons and evidence from the story. Your essay should convince your teacher that you have thought carefully about your interpretation.

High School Sample, California Department of Education, 1991.

SECTION THREE
WRITING

Reflecting on Marriage and Freedom

Writing Situation

In our society, marriage is viewed as an ideal way to achieve lifetime happiness with another person. It is often thought of as a relationship where people develop and grow together to form a lifelong bond. Yet over one half of the marriages in this country end in divorce.

Directions for Writing

Write an essay for your classmates reflecting on marriage and the concepts of marriage and freedom. Consider how marriage affects our ability to be "free." Relate your ideas to yourself, to those you know, and to people in general. Explain your ideas thoughtfully. You do not need to convince your readers that your ideas are best or right, simply explore your ideas thoughtfully.

High School Sample, California Department of Education, 1991.

SCORING GUIDE
FOR
THE CALIFORNIA READING ASSESSMENT

Reading, as defined for the purposes of California's English-language arts assessment, is the process of constructing meaning through transactions with text. In this view of reading, the individual reader assumes responsibility for producing an interpretation of a text guided not only by the language of the text but also by the associations, cultural experiences, and knowledge that the reader brings to the interpretive task. Rather than believing that meaning resides solely within the words on the page, this view of reading emphasizes the role of the individual reader in making meaning through a process that brings together textual and contextual evidence and the distinctive experience and perspective of the reader as meaning-maker.

To assess a student's performance in reading is therefore not only to assess the richness and plausibility of the meaning that the student produces but also the quality of the process through which meaning is produced. In some cases, students may be better readers than the evidence seems to show. Raters must give credit for all evidence of the construction of meaning but, at the same time, be careful not to base a score on rater-inferred meanings. Raters will always be alert to graphic or written clues that show indications of reading performance. Raters should also note that neither length of responses nor negative statements about the assessment provide information about the quality of the reading performance.

A score should not be lowered by a chance or occasional misreading of a word, phrase, or fact in a test performance that would otherwise demonstrate a higher level of reading performance. Similarly, the rater must credit an interpretation that is supported by plausible reasons and/or references to the text, even though the interpretation may differ from the rater's own expectations.

When two passages are paired, one more complex than the other, the best readers interpret both passages and explore implications of the pairing. Less able or emerging readers may be less successful at handling the complexities of the more difficult passage and usually focus on the more accessible one. Looking carefully at the responses to both passages gives raters multiple opportunities to rate the overall performance. For the purposes of this assessment, when two selections are used, they both serve as the basis for the reading assessment.

While every effort has been made to construct a reading assessment approach that gives students multiple opportunities to demonstrate their ability to construct meaning from interacting with given texts, it is important to emphasize that each individual reading score

High School Sample, California Department of Education, 1991.

represents the reading achievement of a particular student on a specific day, reading given text(s) for assessment purposes. No student should be labeled as a "three reader" or a "five reader" on the basis of any single assessment.

Complex factors that affect student responses include the following:

- The purpose of the reading, as established by the prompt and perhaps modified by the student's own needs as established by his or her relationship to the text
- The nature of the questions and activities in the prompt
- Previous experience with the text type or with the subject of the text

Condition Codes

Raters will score every paper that has any evidence of the construction of meaning. However, there may be instances when a student response is scored using condition codes.

Code Definition

A   Unscorable/Uninterpretable Evidence
- Illegible handwriting
- Underlining and highlighting only
- Copied section(s) of text or prompt verbatim with no other response
- "I don't understand."
- Irrelevant doodling (This option is to be exercised only when there is no perceptible relevance to the text(s) in the prompt. If the text is a story that includes a dog sled race and the student draws a picture of a track event, for example, assuming that there is no other evidence available on the assessment, the paper would receive a score point one. The picture shows a personal connection at least to the word *race* in the text; such a connection shows the student is responding at the decoding level, which is score point one.)

B   Off Topic

C   Blank/No Response

D   Language other than English
- Entire paper in language other than English (No score; condition code only)
- Responds in more than one language (Score English portion and enter score; use condition code to flag that a portion of the response is in another language.)

⸗igh School Sample, California Department of Education, 1991.

READING PERFORMANCES

The following list of reading performances shows the range of behaviors that readers may engage in as they construct meaning from a text. Readers are not expected to exhibit all these behaviors, but more effective readers are likely to exhibit a wider range of behaviors. In general, readers also demonstrate more advanced levels of achievement by the degree to which they attend to increasingly more complex structures of meaning.

As readers demonstrate the quality, range, and comprehensiveness of their transactions with texts through their writing and graphic representations, they:

1. Demonstrate intellectual engagement with the text: experiment with ideas; think divergently; take risks; express opinions; speculate, hypothesize, visualize characters or scenes, explore alternative scenarios; raise questions; make predictions; think metaphorically.

2. Explore multiple possibilities of meaning; consider cultural and/or psychological nuances and complexities in the text.

3. Fill in gaps; use clues and evidence in the passage to draw conclusions; make warranted and plausible interpretations of ideas, facts, concepts, and/or arguments.

4. Recognize and deal with ambiguities in the text.

5. Revise, reshape, and/or deepen early interpretations.

6. Evaluate; examine the degree of fit between the author's ideas or information and the reader's prior knowledge or experience.

7. Challenge and reflect critically on the text by agreeing or disagreeing, arguing, endorsing, questioning, and/or wondering.

8. Demonstrate understanding of the work as a whole.

9. Attend to the structure of the text: show how the parts work together; how characters and/or other elements of the work are related and change.

10. Show aesthetic appreciation of the text; consider linguistic and structural complexities.

11. Allude to and/or retell specific passage(s) to validate and/or expand ideas.

12. Make meaning of parts of the text.

13. Make connections between the text and their own ideas, experiences, and knowledge.

14. Demonstrate emotional engagement with the text.

High School Sample, California Department of Education, 1991.

15. Retell, summarize, and/or paraphrase with purpose.
16. Reflect on the meaning(s) of the text, including larger or more universal significances express a new understanding or insight.

Score Point 6—Exemplary Reading Performance

An exemplary reading performance is insightful, discerning, and perceptive as the reader constructs and reflects on meaning in a text. Readers at this level are sensitive to linguistic, structural, cultural, and psychological nuances and complexities. They fill in gaps in a text, making warranted and responsible assumptions about unstated causes or motivations, or drawing meaning from subtle cues. They differentiate between literal and figurative meanings. They recognize real or seeming contradictions, exploring possibilities for their resolution or tolerating ambiguities. They demonstrate their understanding of the whole work as well as an awareness of how the parts work together to create the whole.

Readers achieving score point six develop connections with and among texts. They connect their understanding of the text not only to their own ideas, experience, and knowledge, but to their history as participants in a culture or larger community, often making connections to other texts or other works of art. Exceptional readers draw on evidence from the text to generate, validate, expand, and reflect on their own ideas.

These readers take risks. They entertain challenging ideas and explore multiple possibilities of meaning as they read, grounding these meanings in their acute perceptions of textual and cultural complexities. They often revise their understanding of a text as they re-read and as additional information or insight becomes available to them. They sometimes articulate a newly developed level of understanding.

Readers performing at level six challenge the text. They carry on a dialogue with the writer, raising questions, taking exception, agreeing or disagreeing, appreciating or criticizing text features. They may sometimes suggest ways of rewriting the text. They may test the validity of the author's ideas or information, by considering the authority of the author and the nature and quality of evidence presented. They may speculate about the ideology or cultural or historical biases that seem to inform a text, sometimes recognizing and embracing and sometimes resisting the position that a text seems to construct for its reader.

?h School Sample, California Department of Education, 1991.

Score Point 5—Discerning Reading Performance

A reading performance at score point five is discerning, thorough, and perceptive, but will probably show somewhat less insight or sensitivity to textual nuances and complexities than an exemplary reading. These readers are able to fill in gaps in a text, making plausible assumptions from subtle cues; but they engage in these operations with less acuteness of vision than more expert readers. They recognize and differentiate between literal and figurative meanings. They recognize real or seeming contradictions, exploring possibilities for their resolution or tolerating ambiguities. They demonstrate their understanding of the whole work as well as an awareness of how the parts work together to create the whole.

Readers achieving score point five see connections between their own lives and the world of the text. They connect their understanding of the text not only to their own ideas, experience, and knowledge, but to their history as participants in a culture or community. They often make connections to other texts or other works of art; these connections while always purposeful and connected to the text, may be more predictable than those made by exceptional readers. They also draw on evidence from the text to generate, validate, expand, and reflect on their own ideas.

These readers may explore multiple possibilities of meaning. While they may form firm interpretations early in their reading, they are open to revising their ideas as additional information or insight becomes available to them. They sometimes articulate newly developed levels of understanding.

Readers performing at this level challenge the text. They pose questions, postulate answers, take exception, agree, disagree, speculate; however, the questions and/or issues they raise may not be as insightful or perceptive as those of the reader demonstrating an exemplary reading.

Score Point 4—Thoughtful Reading Performance

Readers at score point four construct a thoughtful and plausible interpretation of a text. They fill in some gaps in a text, making assumptions about unstated causes or motivations or drawing meaning from cues in the text. They usually differentiate between literal and figurative meanings. They may recognize real or seeming contradictions, but are sometimes distracted by these contradictions and by ambiguities. They demonstrate a thoughtful understanding of the whole work.

High School Sample, California Department of Education, 1991.

Readers achieving score point four develop connections with and among texts. They usually connect their understanding of the text to their own experience and knowledge and sometimes to other texts. When directed, these readers may generate, validate, expand, and/or reflect on their ideas about the text, but with less depth than in a score point five or six response. These readers tend to paraphrase or retell, often thoroughly and purposefully. They also see, however, a more general significance in or wider application of the literal facts of the text.

These readers, while confident, rarely take risks. They accept the text without exploring multiple possibilities of meaning. They tend to present their understanding of a text as fixed and rarely revise their interpretation as they re-read and as additional information becomes available.

Readers demonstrating this level of reading performance sometimes challenge or question the text. They may raise questions and may agree or disagree without explaining their reactions.

Score Point 3—Literal Reading Performance

Students performing at score point three are literal readers, constructing a plausible, but superficial interpretation of the whole work. They show little sensitivity to nuances and complexities; they may not respond to some portion of the text. They usually demonstrate a sense of the whole work, but at a simplistic and literal level.

These readers develop few or no connections with or among texts. Sometimes they connect the text associationally with personal experience, but the connection is generally superficial and unexamined.

Score point three readers are not risk takers. They show little tolerance for textual difficulties or lack of closure. Confronted by textual complexities, they may not address the difficulties. Their reading process tends not to be recursive: having made some initial sense of the text, they are inclined to retain their view without testing or revising it.

Readers at the score point three level of reading performance rarely challenge the text or carry on an internal dialogue with the writer. If they raise questions at all, the questions will be largely unproductive expressions of frustration or low level inquiries (e.g., about word meanings). Any expressed appreciations or criticisms are likely to be simplistic and based on literal understanding of the text.

High School Sample, California Department of Education, 1991.

Score Point 2—Limited Reading Performance

A limited reading performance indicates that readers at score point two construct partial and/or reductive meanings for a text. They may demonstrate a superficial understanding of parts of the text. They demonstrate a reductive meaning for the text by overgeneralizing or oversimplifying but seem unable to grasp the whole.

Readers within this range of performance develop few or no connections with texts. They may, as they recognize some idea, continue to write or draw, but their responses will appear to have only a tangential relevance to the text.

These readers seldom ask questions of a text or offer meaningful evaluations of what they read. They tend to abandon or become entangled in difficult sections of a text.

Score Point 1—Minimal Reading Performance

In a minimal reading performance, the reader appears to understand and respond to an individual word, title, and/or phrase but not in ways that demonstrate even a rudimentary understanding of how these words relate to text ideas.

Any connections such readers may make to their own experience will appear in the form of words or drawings that have textual associations only to an isolated word or phrase. Minimal responses may include vague and unsupported evaluations or responses (e.g., "I like/don't like this story" or "It's boring.")

Level one reader responses suggest that these students engage in reading as an act of decoding rather than as a process of making coherent meaning.

High School Sample, California Department of Education, 1991.

HIGH SCHOOL RHETORICAL EFFECTIVENESS SCORING GUIDE INTERPRETATION

In California's writing assessment framework, interpretive writing invites students to say what a text or other data might mean and to justify the meanings they see. It requires thoughtful, patient reading (and rereading) and careful analysis. We classify it as argumentative writing because it occurs in a writing situation where alternative meanings are defensible—where a writer's readers may prefer meanings that are different from the writer's.

Writers of interpretive essays must identify the subject being interpreted but only to the extent that readers may require it; offer meanings by making a claim or claims about the subject; provide evidence from the subject to support or justify the meanings; and maintain a focused, authoritative interpretive stance throughout the essay.

While the *rhetorical* aspect of the assessment focuses on the distinctive features of writing types, the *effectiveness* aspect guides us to look carefully at the more comprehensive features of coherence and style. Coherence, a sense of organization, flow, and focus, is essential to all good writing. The coherent essay has a clear direction, each section flowing naturally from the preceding one. Coherence is demonstrated to readers through emphasis, organization, and repetition achieved through recurrences of language, syntax, and ideas. Style, for the purposes of this assessment, is observable in two written language features: (1) *sentence control* and (2) *word choice* or *diction*. In assessment of the effectiveness of style, the primary considerations are *appropriateness, precision*, and *control*.

The prompts may ask students to decide what a poem might mean, reach conclusions about character relationships in short stories or about data on social phenomena (like TV watching), or make inferences about remembered fictional characters' conflicts or growth in self-knowledge.

With 45 minutes to write one draft, students face a special challenge in announcing early at least some of the claims they intend to make. They also have to orient readers adequately to the essay by presenting the subject and forecasting the purpose and direction of the essay.

In a one-draft test situation, students may have difficulty achieving such a strong start, in large part because they begin writing with only a partial idea of what they want to say.

With or without a strong start, students need to keep readers on track by pointing explicitly to claims they are making about the sub-

᠇h School Sample, California Department of Education, 1991.

ject, and they need to lead readers toward a conclusive interpretation. Most important, along the way, students must amass enough specific relevant evidence from the subject (text or data) itself to convince readers that the claims are justified. Instead of retelling or summarizing, they have to present evidence from the subject in a way that supports their claims. Finally, writers have to maintain throughout the essay an authoritative (though not dogmatic or polemical), interpretive stance, assuring readers that they know the subject well and have some interesting (probably nonobvious) ideas about it.

Score Point 6—Exceptional Achievement

Point of Departure. The writer orients the reader through a clear and concise identification of the subject being interpreted. The writer provides context to help readers follow the interpretation.

The beginning seems purposeful in that it sets up the interpretation, orienting the reader to what is to come, perhaps even forecasting explicitly the direction the essay will take.

Interpretive Claims. The writer presents interpretive claims that are unusually perceptive. The claims may be unexpected or even contrary to a predictable interpretation.

Evidence. The writer supports interpretive claims with various kinds of evidence: in writing about literature, for example, quotations, paraphrases, and citing/reviewing specific events are appropriate. The writer provides substantial evidence to support major claims. The writer goes well beyond the immediate response most writers would give. Each section of the essay is developed coherently. Language is consistently used with precision and appropriateness. The writer exhibits an exceptional control of a variety of sentence structures and maintains connections between ideas. The overall essay has a consistently smooth forward movement. The writer avoids unsubstantiated generalizations and oversimplifications.

The writer uses "data" from the subject as concrete evidence in an explicit, pointed, convincing interpretation. The writer clearly knows the difference between retelling or summarizing and amassing relevant, concrete evidence to support an interpretive claim.

Interpretive Stance. The writer seems authoritative and committed to justifying claims adequately. The writer knows how to write an interpretive essay and clearly wants to persuade readers that the interpretation is reasonable and valid. The reader never loses sight

High School Sample, California Department of Education, 1991.

of the writer's point and can see the argument advances logically to a convincing and satisfying conclusion. The reader is never left to infer the relevance of evidence, examples, or retelling. The writer does not substitute retelling, summary, or brief and general examples for concrete evidence and insightful reasoning.

The writer may acknowledge that readers favor alternative interpretations. The writer may evaluate alternative interpretations, accepting or rejecting them tactfully.

Score Point 5—Commendable Achievement

Point of Departure. Like the writer of a six-point essay, this writer provides a context for the subject of the interpretation. The writer presents an appropriate amount of background information about the subject. The opening announces at least one claim about the subject and may forecast the direction the essay will take.

While a six-point essay always begins with a strong opening claim and focus, a five-point essay may work its way into an idea or claim about its subject. Eventually, though, it reaches a clear focus or point.

Interpretive Claims. As in a six-point essay, the writer presents claims clearly. The writer makes perceptive claims.

Evidence. The writer does not rely on summary and includes adequate evidence to support major claims so that the interpretation seems convincing. Evidence may not be as full or insightful as in a six-point essay. A five-point essay may lack the unfaltering smoothness of the six-point essay. A five-point essay will show the writer's ability to use words appropriately. Word choice may show less versatility than in the six-point essay; however, the diction is still consistently strong and controlled throughout the essay. The writer exhibits sustained control of a variety of sentence structures. The writer clearly knows how to construct an interpretation.

Interpretive Stance. Like the writer of a six-point essay, the writer seems authoritative and attempts to convince readers that the interpretation is reasonable. The writer seems thoughtful and clearly understands how to justify an interpretation. The writer may acknowledge alternative interpretations.

Score Point 4—Adequate Achievement

Point of Departure. The writer of the four-point essay orients readers adequately to the subject but may not always establish an overall structure for the interpretation. The writer identifies the subject and presents enough information about it for the designated readers and may even forecast some part of what is to be discussed. The context usually includes one claim about the subject. The writer of a four-point essay may begin unsteadily but eventually will write his or her way around to a focus, but not so insightfully as a writer of a five-point essay.

Interpretive Claims. The writer of a four-point paper makes at least one clear but sometimes predictable claim.

Evidence. To support the interpretation, the writer offers evidence from the source. The evidence may be general, lacking specific detail. The language in the four-point essay may be somewhat conventional and predictable. The essay shows a sustained control of sentence structure but may have less variety than the five- and six-point essays. The writer may rely too much on generalization or summary.

The writer presents an adequate, expected response.

Interpretive Stance. The writer knows how to go about justifying an interpretation.

1. The writer may not reveal the main point until the conclusion but finally does so; or

2. The writer may set up the interpretation impressively and support it explicitly (as in a five- or six-point essay) but not amass nearly enough relevant evidence to impress readers; or

3. The writer may provide a "reading" of the subject that offers a series of interesting claims but does not consistently connect them to a main point or major claim.

Score Point 3—Some Evidence of Achievement

Point of Departure. The writer may begin with a perfunctory introduction in which the subject is simply identified without additional information. The background and context for the essay are quickly sketched.

High School Sample, California Department of Education, 1991.

Interpretive Claims. The claims seem obvious; or if they are thought-ful, they are developed inadequately.

Evidence. The writer may summarize the work or narrate an event rather than offer concrete evidence. Although the reader can under-stand the major ideas, there may be irrelevant details, digressions, and/or repetitions that hamper the forward movement. The writer shows basic control of simple sentences, but the three-point essay has little sentence variety. The word choice is usually appropriate to the content; however, the writer may rely on general rather than specific language.

Interpretive Stance. The writer of a three-point essay seems to know about some features of supporting an interpretation but cannot yet bring them together in a balanced, convincing way. The writer seems to lack confidence or awareness of readers' needs.

Score Point 2—Little Evidence of Achievement

Point of Departure. The introduction is either brief or unfocused. The writer may identify the subject but usually fails to identify any claims in the opening.

Interpretive Claims. The writer may introduce no explicit interpretive claims anywhere in the essay. Any claims presented seem obvious. Claims may be too broad or general and may be contradictory. The writer relies on generalizations or summaries. The writer may indi-cate some understanding beyond the literal level.

Evidence. Little if any relevant evidence is presented.

Interpretive Stance. The writer seems confused and is clearly struggling to present an interpretation. The essay may be incomplete, out of balance, or superficial.

Score Point 1—Minimal Evidence of Achievement

Point of Departure. Context may be missing, abrupt, or confusing.

Interpretive Claims. The writer fails to present interpretive claims. The writer may merely summarize the subject, usually in a few lines. The writer stays on a literal level.

---

h School Sample, *California* Department of Education, 1991.

Evidence. The writer presents neither specific support nor personal reactions. The reader is frequently confused about relationships between sentences and ideas. There are frequent lapses in sentence sense, resulting in confusion. The writer is on topic but does not refer to a text or to data presented in the prompt.

Interpretive Stance. The writer responds to the prompt but does not seem to understand what is required in interpretive writing situations.

Unscorable—Inappropriate Response

Off topic. No response. Written in a foreign language.

High School Sample, California Department of Education, 1991.

HIGH SCHOOL RHETORICAL
EFFECTIVENESS SCORING GUIDE
REFLECTIVE ESSAY

Reflective essays derive from the personal experience of the writer. But beyond the description and narration involved in communicating that experience, reflection requires probing into what this experience can show about the writer's life in particular and, more importantly, about the writer's ideas of life in general.

The writer of a reflective essay works to see connections between experience and ideas, to test out thinking about an idea in the light of other experiences, and to arrive at new dimensions of the initial thinking.

Reflective essays are grounded in the concrete. An ordinary thing seen, read, or experienced triggers the reflection and leads to exploration of an idea. Occasions for reflections cover the range of personal experience from observations of natural phenomena, to recalling or witnessing events or to encountering a provocative idea in a novel or on the screen.

While the *rhetorical* aspect of the assessment focuses on the distinctive features of writing types, the *effectiveness* aspect guides us to look carefully at the more comprehensive features of coherence and style. Coherence, a sense of organization, flow, and focus is essential to all good writing. The coherent essay has a clear direction, each section flowing naturally from the preceding one. Coherence is demonstrated to readers through emphasis, organization, and repetition achieved through recurrences of language, syntax, and ideas. Style, for the purposes of this assessment, is observable in two written language features: (1) *sentence control* and (2) *word choice* or *diction*. In assessing the effectiveness of style, the primary considerations are *appropriateness, precision,* and *control.*

Unlike observational writing, which focuses on conveying one's personal perceptions, or autobiographical incident, which involves narrating an incident and evaluating its significance, reflective essays move to a different level of abstraction. The writer of a reflective essay ultimately reveals that the subject of the essay is, in fact, an abstraction, such as truth, beauty, patience, injustice. Reflective writers explore the meaning of this abstraction for themselves and for people in general. It is this people-in-general aspect of reflection—exploring the larger social implications of an idea—that is the hallmark of the reflective essay. It involves students in a unique kind of experience-based thinking.

The flow of thinking in exploring an idea may take shapes such as the following:

High School Sample, California Department of Education, 1991.

- The writer may first present the occasion (narrate a full incident or describe an observation), choosing details and images carefully as a way to ground the reflection that follows. The reflection then moves off on its own, perhaps with some reference to the initiating occasion.

- The writer may launch an occasion but then move in and out of it along the way, reflecting on the idea it suggests.

- The writer may construct a web of related, often parallel experiences that serve as the stimulus for reflection.

- The writer may focus first on a single occasion and then draw associations between it and other related experiences that build to an ultimate idea about people or the world at large.

- The writer may being with an idea from a quotation, proverb, or general experience and test concrete personal experience against it, reflecting about how each experience relates to the idea. The reflection is refined more fully with each example until the idea has been tested from various angles.

Whatever thought pattern emerges, the writer's reflections explore the meaning of the occasion beyond the personal to the general.

Students who lack experience reading and writing the reflective essay usually respond in limited ways to prompts: (1) they fail to ground their reflections in concrete observations or personal anecdotes or do so only superficially and then write a conventional "expository" essay about the idea in the topic; (2) they narrate a relevant personal experience but then neglect to explore the idea it suggests or do so only briefly, often in a moralizing way; or (3) they write a meditation rather than a reflection, turning an idea over and over but not grounding their ideas in personal experience.

Score Point 6—Exceptional Achievement

Occasion for Reflection. The writer of a six-point essay memorably presents the occasion for reflection (a thing seen, read, or experienced), often with the fine detail of the naturalist or autobiographer. Though it does not dominate the essay at the expense of reflection, the occasion is nevertheless presented in extended, concrete detail. Whether it be an anecdote or an observation of nature or a literary text, the occasion grounds the entire essay in concrete experience.

Writers of six-point essays may use such strategies as the following to ground their reflections:

High School Sample, California Department of Education, 1991.

- Describe an animal, object, or phenomenon, using concrete language rich in sensory detail.

- Record specific behaviors, properties, or actions, often using narrative strategies such as pacing, dialogue, or movement.

- Cite a quotation—poetry, prose, or proverb.

- Construct a web of related, often parallel experiences that serve as the stimulus for reflection.

Reflection. In a six-point essay the reflection or the idea suggested by the occasion is exceptionally thoughtful and convincing. The reader is impressed by particular insights. The writer is clearly thinking freshly, originally, and honestly about the idea and has left commonplaces and clichés behind. The reflection tends to be extended, reflecting a serious, almost tenacious, probing and exploring of the idea.

The reflection may include generalizations about the writer's personal experience (signaled by "I" and "my") or more abstract commentary (signaled by "people," "they," and the editorial "we") about the idea and its broader implications. (For brevity's sake, these two types of reflections can be referred to as *personal reflection* and *general reflection.*)

Personal reflection may be understood as the first step away from narration of personal experience toward the reflective essay's characteristic idea abstraction of general reflection. Most essays scored six will have some explicit, insightful general reflection. In some notable papers, however, the writer's presentation of the occasion is at the same time a reflection. In these papers the general reflection is implicit, embedded in phrases or clauses that cue the reader to move beyond the specific occasion to the abstraction that underlies it. The tone, established by a distancing of self from occasion, clearly conveys the reflective nature of such essays. Through exploratory, the reflection seems to find a direction and reveals discovery or deepening insight, sometimes expressed as wonder, without a sense of conclusiveness.

The six-point essay shows the writer's exceptional control of a range of sentence structures. These writers consistently use language with precision, appropriateness, and imagination, drawing on specific concrete language, sensory description, and details to draw the reader into the exploration.

Score Point 5—Commendable Achievement

Occasion for Reflection. Like a six-point essay, the five-point essay presents an extended concrete occasion. The occasion does not domi-

igh School Sample, California Department of Education, 1991.

nate the essay at the expense of reflection. A five-point essay lacks only the vividness and impact of a six-point essay.

Reflection. The writer engages in extended, thoughtful reflection. As in a six-point essay, the writer includes at least some general reflection. The occasional five-point essay establishes a reflective tone by an effective distancing of self from the occasion. The five-point essay, however, will not carry it through so conclusively. The personal reflection and general reflection are serious and honest but lack the intellectual leaps and freshness of a six-point essay. The essay reaches beyond obvious statements about the occasion and idea. The reflection is not entirely predictable.

A five-point essay shows the writer's ability to use words appropriately. Word choice may show less versatility and imagination than in the six-point essay; however, the diction is still consistently strong and controlled. The writer exhibits sustained control of a variety of sentence structures, and the essay reveals direction or purpose, although without the insight of the six-point essay.

Score Point 4—Adequate Achievement

Occasion for Reflection. The four-point essay presents a concrete occasion but may lack the detail or specificity of a five- or six-point essay. The language, though appropriate, may be somewhat conventional and predictable. A full-fledged incident may dominate the reflection. It strikes the reader as a strong and interesting occasion.

Reflection. Reflection will indicate a serious attempt to explore the idea suggested by the occasion but may be less well grounded in that specific occasion. Some details may seem extraneous, interrupting the forward exploratory movement of the essay. The essay shows a sustained control of sentence structure, but it may have less variety than the five- or six-point essays. The reflection may be intelligent but predictable or commonplace. The connection may seem tangential. The writer may rely on personal reflections about the occasion but will still include at least a brief general reflection. A four-point essay may be characterized by thoughtfulness rather than by discovery.

Score Point Three—Some Evidence of Achievement

Occasion. The writer presents an occasion, but it may either be brief or dominate the essay. What appear at first reading to be occasions may actually be examples chosen to illustrate an initial generalization. The writer may rely on general rather than specific language.

High School Sample, California Department of Education, 1991.

Reflection. The essay may have a meandering, rather than purposefully exploratory, quality. Although the reader can understand the major ideas, there may be irrelevant details, digressions, and/or repetitions. The three-point essay may rely on personal refection to the exclusion of general reflection. Reflection will seem obvious or even superficial, often taking the form of moralizing.

Some three-point essays will offer only extended reflection about the idea in the prompt, with little grounding in an occasion. The essay may seem generally competent and the reflection may be as interesting as in a four-or five-point essay, but the writer has not yet learned that reflection must be carefully grounded in an occasion.

Other three-point essays will begin with what sounds like the end point of reflection, a conclusion or generalization that becomes the stimulus for recounting one or more illustrative examples.

Score Point 2—Little Evidence of Achievement

Occasion. The occasion may be brief or it may dominate the essay. There may be no occasion or the essay may be all occasion, with little reflection.

Reflection. If there is an occasion, the reflection may be additive or unfocused. It may be very brief and simplistic, and some details are irrelevant. The overall structure of the essay is weak. Some two-point essays may be extended personal or generalized reflections on a topic with no grounding at all in an occasion. The writer exhibits little control of sentence structure, and the word choice is limited. Some words may be inappropriate or inappropriately used.

Score Point 1—Minimal Evidence of Achievement

Occasion. If there is an occasion, it will be very brief and devoid of specificity or concreteness.

Reflection. No reflection is indicated. There may be brief and superficial attempts at definition or statements of opinion rather than reflection. The paper lacks organization, and there are frequent lapses in sentence sense, resulting in confusion for the reader.

Unscorable—Inappropriate Response

Off topic. No response. Written in a foreign language.

---

igh School Sample, California Department of Education, 1991.

APPENDIX B
MEMO TO THE ENGLISH DEPARTMENT

Here you have a memo written to spur a department toward portfolio assessment. As noted in Chapter 1, "Defending a Grade," and Chapter 11, "The Writing Competency Test," portfolios have been shown to improve student writing competence, reflection on progress, and appropriate goal-setting. Collecting and selecting portfolios is consistent with good instructional practice and with newer assessments such as the national portfolio assessment system developed by the New Standards Project.

MEMO TO:	**Members of the English Department**
FROM:	**Mark Larson**
RE:	**Assessment of Writing**

Here as you requested at our meeting last week is my rationale for proposing a new way to assess writing. As I told you then, my discomfort and dissatisfaction with our present system grows out of the fact that the students are not writing with verve or energy. They lack the proverbial "authentic voice." One of my tenth graders expressed my own dissatisfaction well when she wrote:

> For English we are to write a paragraph in what is being called the "hamburger style." Well, after finding out exactly what the hamburger style is, I would like to complain. The hamburger style paragraph consists of one paragraph that holds a topic sentence, three examples, and a conclusion. The problem with this is that it limits us, the writers, to such a strict form that it cuts out room for our imagination. Writing is not about form, it's about life, feeling, and emotions. You just can't put all that in a paragraph! Another problem with this assignment is that it makes the writer worry more

about fitting the form than explaining the answer or opinion. When in a test situation, people do what is required of them and forget that it is themselves that make the paper and its opinion, not the paper's form. I think this hamburger essay thing has got to go.

So that's where I started—with the student's complaint and my goals chiming in my head.

GOALS

I began by reflecting on what has been happening to me. Since I started teaching, I have developed a keen eye for students' errors. I was on a mission, an error-hunt. I believe now that in my zeal I missed the well-turned phrase, the clever choice of words, the unique perspective, the exceptional metaphor, the clear thought. I believe, too, that when I did find something worth noting, my "Good!" in the margin was a tiny voice, lost in the cacophony of screaming red slashes and other complaints. I began to fear that I was doing more harm than good. I grew bored with blaming the kids, perhaps because I got to be so good at it. So I took a long look and found that:

1. The students' writing was consistently bland and uninspired.
2. The kids repeated the same errors again and again, no matter how often I circled them or how many correction sheets the kids completed.
3. Students did not know how to rewrite, often mistaking the correction of mechanical errors for an authentic and thorough revision.
4. More and more students were not turning in the required work.

My long look brought me to recognize, along with Tom Romano,[1] that the "first and constant order of business [for the writing teacher] is to enable all students to establish and develop their individual voices." I wanted above all for the students to become invested in their writing and, though it may sound sentimental, to find it a source of satisfaction, even pride. So, to that end, I established the following goals for myself and looked for ways to achieve them:

1. To respect differences in student learning and therefore to individualize my instruction

---

[1] *Clearing the Way: Working with Teenage Writers*, (Portsmouth, N.H.: Heinemann, 1987), 7.

2. To allow students to work at their own pace

3. To help students realize what rewriting is really about

4. To eliminate letter grades as a way to evaluate each paper (for most students, grades are too abstract and difficult to translate into concepts students can use to improve their writing)

5. To help students learn how to manage their time

METHOD

To achieve my goals, I set up the following procedures:

Requirements

Each student was responsible for developing and maintaining a portfolio to present to me at the end of each quarter. It contained written work that the students felt represented and demonstrated their strengths and their growth as writers.

Students created their own topics, but for those who had trouble coming up with topics, I devised a list of eighty suggestions. I started most classes with some sort of writing prompt, usually relating to something from the newspaper, as a lure to those who still had trouble generating their own topics.[2]

They worked constantly all term on their papers. I tried to get them into the computer lab every Friday to make it easier for them to get their papers finished.

Acceptance Policy:

1. First, students tried out an idea. Some were rough drafts, others scratch outlines or lists, others a full-blown sentence, paragraph, or poem. At the top of the paper they wrote, "Comments?" and dropped the paper in a wire basket in my room. They frequently wrote questions in the margins: "Does this sound stupid, do you think?" "Like my alliteration?" "How can I make this clearer?" This focused their attention and mine on their concerns. I could directly respond to those elements they wanted me to respond to. I might also note what I liked and what I would have liked to see developed further, or shortened—whatever. Unless they specifically asked me to do so, I did not comment on mechanics

---

[2]See Appendix F for a listing of the range of genres a teacher could present for student choice.

at this point. They were still experimenting with ideas, not mechanics. When I was finished, I put their papers in a different basket for pick up.

2. They then went back to work on the same piece, started something new, or returned to a piece they had previously begun.

3. When they thought a piece was ready, they polished it and wrote "Portfolio?" at the top. At this point I focused on mechanics, logic, organization, style, etc. I underlined errors; I didn't label them. If the kids couldn't figure out what the error was or how it could be changed, they could turn to a friend, a relative at home, or me. When they came to me with a specific question, we had a proverbial "learning moment." Because I received from zero to fifteen papers a day, I could focus on those few writers, teaching to individuals, not to the class as a whole.

4. If we both agreed the writing was completed, I stamped it with the word *File* and the date. It then became a candidate for the final portfolio. If the paper needed more work, I was very specific about what I wanted done before I would certify it as ready for the portfolio. Usually, I would not focus on more than one aspect of the paper's limitations at a time: development, organization, spelling, run-ons, etc. Most papers went through at least two revisions. Each time a new version was turned in, the student stapled it on top of previous drafts so he or she and I could note progress.

Grading

I had two writing conferences each quarter. While students were writing and revising their papers for their portfolios in class, I conducted conferences. At the first conference, halfway through the quarter, they showed me what they had done so far and filled out a progress report. Before they came to me, for their second conference, they filled out a self-evaluation sheet, which asked them to reflect on their progress and to arrive at a letter grade based on the skills they had learned as shown in their four accepted pieces. They needed to consider these questions:

1. Did I experiment with different types of writing?
2. Is there evident improvement in my writing? In which areas?
3. Did I allow time for rewrites?
4. Did I "stretch" myself?

5. Do I like what I wrote? Which piece do I like best?

6. Did I work on mechanical errors that have given me trouble in the past?

To the second conference (during the last week of the quarter), they brought this self-evaluation and a portfolio with the four accepted essays stapled to the previous drafts, works in progress, and any other written work, like essay tests and worksheets. We discussed their responses to the questions above and looked through their portfolio of four papers, which they presented as support for their proposed grade. After discussion, we agreed on a quarter grade and we both signed the sheet. I found that the majority of students were extremely humble. A great surprise. If they felt they merited an A, they usually deserved it. Frequently, students asked for grades that were lower than I would have given them. I tried to talk them up. But the focus always was on the writing. We never argued averages, points, penalties—we just evaluated their writing and the progress we saw in it and the risks they took on the page.

KINKS AND FLAWS AND WHAT I'M DOING ABOUT THEM
Problem 1

It was difficult to give parents a progress report. When a kid said, "I've got three works-in-progress," I had to trust that, or the method fell apart. A work-in-progress could take the form of notes, a draft still in the computer, or a notion still taking shape in the mind. All of these stages are perfectly valid and acceptable—and necessary. So far, I have been scolded only once by a parent who wanted a more concrete form of evaluation. (That wasn't bad. I expected more.)

A lot of parents actually liked the personalized attention their son or daughter was receiving, as well as the opportunity I gave the students to explore their writing, their styles, their thoughts, and themselves.

Possible Solution

I'd like to develop a mid-quarter progress report in which students indicate to their parents the progress they are making. In conjunction with that, I'd send home a note at the beginning of the year that explained my new method of evaluation.

Problem 2

At the end of the first quarter, I received a flood of last-minute work. This was obviously overwhelming for me and did not allow the kids who procrastinated enough time to do necessary rewrites.

Possible Solution

First, I think that it is important for students to run into this type of trouble if they are going to learn to manage their time. I did provide them with quarter schedules and many reminders. If they did not heed my warnings, they had trouble and their grade suffered. So they learned something. As for my dilemma, I put together a committee of three students who reviewed the flooding problem and offered several solutions. They suggested, for example, that I have two papers due by mid-quarter and the other two by the end of the quarter. We're still ironing out this one. Many students still want the flexibility of turning in more than the last two papers at the end of the quarter.

Problem 3

Some kids have more trouble than others managing their time. Some obviously have more experience or guidance or support at home than others.

Possible Solution

This highly individualized method of teaching does offer me opportunities to work with those students who need more structure. I involved some students in working out a mutually-agreed-upon schedule, which I held them to. I did not want to impose it, however. I need to find a way to spot such kids earlier and offer intervention if necessary.

Problem 4

I didn't spend much (any?) time on grammar from the book which, unfortunately, is necessary to prepare them for the language proficiency test. Trouble is, the only way to teach grammar so students retain it is, I think, through writing practice (with feedback), reading, and talking. I give them plenty of that.

Possible Solution

I, frankly, don't see the value of the test, so I have trouble with this.

WHAT THE STUDENTS SAY

As part of the evaluation process, they wrote what they have learned about their writing. Here are some of their untouched answers:

I have learned that I have expressed myself very deeply through my writing. I am honest and true to my writing. When I read it out loud or to myself, I can't believe I actually wrote it, and on my final drafts it sounds so professional, like I've been writing for years!

I like to write about things that pertain to me. I like to do this because it feels good to get out what I have bottled up inside me.

I have learned that the more honest and the closer it is to my heart, the better it is.

I have found by writing I find out more about myself, good or bad. And I have discovered that by writing my feelings down I can better understand what confushes me.

I like the way I can be creative one moment and the next moment be addressing a very serious subject.

Writing is becoming more and more pleasurable to do, and I recently decided that I would love to be an author.

I used to look at writing as a chore, but now I don't mind writing.

At first I wasn't crazy about doing a lot of writing, but I've grown to love it.

Through my writing I've learned that I love my country [Pakistan] very much.

I have learned that I feel strongly about many things and that I care about the world.

I like writing. That's about it.

APPENDIX C
ABRIDGED TRANSCRIPT
OF TEACHER-STUDENT
LITERATURE CONFERENCE

BY MARILYN J. HOLLMAN

Book: *The Awakening* by Kate Chopin[1]

Teacher: You wrote a really good card, Brigit. Well . . .?

Brigit: I never expected it would end like this. I mean where she went off into the sea. I knew she didn't know what she was going to do. . . .

[Brigit's elaboration omitted here]

Teacher: The only thing you didn't mention on your card or in your notebook is Arobin.

Brigit: Well, I didn't know what to do with him. I did mention Robert. She [Edna] fell in love with Robert during that summer and likewise, Robert with her. That's why he left.

Teacher: He was afraid?

Brigit: Yes. He wasn't used to that. He had a different "pretty woman" every summer, but this was different, and when he came back, he left again. When she was with him was when she enjoyed beautiful things of life. Like the swimming and their trip off the island. But somehow he made her feel she had to find her real self. But she realized when he left again that things would never be possible the way she wanted them. . . .

[Brigit's elaboration omitted here]

Teacher: Yes, I remember the night she learned to swim.

Brigit: And that's where she ended up, in the ocean. Her children posed a big problem, and she knew to take care of them she

---

[1] Holt, Rinehart, & Winston, 1970.

would have to stay with her husband and be who she did-
n't want to be. She couldn't sacrifice herself for her children—that's what she said, I remember—so she gave up. I
don't know for sure if she intentionally killed herself or
not.

Teacher: She went out there in spring alone.

Brigit: Yes. It was the place Robert's mother managed.

Teacher: "... and she saw his brother Victor." (Both she and Brigit
smile.)

Brigit: And there was that other woman, that artist who she went
to see back in New Orleans, who wasn't very nice, but she
knew who she was. . . .

[Brigit's elaboration omitted]

Teacher: And Edna's husband?

Brigit: Oh, she began to realize her husband was not something
she needed in her life. She first really expressed this when
she stayed outside when he asked her to come in and go to
bed. . . . Well, he wasn't so bad as he could have been for
the time. . . . She didn't appreciate the same things about
her life as other women did, such as all her material
belongings that her husband bought her that other women
were jealous of. . . .

Entry from Brigit's Notebook

. . . .The yellow parrot is in a cage as Edna seems to be and feels like
she's trapped. It says the bird speaks a language that no one understands and that is how Edna felt, I think, that no one understood
who she really was at all she tried to say. When Mr. Pontellier left
because he had the privileges of leaving—when the bird ceased to be
entertaining is familiar as several times in the book when Edna
wasn't agreeable to him or didn't want to do things his way, he
simply left and went to the Club not explaining why or when he'd
be back. Edna wants out of the "cage" and either the scream could
be directed toward Mr. Pontellier to leave Edna's life or to Edna to
get out of her cage.

APPENDIX D
ASSIGNMENT FOR
READER'S NOTEBOOK

Some ideas for your Reader's Notebook.

1. Write down **basic information** such as title, author, publisher, date of publication, number of pages. You may need this information later in the course when you write your semester essay.

2. Record the names of **characters** or persons you think are important for one reason or another. You might also write mini character sketches for some of them or cite passages that you think show them off effectively.

3. A **summary of action or a list of events/segments** might prove useful to your instructor and to you. This need not be very long—five to ten lines is probably sufficient. You want to distill the essence of action and/or conflict here.

4. What follows are some questions/prompts that may help you surface some of your insights and feelings about your reading. You may choose to respond to all of them, or you may decide to use one or two for a selection. See if you can allow your writing to explore and explain what it is that's important for you in your reading.

   a. **The thing(s) that strikes me most about this book is/are . . .**

   b. **This book is like others** I've read in that . . . and **different . . .**

   c. A **personal connection** I can make with this book is . . .

5. **Commentary:** Write anything that you notice or that interests you. If you have questions about your reading, pose them and try to answer them for yourself in writing. Passages from the book that you like or that you think are important might appear here, too, with your comments. This is your time to respond to and deal with the novel in your own way. It may not take the same form in each entry.

APPENDIX E
SAMPLE STUDENT WORK

Figure E.1
Sample Student Summary Index Cards

"The Good Mother" by Sue Miller
   This book totally caught my attention
I just couldn't put it down. Anna seems
so real. After I finished reading this book
I had the urge to call my mom + just hear
her talk to me. I couldn't imagine if I
would've had to live w/ my dad. I feel
so bad for Molly. It was clear that she
wanted to stay w/ her mom. At first
I didn't like the way the book kept
jumping around but as I get further

**Figure E.2
Index Cards, continued**

---

ana further into it I envied
Miller's ability as a writer.
Sometimes I felt as though
she went on + on with
background stories but
I realized that every
word Miller wrote was
essential to the story.
The first few chapters
are the background info
about Molly & Anna's
relationship and Anna's
independence due to the
divorce from Brian. Anna
+ Molly's relationship
is a sweet, special, and
intimate relationship. who
Leo came along - Anna
didn't focus as much on
her relationship with
Molly. Molly sensed this
and became aware
that she wanted more
attention so she became
interested in Anna's + Leo's

Figure E.3
Conclusion of Index Cards

---

sex life. she tell's her Dad about it
and he gets furious + takes Anna to court
to fight for custody. Anna goes nuts
especially when Brian wins. she
took Leo's gun and drove out to go get
Molly. she knew she couldn't get through
the airport w/ it so she drove to the dunes
after inflicting self wounds to her head. I
thought she was going to kill herself but
she just had a mental lapse of irrationalization
she then went back to Leo's apartment while
he was in New York. Anna tried then to rational
she decided to move out to Washington and follow
Molly. Then back to Boston to follow Molly. she
broke up w/ Leo and she ends up living
her life for Molly. I think something died inside her

Figure E.4
Sample Student Quotations from *The Good Mother*

---

pg 47 The memory, the moment of sight behind
closed lids, is a memory too of the
disease, the tragedy which took sight away
the beloved face is also a talisman of that
disorder, the panic of that loss

pg 190 "Anna I'm sorry" Leo said, "please don't sa
that, it's what you meant. You're only sorry
it hurt me, not that you feel it."

pg 332 Ursula - "EVERYONE knows you're a
good mother Anna." No one except
Ursula has said anything positive about m
being a mother since Brian had set this
whole machine in motion.

Figure E.5
Sample Student Notebook Entry

SEVENTH HEAVEN

Author: Alice Hoffman
Publisher: G.P. Putnam's Sons
Date: 1990

Characters:
Nora Silk - a woman a little ahead of her times
    comes to suburb w/ boys ; has new ideas - at
    first rejected, later loved
Billy Silk - Nora's introvert son - rejected by peers
    until he makes baseball team
James Silk - youngest of Nora's boys.
"Saint" McCarthy - owner of gas station - has 2
    sons (one good/one devious)
Ace McCarthy - good son ; makes love to Nora ; feels
    left out of home; adopts Cathy's dog ; sees her ghost
Jackie McCarthy - devious son of "Saint" - created
    car accident in which Cathy dies ; sees her ghost ;
    changes for the better
Joe Hennessy - suburban head of police ; secretly
    loves Nora
Mrs. Hennessy - wife of Joe ; suburb snob
Stevie Hennessy - son of Joe ; torments Billy until
    by withdraft is reduced ~~to~~ in size
    +Mrs.   suburb couple that
Mr. Shapiro - end up divorcing
Danny Shapiro - best friend of Ace, ↑son, runs
    away to get in the major league.
Rickie Shapiro - daughter of ↑; loves Ace, but
    won't sleep w/ him.

Figure E.5
Sample Student Notebook Entry, continued

Cathy Corrigan- school slut ; killed in car accident
Donna Durgin- left family one day to start over.;
   lost a lot of weight
Rudy- Cathy's dogs

SUMMARY:
The story is about how a woman named Nora
Silk and her two boys move to a small
suburb to start a new life. Nora is a little
ahead of her time and as a result is
rejected by her neighboors at first. In the
meantime Billy is harrassed and beaten up
at school, Joe Henessy is preparing to leave
his wife for Nora, Donna Durgin becomes sick
of her wife weight and decides to leave her
family., Ace starts sleeping with Nora, Billy
is being taught by Ace to play baseball,
Cathy's ghost appears on her lawn, Rudy
adopts Ace as his owner, Danny Shapiro
leaves home to try out for the majors, Stevie
shrinks because of witchcraft, and Mrs.
Henessy sleeps with her husband in
order to get a job. By the end the
town is somewhat happy and Nora is
accepted.

Figure E.5
Sample Student Notebook Entry, continued

Major ideas :

Seventh Heaven is sort of like a "Dallas" in
a book. It was just a story of a town and
its people. One person that it really focused
on was Nora Silk. She moved to this suburb
in the late 1950's, a little ahead of her time,
but she was eventually accepted. Because
she didn't posses the same conservative
attitude as the rest of the town, she wasn't
readily liked. The reader (myself in this case)
can see that the differences in Nora are
signs of the future and eventually everyone
would conform to Nora's behavior

Likes/Hates ?

One of the things I liked most about
Seventh Heaven was the style in which it
was written. The description wasn't abstract
and majestic, but rather it was down
to earth and realistic — example : the kitchen
was described as scum on the wall edges,
dirty mouse foot prints on the floor and
cheerios scattered across the table. It
made the reading a lot easier than the
over descriptive scene settings in some
books. One thing I didn't like at first
was the fact the the story didn't seen

Figure E.5
Sample Student Notebook Entry, continued

to be heading anywhere. There was no real plot to the story, but once the reader really gets into the characters, the book becomes really good. Also, I didnt overly like the ending to the story. Some things got resolved, but not everything. I guess Im just one of those people who likes everything tied up in a neat little bow. Its a story about people, though, so I guess if life isnt always perfect neither should the story be.

Comparisons:
This book reminded me a lot of Second Heaven. Both were really easy written in that the description was light and made the story more interesting. If Alice Hoffman wrote any other books Id really like to read them.

post confrence entry:
One thing I didnt realize after reading Seventh Heaven was the abundance of withcraft and magical pressence throughtout the book. Nora, this good witch like person, and labelled as such, comes and changes the town.

Figure E.6
Sample Student Reflective Essay

Semester's Thoughts

During this semester I have read nine books all on verying subjects, and authors. I've read from Shakesphere to march three flights in the stratosphere.

I have to admit that my journals suffer from consistantcy and effort but I have never been one to keep long records of any reciding. I read for the moment in the book. I like to be entertained in some instances such as my Stephan King writings or I like to be informed like Secret Armies and Her Name, Titanic. I don't find much interest in books with hidden stories or many sub plots. I am the type of person who prefers the above board and show you cards type approach. If you have something to convey in your writting, say the

Figure E.6
Sample Student Reflective Essay, continued

message or a moral don't
hide it between the lines.
A Midsummers Dream was an
interesting story but not
being an expert on his
stories I found myself
constantly second guessing
everything I read and
wondering what I missed. I
do a large amount of reading
on many different levels of
difficulty but I don't care
for writing that has to
many questions. A question
of self confidence is the
absolute worst thing for a person
in any experience.

I found every conference
different and interesting in
a different way. Sometimes
they answered my questions
and others it was just nice
to talk about what I had
read without worrying if
the book topic was of common
interest to whom I was
speaking with. In all
I found this class to
be a good experience and
a good opportunity to read.

APPENDIX F
MATRIX OF PURPOSES, PROCESSES, AND GENRES

This matrix lists a wide range of genres or types of reading matter and writing formats that can be experienced. Each genre of literature and purpose can be achieved orally or in writing and is embedded in the author's purposes. Often when students have difficulty writing a particular genre of literature it is because they have not read or listened to enough of that type of discourse.

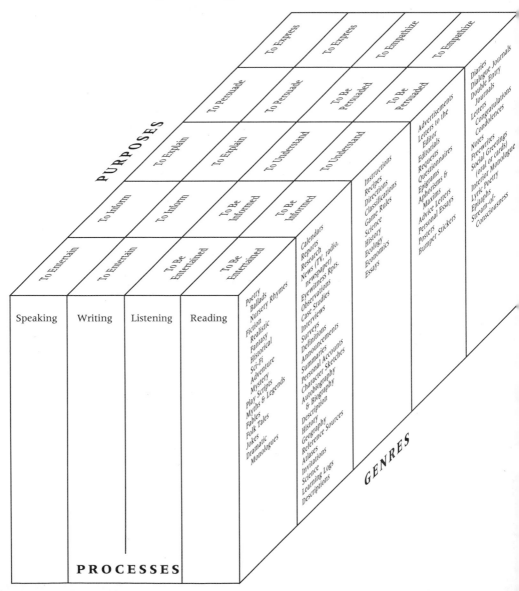

CONTRIBUTING AUTHORS

Marilyn J. Hollman learned to read in Iowa and has been reading ever since. She has read at the University of Iowa, DePaul University, and at Northwestern University where she received her Ph.D. in English Education. Hollman continues to read books she chooses and teaches writing and literature at Naperville Central High School in a suburb of Chicago. She is Co-Director of the Chicago Area Writing Project and adjunct professor at National-Louis University.

Kristin Lems started out as a secondary school English teacher and then heard "the call of ESL," and went off to teach in an Iranian university. After five years as a full-time folk singer, she enrolled in the University of Illinois where she earned a Master of Arts in Teaching English and a Second Language degree. On a Fullbright Scholarship to Algeria, she taught ESL teacher training. Then she came to National-Louis University, where she is an Assistant Professor. She still sings part time.

Brenda M. Landau grew up in the Chicago Public Schools. At George Williams College in Downers Grove, Illinois, she majored in social studies, with minors in secondary education and public administration. After receiving her M.A. in Political Science and Public Administration from Roosevelt University, she received a DeWitt Wallace Fellowship in History to the Woodrow Wilson Institute at Princeton. She teaches at Kenwood High School in Chicago and has taught at Lewis University in Lockport, Illinois and at Chicago State University. She has been Acting Director of the Child Abuse Prevention Program in Chicago.

DATE DUE			
OCT 1 3 1997			